CRITICALLY RESEARCHING YOUTH

critical qualitative research

CRITICAL ISSUES FOR LEARNING AND TEACHING

Shirley R. Steinberg
Series Editor

Vol. 16

The Critical Qualitative Research series is part of the Peter Lang Education list.
Every volume is peer reviewed and meets
the highest quality standards for content and production.

PETER LANG
New York • Bern • Frankfurt • Berlin
Brussels • Vienna • Oxford • Warsaw

CRITICALLY RESEARCHING YOUTH

EDITED BY
SHIRLEY R. STEINBERG & AWAD IBRAHIM

PETER LANG
New York • Bern • Frankfurt • Berlin
Brussels • Vienna • Oxford • Warsaw

Library of Congress Cataloging-in-Publication Data

Critically researching youth / edited by Shirley R. Steinberg, Awad Ibrahim.
pages cm. — (Critical qualitative research; v. 16)
Includes bibliographical references and index.
1. Youth—History. 2. Youth—Research.
I. Steinberg, Shirley R., editor. II. Ibrahim, Awad, editor.
HQ796.C8635   305.235—dc23   2015016454
ISBN 978-1-4331-2710-6 (hardcover)
ISBN 978-1-4331-2709-0 (paperback)
ISBN 978-1-4539-1647-6 (e-book)
ISSN 1947-5993

Bibliographic information published by **Die Deutsche Nationalbibliothek**.
Die Deutsche Nationalbibliothek lists this publication in the "Deutsche
Nationalbibliografie"; detailed bibliographic data are available
on the Internet at http://dnb.d-nb.de/.

Cover photos by Shirley R. Steinberg

We dedicate this volume and our love of work with
youth to the life and celebration of Eva Esther Buitenhuis.
Eva defined the notion of youth, excited about every
aspect of the universe; Eva was an investigator,
curious and interested in life.

As our muse, Eva constantly reminded us of the
intricacies of happiness, of embracing the air,
of moving with confidence, and of love.

We celebrate her life and the impact she made on
everyone she met in her 21 years; we miss her always.

Eva Esther Buitenhuis, Amersfoort, Netherlands, 1994–2015.

CONTENTS

Preface   xi
Awad Ibrahim

Part I Theorizing Youth and Research   1

Chapter 1.   Contextualizing Corporate Kids: Kinderculture
                as Cultural Pedagogy   3
                Shirley R. Steinberg

Chapter 2.   Cipher5 as Method: Aesthetic Education,
                Critical Youth Studies Research, and Emancipation   27
                Michael B. MacDonald

Part II Economics and Youth Research   **47**

Chapter 3.   Trapped Inside a Poisoned Maze; Mapping Young
                People's Geographies of Disposability in Neoliberal
                Times of School Disinvestment   49
                Patricia Krueger-Henney

Chapter 4.   Resisting Marginalization: Students' Conversations
                About Life in University   71
                Carl E. James

Chapter 5. The Standpoint Project: Practitioner Research
            and Action When Working With Young People
            From Low-Income Families   89
            Tony Kruger, Jo Williams, and Marcelle Cacciattolo

Part III Youth Identity and Research   109

Chapter 6. Kinship Narratives: *Beat Nation*, Indigenous
            Peoples (Hip Hop), and the Politics of
            Unmasking Our Ignorance   111
            Haidee Smith Lefebvre and Awad Ibrahim

Chapter 7. "Too Much Drama": The Effect of Smartphones
            on Teenagers' Live Theater Experience   129
            John M. Richardson

Chapter 8. Macklemore: Strong Poetry, Hip Hop Courage,
            and the Ethics of the Appointment   151
            Awad Ibrahim and Adriana Alfano

Chapter 9. Immigrant Canadian New Youth: Expressing and
            Exploring Youth Identities in a Multicultural Context   167
            Handel Kashope Wright and Maryam Nabavi

Part IV Researching Youth and Place   179

Chapter 10. Hispanic Youth Leadership in Texas:
             Creating a Mexican American
             College-Going Culture in West Texas   181
             Mary Frances Agnello

Chapter 11. Conocimiento: Mixtec Youth *sin fronteras*   191
             Elizabeth Quintero

Chapter 12. The Schooling of African Youth in
             Ontario Schools: What Have Indigenous
             African Proverbs Got to Do With It?   205
             George J. Sefa Dei

Part V Youth Living Life and Research   233

Chapter 13. Making Sense of Non/Sense: Queer Youth
             and Educational Leadership   235
             Mark Vicars and Tarquam McKenna

Chapter 14. Where We @? Blackness, Indigeneity,
and Hip Hop's Expression of Creative Resistance 249
Audrey Hudson and Emmanuel Tabi

Chapter 15. Interracial Conscientization Through Epistemological
Re-Construction: Developing Autobiographical
Accounts of the Meaning of Being Black
and White Together 267
Paul R. Carr and Gina Thésée

About the Contributors 285
Index 291

PREFACE

Critically Researching Youth as an Act of Radical Love: Let Them Speak and Let Us Shut Up and Listen!

Critically researching youth requires different epistemologies and a mind shift, where the very terms we use have to be re-labeled. As the authors in this book demonstrate, critically "researching" youth is now approached as a critical *dialogue* with youth, where youth speak, make sense of their lives, and radically envision their own futures. Critically researching youth is now turned into an act of *radical love*, where we researchers/adults shut up and listen (clearly in the most active and caring sense), and in doing so help young people think through their ideas and lives and hence materialize that which is yet to come, their futures.

However, for research to qualify as critical dialogue, it has to first, wrap itself in what Buber (2002) called "genuine dialogue," and second, be conscious of three things: first, there is no humanity without dialogue; second, dialogue can and does take place in and through language (linguistic) but also sacramentally and holistically in silence (outside language and speech act, or para-linguistic); and third, in most relationships, especially those of domination (oppressor/oppressed, adult/youth, guard/inmate, etc.), what is conceived as dialogue is actually monologue. Monologue is when one hears one's own voice and echo, and dialogue, especially when it is genuinely done, requires: a quality of communion; a sense of time, place, and above all love; an ethics of care (Noddings, 2005); a transformative act of love and intellectual rigor.

This volume, is a follow-up to our earlier book, *Critical Youth Studies Reader* (Ibrahim & Steinberg, 2014), brings together a group of scholars who are seeking genuine dialogue with youth. They challenge the notion of youth as an object of study, whose utility stops when the research finishes. They are aware and wide-awake (Ibrahim, 2014) of the powerful possibilities of our research findings and their social, historical, and pedagogical implications.

In *becoming aware*, the authors in this volume are completely open to being addressed by youth. Here, research is no longer about collecting data, organizing notes, testing theories, but an act of love. In researching (*with*) youth, we have to live the tension between being conscious, systematic, organized, and thoroughly ethical, respectful, trustworthy, and committed. The authors cover broad fields and areas of study, from music to arts to language, and from First Nations to immigrants to Mexican Americans. What is clear in all the chapters is the need for different epistemologies (moving from research to radical love) and methodology (moving from data collection to dialogue). Welcome to the new ethics of doing research with youth. WORD!

Awad Ibrahim

References

Buber, M. (2002). *Between man and man.* New York, NY: Routledge.

Ibrahim, A. (2014). Research as an act of love: Ethics, émigrés and the praxis of becoming human. *Diaspora, Indigenous and Minority Education, 8*(1), 7–20.

Ibrahim, A., & Steinberg, S. (Eds.). (2014). *Critical youth studies reader.* New York, NY: Peter Lang.

Noddings, N. (2005). *The challenge to care in schools: An alternative approach to education.* New York, NY: Teachers College Press.

PART I

THEORIZING YOUTH AND RESEARCH

CONTEXTUALIZING CORPORATE KIDS*

Kinderculture as Cultural Pedagogy

Shirley R. Steinberg

With our crashing tidal waves of war, politics, religious influences, struggles, and advancing web 3.0 globalization come an incredible phenomenon, *kinderculture*. Joe Kincheloe and I introduced this phenomenon in 1997 (Steinberg & Kincheloe, 1997) as a socio-theoretical conversation about (and with) the children and youth of the late twentieth century. Our points were underpinned by the notion that kids were being infantilized by a corporate/ media agenda from popular culture, schools, and adults. Yet, while being considered "too" young for almost anything, at the same time, these young consumers were being marketed to as seasoned adults. Almost 20 years later, the result is a consumer public of little girls, for example, who wear chastity rings and hip-clinging jogging pants with "Kiss My Booty" in glitter on the backside. With one voice, adults tell kids to stay clean, avoid sex and drugs, go to Disneyland, and make vows of celibacy … with another voice, the corporate side markets booty clothing, faux bling, and sexualized images of 12-year-olds. After three editions of *Kinderculture: The Corporate Construction of Childhood* (Steinberg & Kincheloe, 2006, 2012), this chapter adds

---

*This chapter first appeared in *Communication and Social Change* (2014, October 31). *2(1)*, 35–57. doi: 10.4471/csc.2014.07. Permission granted by Hipatia Press.

to that notion by continuing to insist that new times have created a new childhood. However, paradoxically the current new times are conservative and liberal, sexual and celibate, and innocent and seasoned. Evidence of this dramatic cultural change surrounds each of us, but without a cultural lens, it is easy to ignore. In the mid-90s many people who made their living studying or caring for children had not recognized this phenomenon. However, in the middle of the first decade of the twenty-first century, more and more people had begun to understand this historic change, *and* other child professionals remained oblivious to these social and cultural alterations. Now, in the second decade of the twenty-first century, the notions of childhood and youth are more complex, more pathologized, and more alien to adults who educate and parent.

In the domains of psychology, education, and to a lesser degree sociology, few observers have seriously studied the ways that the information explosion so characteristic of our contemporary era has operated to undermine traditional notions of childhood. Those who have shaped, directed, and used contemporary information technology have played an exaggerated role in the reformulation of childhood. *Kinderculture* analyzes these changes in childhood, including the role that information technology and media have played in this process. To say that technology and media had created an entirely new childhood would be simplistic; numerous social, political, and economic factors have operated to produce such changes. My focus here is not to cover all issues but to question the ways media, in particular, have helped construct what I will continue to call *the new childhood*. Childhood is a social and historical artifact—not simply a biological entity. Many argue that childhood is a natural phase of growing up, of becoming an adult. The cardinal concept here involves the format of this human phase that has been produced by social, cultural, political, and economic forces operating upon it.

Childhood is a creation of society that is subject to change whenever major social transformations take place. What is labeled as "traditional childhood" is only about 150 years old. The concept of *children* as a particular classification of human beings demanding special treatment differing from adults had not yet developed as a social construct until the twentieth century. From the 1600s, children were considered mini-adults, a chronological definition, which didn't define their social or labor status. In the Middle Ages, for example, children participated daily in the adult world, gaining knowledge of vocational and life skills, working as young as 7 or 8. The zenith of the traditional childhood lasted from about 1850 to 1950. Protected from the dangers of the adult world, many children (up until the twentieth century, boys) during this period were removed from factories and placed into schools.

As the prototype of the modern family developed in the late nineteenth century, "proper" parental behavior toward children coalesced around notions of tenderness and adult accountability for children's welfare. By 1900 many believed that childhood was a birthright—a perspective that eventuated in a biological, not a cultural, definition of childhood. Emerging in this era of the protected child, modern child psychology was inadvertently constructed by the tacit assumptions of the period. The great child psychologists, from Erik Erikson to Arnold Gesell to Jean Piaget, viewed child development as shaped by biological forces.

Piaget's brilliance was constrained by his non-historical, socially decontextualized scientific approach. What he observed as the genetic expression of child behavior in the early twentieth century he generalized to all cultures and historical eras—an error that holds serious consequences for those concerned with children. Considering biological stages of child development fixed and unchangeable, teachers, psychologists, parents, welfare workers, and the community at large view and judge children along a fictional taxonomy of development. Those children who didn't measure up would be relegated to low and self-fulfilling expectations. Those who made the grade would find that their racial and economic privilege are confused with ability (Polakow, 1992; Postman, 1994). *Kinderculture* joins the emerging body of literature that questions the biological assumptions of "classical" child psychology (Kincheloe, 2008).

Living in a historical period of great change and social upheaval, critical observers are just beginning to notice changing social and cultural conditions in relation to this view of childhood. Categories of child development appropriated from modernist psychology may hold little relevance for raising and educating contemporary children. In the 1950s, 80 percent of all children lived in homes where their two biological parents were married to each other (Lipsky & Abrams, 1994). No one has to be told that the family unit has changed in the past 60 years. Volumes have been written specifying the scope and causes of the social transformation.

Before the 1980s ended, children who lived with their two biological parents had fallen to merely 12 percent. Children of divorced parents (a group made up of more than half of the North American population) are almost three times as likely as children raised in two-parent homes to suffer emotional and behavioral difficulties … maybe more the result of parental conflict

than the actual divorce (Mason & Steadman, 1997). Despite such understandings, social institutions have been slow to recognize different, nontradi-
tional family configurations and the special needs they encounter. Without
support, the contemporary "postmodern" family, with its plethora of working
and single mothers and deadbeat dads, is beset with problems emanating from
the feminization of poverty and the vulnerable position of women in both the
public and private spaces (Polakow, 1992).

Positivist Notions of Children

It is important to place *Kinderculture* in paradigmatic context, to understand
what I am discussing in relation to other scholarship on childhood studies and
childhood education. Kinderculture directly challenges the positivist view of
children which is promoted in mainstream articulations of psychology, sociology, education, and anthropology. Positivism is an epistemological position
maintaining that all knowledge of worth is produced by the traditional scientific method. All scientific knowledge constructed in this context is thus
proclaimed neutral and objective. Critics of positivism (see Kincheloe, 1993,
2001, 2003, 2004, 2008) argue that because of the narrow nature of what
positivist research studies (what it *can* study given its rules of analysis), it
often overlooks powerful normative and ideological assumptions built into its
research design. In this naïve context positivists often seek empirical proof of
what are normative and/or political assertions that *adults always know better*
when it comes to issues involving children.

A key goal of critics of positivism involves bringing these normative and
ideological assumptions to the surface so observers can gain a much more tex-
tured perspective of what research involves and indicates. Indeed, critics of
positivism insist that one dimension of research involves the researcher's analysis of his or her own assumptions, ideologies, and values, and how they shape
the knowledge produced. In such a spirit, I openly admit my anti-positivist,
hermeneutic epistemological orientations. Concurrently, I admit my critical
democratic values, my vision of race, class, gender, and sexual equality, and the
necessity of exposing the effects of power in shaping individual identity and
political/educational purpose. This is not an act of politicization of research;
research has always been politicized. Instead, I am attempting to understand
and act ethically in light of such politicization.

In the positivist perspective, children are assumed to be subservient and
dependent on adults as part of the order of the cosmos. In this context, adults

are seen as having a "natural" prerogative to hold power over children. Positivists turn to biology to justify such assumptions, contending that the physical immaturity of children is manifested in other domains as inferiority, an absence of development, incompleteness, and weakness. One does not have to probe deeply into these biological assumptions to discern similarities between the positivist hierarchy of adults and children and the one subordinating *emotional* women to *rational* men. In my challenge to the positivist view of children, I focus on age and generation to depict children as different from adults but not inferior to them. Children are not merely entities on their way to adulthood; they are individuals intrinsically valuable for who they presently are. When positivists view children as lesser than adults, they consistently ignore the way power operates to oppress children around the axes of race, class, gender, sexuality, ability, etc. The positivist construction of the "vulnerable" child in this context actually becomes more vulnerable as real and specific threats are overlooked because childhood is viewed as a naturally vulnerable state. The threats of different social, economic, political, and cultural "childhoods" are erased (Mason & Steadman, 1997).

The positivist view of childhood has been firmly grounded in developmental psychology's universal rules of child development. Regardless of historical or social context, these rules lay out the proper development of *normal* children. This mythos of the universal innocent and developing child transforms cultural dimensions of childhood into something produced by nature. By the second decade of the twentieth century, this universal norm for the developing child had been established on the basis of scientific authority, drawn almost exclusively from North American white, middle-class norms and experiences. Schools fell into line, developing a white, middle-class, patriarchal curriculum that reflected the norms of proper development. Reformers, blessed with the imprimatur of science, based their efforts to regulate play on the principles of developmental psychology. Advocates of municipal playgrounds, the Boy Scouts and Girl Scouts worked to make sure that children made *appropriate* use of leisure time (Spigel, 1998).

The decontextualized aspect of the positivist view of childhood shapes numerous problems for those who don't fit into the dominant cultural bases of the proper development of normal children. In failing to understand the impact of race, class, gender, linguistics, national origin, etc., positivism fails to understand the nature of, and the reasons for differences between children. Positivism is often drawn by the obsession with standards, standardization, and testing ... wherein differences are viewed as deficiencies. In this positivist regime, children from lower socioeconomic, nonwhite, or immigrant back-grounds are relegated to the lower rungs of the developmental ladder. The idea that life experiences and contextual factors might affect development is not considered in the positivist paradigm because it does not account for such social and cultural dynamics (Mason & Steadman, 1997).

As positivism came to delineate the scientific dimensions of child development, male psychologists replaced mothers as child-rearing experts. In the early part of the twentieth century, the psychologist took on a socially important role. Many people believed that if scientific principles were not followed, innocent, malleable children would be led en masse into immorality and weakness. A significant feature of these scientific principles involved exposing children only to developmentally appropriate adult knowledge. The secret knowledge of adulthood, the positivist psychologists believed, should only be delivered to children at appropriate times in their development. One can understand the impact TV made on nations that bought into major dimensions of the positivist mythos. TV became a window to adult knowledge that could undermine the nation's strength and moral fiber. The positivist view of childhood could be maintained only through constant social regulation and surveillance of the young. Since childhood is vulnerable and socially unstable, the control of knowledge becomes especially important in the maintenance of its innocent format. In positivism, childhood no longer exists if the young gain access to certain forms of adult knowledge. No wonder the last half of the twentieth century witnessed so many claims that after TV and other electronic media, childhood was dead. The positivist position has been deemed by many as an elitist perspective, as adults are deemed the guardians under the bridge of childhood. Adults decide what children should know and how they should be socialized. The idea that children should be participants in making decisions about their own lives is irrelevant. In the positivist paradigm children are passive entities who must be made to submit to adult decisions about their lives (Spigel, 1998).

Naming a New Paradigm for Childhood

With the advent of a plethora of socioeconomic changes, technological developments, globalization, and the perceived inadequacy of the old paradigm, Western societies and increasingly other parts of the world have entered into a transitional phase of childhood. This transitional phase has been accompanied by a paradigm shift in the study of childhood and situates it within social, cultural, political, and economic relations. This scholarly shift takes direct exception to the positivist view of childhood and its expression of a universal, uniformly developmentalist conception of the normal child. This conception of the child as a passive receiver of adult input and socialization strategies has been replaced by a view of the child as an active agent capable of contributing to the construction of his or her own subjectivity. For those operating in the parameters of the new paradigm, the purpose of studying and working with children is not to break the borders between childhood and adulthood but to gain a thicker, more compelling picture of the complexity of the culture, politics, and psychology of childhood.

With its penchant for decontextualization and inability to account for contemporary social, cultural, political, economic, and epistemological changes, the positivist paradigm is not adequate for this task (Cannella, 1997; Cannella, 2002; Cannella & Kincheloe, 2002; Cook, 2004; Hammer & Kellner, 2009; Hengst, 2001; Steinberg, 2010, 2012). Insisting that children existed outside society and could be brought in from the cold only by adult socialization that led to development, the positivist view constructed research and childhood professional practices that routinely excluded children's voices. Advocates of this new paradigm have maintained time and again that such positivist silencing and general disempowerment is not in the best interests of children. In the name of child protection, advocates have argued, children are often rendered powerless and vulnerable in their everyday lives. As they construct their view of children as active constructors of their own worlds, proponents of the new paradigm work hard to emphasize the personhood of children. The children of the new paradigm both construct their worlds and are constructed by them. In ethnographic and other forms of new paradigm childhood study, children, like adults, are positioned as co-participants in research—not as mere objects to be observed and categorized. Advocates of the new paradigm operating in the domain of social and educational policy-making contend such activity must take into account the perspectives of children to inform their understanding of particular situations (Cook, 2004; Mason & Steadman, 1997; Seaton, 2002; Steinberg, 2010). Central to the new paradigm is the effort to make sure children are *intimately involved* in shaping their social, psychological, and educational lives. Unfortunately, child-empowerment advocacy is represented by media and psychologists as a permissive relinquishment of adult power over impudent and disrespectful children (Mason & Steadman, 1997; Ottosen, 2003).

Undoubtedly, it will be a difficult struggle to reposition the child in twenty-first-century social relationships. In this context Henry Jenkins (2002) argues, as an advocate of the new paradigm, that his work seeks to provide children with tools that facilitate children's efforts to achieve their own political goals and help them construct their own culture. In rejecting the positivist paradigm of childhood passivity and innocence, I am not contending that there is no time when children need adult protection—that would be a silly assertion. Children, like human beings in general, often find themselves victimized by abuse, neglect, racism, class bias, and sexism. The salient point is that instead of further infantilizing children and rendering them more passive, critical scholars try to employ their perspectives in solving their problems (Mason & Steadman, 1997). Transformative researchers and child professionals work to help children develop a critical political consciousness as they protect their access to diverse knowledge and technologies. Using a critical lens, I argue that children in social, cultural, psychological, and pedagogical contexts need help in developing the ability to analyze, critique, and improve their position in the world … to employ an understanding of kinderculture.

It is also essential to involve the explicit rejection of positivism's universalist conception of childhood and child development. When we enter diverse class and racial/ethnic cultures, we find childhoods that look quite different from the white, middle- and upper-middle-class, English-speaking one presented by positivism. In these particularistic childhoods researchers find great complexity and diversity within these categories. The social, cultural, and political structures that shape these childhoods and the children who inhabit them are engaged in profoundly different ways, depending on specific circumstances. Such structures never determine *who* children are, no matter how much consistency in macrostructures may exist. The particular and the general, the micro and the macro, agency and structure always interact in unpredictable ways to shape the everyday life of children. A central theme of the new paradigm reemerges: *children shape and are shaped by the world around them.*

Kinderculture maintains that the delicate and complex balance between these constructive forces must be carefully studied and maintained. If we move too far in our emphasis of structure over agency, we lapse into a structural determinism that undermines the prerogative of individuals—thus, there is nothing a child can do to escape the ravages of poverty. If we move too far in our emphasis of agency, we often lose sight of how dominant power operates to undermine children's role in shaping their own lives and constructing their own subjectivities. The overemphasis of particularism and agency will often obscure just how powerless children can be. To develop our thicker and more complex view of childhood, we must constantly work to integrate the micro and the macro, to discern new cultural and political economic contexts in which to view and make sense of child behavior (Garey & Arendell, 1999; Ottosen, 2003). In this context, new paradigmatic researchers must not only nurture these macro (social, political, economic), meso (institutional, e.g., school, media, religious institution, welfare agency), and micro (individuals) interactions, but also attend to the ways such levels connect to one another.

Some scholars of childhood make distinctions between proponents of the new paradigm who emphasize structural issues and those who stress the agency of individual children. In this dichotomy scholars who emphasize the importance of commercial relations and corporate marketing in shaping children's culture have been relegated to the "structuralist" camp. Structuralists are represented in this configuration as emphasizing the corporate invasion of childhood and its resulting exploitation. Structuralists are said to view such exploitation as similar in nature to the exploitation of women. The agential perspective often focuses not on the exploitative but the *empowering* dimensions of children's participation in commercial culture.

By arguing that children construct their own lives, such agential scholars maintain that children are capable of avoiding the manipulations of corporate advertising and making positive use of the consumptive act and consumer products. Illustrating the divergence of the agential and structuralist positions, those labeled structuralists contend that while such creative appropriation certainly does take place, it often does nothing to subvert the ideological meanings inscribed on corporate constructions. When children appropriate toys and media productions, they often make meanings that subvert ideological inscriptions, while at other times their appropriations operate to validate the status quo. Such appropriations are complex and must be studied on a case-by-case basis. Kinderculture is dedicated to the notion that often the separation of structural and agential interpretations creates a false binarism. Indeed, in every situation we study (see Joe Kincheloe's 2002 *Sign of the Burger: McDonald's and the Culture of Power* for an expansion of these ideas) we discern both structural and agential dimensions at work. A child, like an adult, can concurrently be exploited and possess agency. Whenever individuals deal with hegemonic and ideological productions, they deal with these competing dynamics (Cook, 2004; Mason & Steadman, 1997; Ottosen, 2003).

As in any sociopolitical situation with the potential for hegemonic and ideological exploitation, one can learn to be more sensitive to the ways exploitation takes place while developing strategies for avoiding it. And, as in any pedagogical situation, we can develop these strategies on their own or, in a Vygotskian sense, in cooperation with teachers who provide a new zone of proximal development that allows for a deeper understanding of the way power operates. This, of course, is the basis of critical media literacy of kinderculture (Steinberg, 2007).

David Buckingham (2003) dismissed the value of structuralist concerns with exploitation and argues that pedagogies of empowerment such as an understanding of kinderculture have "increasingly been seen to amount to little more than rhetoric." By denying the possibility of a media literacy of power, Buckingham lapsed into a pedagogy of nihilism that provides need for scholarly activity in the area of children's culture. Power and exploitation are erased in Buckingham's articulation, and any effort to alert children to the ways the social, cultural, political, and economic domains operate to harm both them and other individuals is represented as a misguided form of "salvationism." Buckingham equated this so-called salvationism with right-wing attempts to protect childhood innocence via forms of censorship and moralistic regulation.

Most discussions between the agential and structuralist positions in the new paradigm of child studies should be this contentious. It is important to specify kinderculture's location in this conceptual matrix. The notion of kinderculture represents the critical theoretical new paradigm in childhood studies and childhood education. Criticality indicates a concern with power structures and their influence in everyday life. In the case of contemporary children, the sociopolitical and economic structures shaped by corporate power buoyed by the logic of capital as well as patriarchal structures, with their oppressive positioning of women and children, are central concerns of the critical paradigm (Garey & Arendell, 1999; Scott, 2002). Using the production of pleasure as its ultimate weapon, "the corporate children's consumer culture labeled kinderculture commodifies cultural objects and turns them into things to purchase rather than objects to contemplate. Kinderculture is subversive but challenges authority in its effort to maintain, rather than transform, the status quo. It appeals to the agential child and agential child advocates as it offers children identities that Jane Kenway and Elizabeth Bullen (2001) labelled as autonomous, rational, and hedonistic.

Kinderculture is produced by ingenious marketers who possess profound insights into the lives, desires, and cultural context of contemporary children. Such marketers know how to cultivate intense affect among children and use such emotion to elicit particular consumptive and, in turn, ideological reactions.

A key dimension of this consumptive-ideological dimension of kinderculture involves the marketers' understanding that children, particularly middle-class children, are especially interested in TV; movies, Internet, toys, and even foods (Kincheloe, 2002) that transgress parental norms of "good taste," social status, and educational development. This ideology of opposition is central in many cases to what separates contemporary children from their parents and other adults. Such oppositionality operates to subvert the bourgeois educational project of modernity—rational child development based on the achievement of universal stages of reason reflecting adult behavior and ways of being. As it commodifies and lures children into this oppositional conspiracy, it meshes consumption, education, information, knowledge, cultural capital, emotional bonding, entertainment, and advertising (Hengst, 2001; Kenway & Bullen, 2001; Steinberg, 2007). As an advocate of the critical new paradigm of childhood studies, I argue that kinderculture can no longer be ignored in the effort to understand the social, psychological, and educational dimensions of children. Corporate children's culture has replaced schooling as the producer of the central curriculum of childhood.

Is Childhood in Crisis?

Changing economic realities coupled with children's access to information about the adult world have drastically changed childhood. Recent writing about childhood in both the popular and scholarly presses speaks of the lost childhood, children growing up too fast, and fragmented homes. Images of mothers killing children, babysitters torturing infants, kids pushing kids out of 14-story windows, and trick-or-treat razor blades in apples saturate the contemporary conversation about children. Popular culture/kinderculture provides haunting images of this crisis of childhood that terrify and engage our worst fears. The film *Halloween*, for example, is at one level a story of the post-modern childhood-fear in isolation. The isolation referenced here involves separation from both absent parents and a nonexistent community. No one is there to help; on the once-festive Halloween night, children are not present.

Even in "safe" suburbia, the community has fragmented to the point that the safety of children trick-or-treating cannot be guaranteed (Ferguson, 1994; Paul, 1994). The crisis of contemporary childhood can be signified in many ways, all of which involve at some level the horror of danger faced in solitude.

This crisis of childhood is part imagination, part reality. While children are vulnerable to social ills and the manipulations of unscrupulous adults and power-wielders, there is a degree of moral panic and general hyperbole in the view that children are facing threats from predators unlike anything they have experienced in the historical past. While certainly not dismissing everyday threats to childhood in the twenty-first century, we should be careful not to let hysterics from diverse ideological perspectives paint a fear-driven portrait of the social landscape. A balanced view would demand that we position the crisis of childhood within the twenty-first-century social, cultural, and economic context. There is no doubt that childhood in Western societies is affected by the decline of industrialized economic arrangements.

In such industrialized societies labor was the most important social force for social integration. In a post-industrial condition people make life meanings outside the boundaries of their work lives. The labor process in this new context plays less and less of a role in shaping identity and constructing life experiences. As industrial jobs that lasted a lifetime with pensions and social benefits decline, more women have entered the workforce. More mothers have sought work outside the home, subsequently placing more pressure on their partners or babysitters to participate in child-rearing activities. In such contexts children learn to cope with busy and often preoccupied parents. Consequently, they become more self-reliant than children from previous generations earlier in the twentieth century.

The changing role of women profoundly changes the role of children in contemporary Western societies. Even though women work outside the home, this does not lead to an equal sharing of domestic work: women work both in the home and out of the home (Du Bois-Reymond, Suenker, & Kruger, 2001). Increasing numbers of single poor women combine both paid labor and childcare without the help of a partner and with little or no assistance from the state. Without economic or social support, women and children in these categories have experienced increasingly harsh conditions and no hope for upward mobility. For middle- and upper-middle-class children, these social, economic, and cultural trends have sometimes provided them more independence and influence in the family. In lower socioeconomic circumstances, the trends exacerbate the effects of poverty and sometimes lead to more neglect and alienation.

In many middle- and lower-class homes, these larger socioeconomic trends operate to make children *more useful* than they had been throughout much of the twentieth century. As women become embedded in the workplace, traditional role expectations continue to erode. In order to adjust to these modified familial relationships, children and youth have taken on more responsibilities for caring not just for themselves but for their parents as well. Studies (Hengst, 2001) illustrate that children buy the family food. Indeed, the home appliance industry, understanding this trend, is directing more and more of its advertising budget toward children and youth magazines. Industry demographics tell them that a growing segment of those who buy food, microwaves, and other kitchen appliances are youth (Du Bois-Reymond, Suenker, & Kruger, 2001). This represents a profound change in the way children are positioned in the social order and it holds dramatic implications for the education of children. As age boundaries blur, age becomes less important in shaping human abilities and role expectations; the crisis of childhood becomes the crisis of education. Children emerging in the new social conditions no longer reflect the expectations for childhood embedded in the structures and organization of schools. *New children* who experience more adult-like roles in other phases of their lives may not react positively to being treated like "children" in the classroom. Teachers voice complaints about children who talk like adults and have little or no respect for their demands. What teachers sometimes perceive as impudence and a lack of respect is often a reflection of independent, self-sufficient children reacting to forms of regulation that they experience in no other aspect of their lives. This redirection of anger with adults is found in many media representations of children and youth. A savvy kid is often in complete control of not only her or his own destiny but that of a family or possibly the school or entire community. The knowing *kinderculturated* kid of the new millennium balances complexity as the naive being promoted by caregivers and teachers, and as the in-control leader of the tacit life of a kid in today's society.

In this changing social context many scholars (Casas, 1998; Hengst, 2001) are making the argument that children are far more cognitively capable than traditionally maintained by developmental psychology. The world of technology and media, along with these changing notions of the social role of the child, has expanded what Lev Vygotsky referred to as the ZPD (zone of proximal development: the context that facilitates the learning process of contemporary children). In the ZPD, individuals learn to take part in social and cultural activities that catalyze their intellectual development. In the media-created electronic ZPD, with its social media, TV, computers, video games, Internet, popular music, and virtual realities, children learn to use the tools of culture (language, mathematics, reasoning, etc.) effortlessly (Fu, 2003).

When sociologists, psychologists, and cultural scholars examine what children and youth are able to construct employing the symbols and tools of mediated culture, it is clear how sophisticated and intellectually advanced children's abilities can become in this new ZPD. Kinderculture has quickly become a new culture of childhood learning. The space within which many contemporary children play is the same domain in which their parents work. Children access national and international information networks using the same tools as their parents. In this domain of learning, many children free themselves from the educational project of modern Western societies; they are not learning by preplanned program lesson plans taught by deskilled teachers.

Childhood is perceived in crisis because it resembles no thing most people have ever seen before. The corporate production of popular kinderculture and its impact on children is serious. The discussion falls under cultural pedagogy, which refers to the idea that education takes place in a variety of social sites including but not limited to schooling. Pedagogical sites are those places where power is organized and deployed including music, social networking, TV, movies, newspapers, magazines, toys, advertisements, video games, comics, sports, etc. This work demands that we examine both school and cultural pedagogy if we are to make sense of the educational process (Giroux, 1994). Operating on the assumption that profound learning changes one's identity, we see the pedagogical process as one that engages our desire, captures our imagination, and constructs our consciousness. The emergence of cultural studies (Grossberg, 1995) has facilitated our effort to examine the cultural practices through which individuals come to understand themselves and the world that surrounds them (Steinberg, 2007). Supported by the insights of cultural studies, we are better equipped to examine the effects of cultural pedagogy, with its identity formation and its production and legitimation of knowledge: the cultural curriculum (Kasturi, 2002).

The organizations that create this cultural curriculum are not educational agencies but rather commercial concerns that operate not for the social good but for individual gain. Cultural pedagogy is structured by commercial dynamics, forces that impose themselves into all aspects of our own and our children's private lives (Giroux, 1994). Patterns of consumption shaped by corporate advertising empower commercial institutions as the teachers of the contemporary era. Corporate cultural pedagogy has produced educational forms that are wildly successful when judged on the basis of their capitalist intent. Replacing traditional classroom lectures and seatwork with magic kingdoms, animated fantasies, interactive video games, virtual realities, kickboxing TV heroes, action figures (complete with their own recorded "history"), and an entire array of entertainment forms produced ostensibly for adults but eagerly consumed by children, corporate America has helped rev-olutionize childhood. Using fantasy and desire, corporate functionaries have created a perspective on the world that melds with business ideologies and free-market values. The worldviews produced by corporate advertisers to some degree always let children know that the most exciting things life can provide are produced by their friends in corporate America.

We have become seasoned in the corporate interventions by brands like Pizza Hut (reading program), McDonald's (A students), and Nike (most school sports teams). It is also a time when publishing companies create cur-ricula for students, with little or no educational or academic input. New curricula is a reflection of the agenda created by McGraw-Hill in the 1990s. Pearson Publishing redesigned the New York State primary curriculum in the early 2002, without one academic or schoolteacher on the design team. In less than a decade, Pearson now has complete economic access to the Common Core through texts and tests created to meet the Pearson cur-riculum. Up until this point, Disney has always had a hegemonic hold on children's culture through the participation of both families and teachers. It has never been unusual to walk into a primary school, really anywhere in the world, and spy bulletin boards, reading charts, and classroom assignment ledgers thematically displayed by Mickey, Donald, or a princess. In schools that claim a diverse and multicultural view, one will see representations of *Mulan*, *Pocahontas*, and *Aladdin* proclaiming that "It's a small world after all." Disney has recently taken the grandiose step of creating *Disney English Schools*. Disney claims an expertise in English, as it has been writing chil-dren's books for more than three-quarters of a century. These "qualifications" opened a market in Asia for English-language teaching. Disney English is a billion-dollar enterprise that has blurred the boundaries of education and corporate book-making.

One of the most profound events of the last century in world history in general and certainly in the history of childhood involves the successful commodification of childhood. Not only did corporate marketers open a new market but they helped generate a body of meanings, cultural practices, and ideological understandings that continues to shape our world and children around the planet (Cook, 2004). By gaining access to children, advertisers found out early in the twentieth century not only that they could induce children to buy more but that they could get children to nag their parents to consume more (Spigel, 1998). Though many argue to the contrary, it seems increasingly obvious that a large percentage of children and young people in the twenty-first century are enthusiastic participants in consumer society. In recent polls they express the belief that having more money would most improve their lives. Concurrently, they express great faith in the American economic system. Increasing numbers of children and young people own more than one credit card, and many own stocks. It is not uncommon for a 10-year-old to find a pre-paid Visa or Master Card in a gift card.

Corporate power wielders have worked hard to win such perspectives and orientations among the young. Indeed consumer capitalism has succeeded in ways unimagined by previous advocates, as more and more children and young people come to hold the values and ideological dispositions that serve the best interests of corporate leaders (Allen, 2003; Spigel, 1998). In an interesting and insidious way, the marketers and children enter into an unspoken alliance that helps children escape both the control and the educational-developmental agenda of middle- and upper-middle-class parents. Social media and technology help create a personal, secluded domain for children free from direct parental regulation. Of course, many parents find such independence frightening, and many understandably worry about children becoming targets for advertising and marketing. While many concerned individuals have expressed anxiety over what they thought was corporate advertising's violation of the social contract protecting the sanctity of childhood, others such as David Buckingham (2003) have argued that such fears are overblown. Children, Buckingham maintains, possess the ability to discern advertising strategies early in their lives and can thus protect themselves from corporate exploitation. Moreover, Buckingham posits, there is no evidence that indicates that advertising makes children more materialistic than they would have been otherwise. In an empirical research context Buckingham's assertion is a safe one. Since no one knows how children would have been otherwise, it is empirically impossible to prove such an assertion either true or false. I could not disagree more.

The arguments I make for kinderculture maintain that it is our parental, civic, and professional responsibility to study the corporate curriculum and its social and political effects. Indeed, we maintain that as parents, citizens, and teachers we must hold corporations accountable for the pedagogical features of their activities, for the kinderculture they produce. We must intervene in the cozy relationship between popular culture and pedagogy that shapes our identities. In the interest of both our children and the larger society, we must exercise our personal and collective power to transform the variety of ways corporate power (gained via its access to media) oppresses and dominates us.

We must cultivate an awareness of the ways cultural pedagogy operates so that we can scold when appropriate and rewrite popular texts when the opportunity presents itself. Kinderculture is primarily a pedagogy of pleasure, and as such it cannot be countered merely by ostracizing ourselves and our children from it. Strategies of resistance must be formulated that understand the relationship between pedagogy, knowledge production, identity formation, and desire. In this chapter, I attempt to open a public conversation about the effect of kinderculture as the central curriculum of contemporary childhood.

Culturally Studying Kinderculture

Questions concerning kinderculture and its relationship to cultural pedagogy can be clarified and discussed within the academic field of cultural studies. Kinderculture resides at the intersection of educational childhood studies and cultural studies. Attempts to define cultural studies are delicate operations in that the field has consciously operated in a manner that avoids traditional academic disciplinary definitions. Nevertheless, cultural studies has something to do with the effort to produce an interdisciplinary (or counterdisciplinary) way of studying, interpreting, and often evaluating cultural practices in historical, social, and theoretical contexts. Refusing to equate "culture" with high culture, cultural studies attempts to examine the diversity of a society's artistic, institutional, and communicative expressions and practices. Because it examines cultural expressions ignored by the traditional social sciences, cultural studies is often equated with the study of popular culture. Such an equation is misleading; while popular culture is addressed by cultural studies, it is not the exclusive concern. Indeed, the interests of cultural studies are much broader, including the "rules" of academic study itself: the discursive practices (tacit regulations that define what can and cannot be said, who speaks and who must listen, and whose constructions of reality are valid and whose are unlearned and unimportant) that guide scholarly endeavor.

Thus, cultural studies holds exciting possibilities for new ways of studying education: specifically childhood education, with its attention to the discursive dynamics of the field. How do children embody kinderculture? How do the power dynamics embedded in kinderculture produce pleasure and pain in the daily lives of children? How do critically grounded parents, teachers, child psychologists, and childhood professionals in general gain a view of children that accounts for the effects of popular culture in their self-images and worldviews?

Such questions open new domains of analysis in childhood studies, as they seek out previously marginalized voices and the vantage points they bring to both the scholarly and practitioner-based conversation (Grossberg, 1995; Nelson, Treichler, & Grossberg, 1992). While we are enthused by the benefits of cultural studies of childhood, we are simultaneously critical of expressions of elitism within the discourse of cultural studies itself—a recognition made more disturbing by cultural studies' claim to the moral high ground of a politics of inclusivity. Unfortunately, the study of children has traditionally been regarded as a low-status exercise in the culture of academia. The field of cultural studies has reproduced this power/status dynamic in its neglect of childhood study. Indeed, few students of cultural studies have targeted children as the subjects of their scholarship. *Kinderculture* attempts to address this absence and promote new literature and research focus.

Popular Culture as a Serious Discipline

The study of traditional forms of kinderculture, for instance fairy tales, has granted scholars insights into hard-to-reach domains of child consciousness. Moreover, the more disturbing and violent the fairy tale, some would argue, the more insight into the "primitive" feelings that arise and shape us in early childhood and, in turn, in adulthood. The connection between kinderculture and childhood desires and feelings blows the rational cultural fuse, thus connecting adults to childrens' *lebenswelt* and granting them better access to childhood perceptions (Paul, 1994). Not only does the study of children's popular culture grant insights into childhood consciousness; it also provides new pictures of culture in general. Kinderculture, in this context, inadvertently reveals at a very basic level what is disturbing us in our everyday lives, what irritants reside at the level of our individual and collective subconsciousness.

Exposing Power

My objective is to promote understandings of kinderculture that lead to smart and democratic pedagogies for childhood at the cultural, familial, and school levels. Cultural studies connected to a democratic pedagogy for children involves investigations of how children's consciousness is produced around issues of cultural expectations for children, social justice, and egalitarian power relations. An analysis must focus on exposing the footprints of power left by the corporate producers of kinderculture and their effects on the psyches of our children. Appreciating the ambiguity and complexity of power, our democratic pedagogy for children is committed to challenging ideologically manipulative and racist, sexist, and class-biased entertainment for children. It is equally opposed to other manifestations of kinderculture that promote violence and social and psychological pathologies. Children's entertainment, like other social spheres, is a contested public space where different social, economic, and political interests compete for control.

Unfortunately, many are uncomfortable with overt discussions of power. Such unease allows power wielders to hide in the recesses of the cultural and political landscape all the while shaping cultural expression and public policy in their own interests—interests that may conflict with those of less powerful social groups such as children. We are not good students of power. All too often references to power are vague to the point of meaninglessness in the worst literature produced by critical scholars. For the purpose of clarification, when we refer to power-wielders, we are not merely referencing a social class or a category of human beings. Picking up on John Fiske's (1993) use of the term, *power bloc*, we are referring to particular social formations designated by race, class, gender, and ethnicity that hold special access to various resources (e.g., money, information, cultural capital, media, etc.) that can be used for economic or political gain. Power, as we use the term, involves a panoply of operations that work to maintain the status quo and keep it running with as little friction (social conflict) as possible.

It is beneficial to those individuals and groups that profit most from existing power relations to protect them from pests like us. When studying this power bloc, we employ Fiske's (1993) notion that it can be better understood by "what it does than what it is" (p. 11). Our use of the concept of the power bloc in the production of kinderculture is not meant to imply some conspiracy of diabolical corporate and political kingpins churning out material to harm our children. Rather, our notion of the power bloc revolves around alliances of interests that may never involve individual relationships between representatives of the interests or organizations in question. Power bloc alliances, we believe, are often temporary, coming together around particular issues but falling apart when the issue is no longer pertinent. Those who perceive power to be a complex issue will encounter little disagreement from us. Power and power bloc alliances are nothing if not complex and ambiguous. But because of the power bloc's contradictions and ephemerality, it is never able to dominate in some incontestable manner. Along the lines of its contradictions may exist points of contestation that open possibilities of democratic change. Larry Grossberg (1995) contended that since power never gets all it wants, there are always opportunities to challenge its authority. In this context we begin our study of the corporate production of kinderculture, analyzing the ways power represses the production of democratic artifacts and produces pleasure for children. If power was always expressed by *just saying no* to children's desires, it would gain little authority in their eyes.

The power of Disney, Microsoft, Apple, Dreamworks, Pixar, and McDonald's is never greater than when it produces pleasure among consumers. Recent cultural studies of consumption link it to the identity formation of the consumer (Kincheloe, 2002; Warde, 1994), meaning that to some degree we are what we consume. Status in one's subculture, individual creations of style, knowledge of cultural texts, role in the community of consumers, emulation of fictional characters, and internalization of values promoted by popular cultural expressions all contribute to our personal identities. Popular culture provides children with intense emotional experiences often unmatched in any other phase of their lives. It is not surprising that such energy and intensity exert powerful influences on self-definition, on the ways children choose to organize their lives. Obviously, power mixed with desire produces an explosive cocktail; the colonization of desire, however, is not the end of the story. Power enfolds into consciousness and unconsciousness in a way that evokes desire, no doubt, but also guilt and anxiety. The intensity of the guilt and anxiety a child may experience as a result of her brush with power is inseparable from the cultural context in which she lives. Desire in many cases may take a back seat to the repression of desire in the construction of child consciousness/unconsciousness and the production of identity (Donald, 1993). The cocktail's effects may be longer-lasting than first assumed, as expression of the repression may reveal itself in bizarre and unpredictable ways. To make this observation about the relationship among power, desire, and the way that the repression of desire expresses itself at the psychological level is not to deny human agency (self-direction). While the power bloc has successfully commodified kinderculture, both adults and children can successfully deflect its repressive elements. The role of the critical childhood professional involves helping children develop what Fiske (1993) calls the affective moments of power evasion. Using their abilities to re-read Disney films along fault lines of gender or to re-encode Barbie and Ken in a satirical mode, children take their first steps toward self-assertion and power

resistance. Such affective moments of power evasion certainly do not constitute the ultimate expression of resistance, but they do provide a space around
which more significant forms of critical consciousness and civic action can
be developed (Steinberg, 2007).

Critical Literacies

The information explosion—the media saturation of contemporary Western
societies, with its access to private realms of human consciousness—has created a social vertigo. This social condition, labeled by Baudrillard as hyperreality, exaggerates the importance of power wielders in all phases of human
experience. Hyperreality's flood of signifiers in everything from megabytes to
TV advertising diminishes our ability to either find meaning or engender passion for commitment. With so much power-generated information bombard-
ing our senses, adults and children lose the faith that we can make sense of
anything (for an expansion of these themes, see Kincheloe, 1995). Thus, the
existence of hyperreality forces us to rethink our conversation about literacy.
Children, who have been educated by popular culture, approach literacy from
a very different angle. Media literacy becomes not some rarefied add-on to a
traditional curriculum but a basic skill necessary to negotiating one's identity,
values, and well-being in power-soaked hyperreality. In many schools such
ideas have never been considered, not to mention seriously discussed. Media
literacy, like power, is not viewed in mainstream circles as a topic for children
(or even adults). The same educators who reject the study of media literacy or
kinderculture are the ones who have to cope with its effects.

As I contend in *Media Literacy: A Reader* (Steinberg, 2007), a critical
understanding of media culture requires students not simply to develop the
ability to interpret media meanings but to understand the ways they consume
and affectively invest in media. Such an attempt encourages both critical
thinking and self-analysis, as students begin to realize that everyday decisions
are not necessarily made freely and rationally. Rather, they are encoded and
inscribed by emotional and bodily commitments relating to the production
of desire and mood, all of which leads, in Noam Chomsky's famous phrase, to
the "manufacture of consent." These are complex pedagogical and ideological
issues, and they demand rigorous skills of questioning, analyzing, interpreting,
and meaning-making. Contrary to the decontextualized pronouncements of
developmental psychology, relatively young children are capable of engaging
in these cognitive activities (Nations, 2001). Of course, in the contemporary

right-wing, test-driven educational context, such abilities are not emphasized, as memorization for standards tests becomes more and more the order of the school day.

The political dimension of our critical pedagogy of childhood requires developing and teaching this media literacy. Such a literacy respects children's intellectual ability to deal with the complexities of power, oppression, and exploitation, as it refuses to position them as innocent, passive, and helpless victims. In an era when children can instantaneously access diverse types of information, they need the ability to traverse this knowledge terrain in savvy and well-informed ways. A critical pedagogy of childhood finds this approach much more helpful than pietistic right-wing efforts to censor potentially offensive data from innocent childhood eyes. In their effort to perpetuate the discourse of childhood innocence, right-wing child advocates maintain a positivist developmentalist view that media literacy is irrelevant because children do not have the intellectual and emotional maturity to understand TV advertising or subtle marketing appeals (Cassell & Jenkins, 2002). As much as the advocates of childhood innocence might wish for it, children in the twenty-first century are not going to return to the mythical secret garden of innocence. For better and worse children now live in a wider, information-saturated adult world. I believe that the best thing we can do in this circumstance is to prepare children to cope with it, make sense of it, and participate in it in ways that benefit everyone (Vieira, 2001).

Ideas expressed in this chapter originate from research stemming from all three editions of *Kinderculture: The Corporate Construction of Childhood*.

References

Allen, D. (2003). *Is childhood disappearing?* Paper presented at the International Social Theory Consortium Second Annual Conference at Sussex University, England.

Buckingham, D. (2003). *Media education, literacy learning, and contemporary culture*. London, England: Polity Press.

Cannella, G. (1997). *Deconstructing early childhood education: Social justice and revolution*. New York, NY: Peter Lang.

Cannella, G. (2002). Global perspectives, cultural studies, and the construction of a postmodern childhood studies. In G. Cannella & J. L. Kincheloe (Eds.), *Kidworld: Childhood studies, global perspectives, and education*. New York, NY: Peter Lang.

Cannella, G., & Kincheloe, J. L. (Eds.). (2002). *Kidworld: Childhood studies, global perspectives, and education*. New York, NY: Peter Lang.

Cassell, J., & Jenkins, H. (2002). Proper playthings: The politics of play in children. Retrieved from http://www.web.media.mit.edu/~andrew_s/andrew_sempere_2002_politics_of_play.pdf

Cook, D. (2004). *The commodification of childhood: The children's clothing industry and the rise of the child consumer.* Durham, NC: Duke University Press.

Donald, J. (1993). The natural man and the virtuous woman: Reproducing citizens. In C. Jenks (Ed.), *Cultural reproduction.* New York, NY: Routledge.

Du Bois-Reymond, M., Suenker, H., & Kruger, H. (Eds.). (2001). *Childhood in Europe.* New York, NY: Peter Lang.

Ferguson, S. (1994, July/August). The comfort of being sad. *Utne Reader, 64,* 60–61.

Fiske, J. (1993). *Power plays, power works.* New York, NY: Verso.

Garey, A., & Arendell, T. (1999). Children, work, and family: Some thoughts on "mother blame" (Working Paper No. 4). Retrieved from https://workfamily.sas.upenn.edu/sites/workfamily.sas.upenn.edu/files/imported/new/berkeley/papers/4.pdf

Giroux, H. (1994). *Disturbing pleasures: Learning popular culture.* New York, NY: Routledge.

Grossberg, L. (1995). What's in a name (one more time). *Taboo: The Journal of Culture and Education, 1,* Fall, 11–37.

Hammer, R., & Kellner, D. (Eds.). (2009). *Media/cultural studies: Critical approaches.* New York, NY: Peter Lang.

Hengst, H. (2001). Rethinking the liquidation of childhood. In M. Du Bois-Reymond, H. Suenker, & H. Kruger. *Childhood in Europe.* New York, NY: Peter Lang.

Kasturi, S. (2002). Constructing childhood in a corporate world: Cultural studies, childhood, and Disney. In G. Cannella & J. L. Kincheloe (Eds.), *Kidworld: Childhood studies, global perspectives and education.* New York, NY: Peter Lang.

Kellner, D. (1990). *Television and the crisis of democracy.* Boulder, CO: Westview Press.

Kellner, D. (1992). Popular culture and the construction of postmodern identities. In S. Lash & J. Friedman (Eds.), *Modernity and Identity.* Cambridge, MA: Blackwell.

Kenway, J., & Bullen, E. (2001). *Consuming children: Entertainment, advertising, and education.* Philadelphia, PA: Open University Press.

Kincheloe, J. L. (2002). *The sign of the burger: McDonald's and the culture of power.* Philadelphia, PA: Temple University Press.

Kincheloe, J. L. (2003). *Teachers as researchers: Qualitative paths to empowerment* (2nd ed.). London, England: Falmer Press.

Lipsky, D., & Abrams, A. (1994). *Late bloomers.* New York, NY: Times Books.

Mason, J., & Steadman, B. (1997). The significance of the conceptualisation of childhood for child protection policy. *Family Matters, 46,* 31–36.

McLaren, P., Hammer, R., Sholle, D., & Reilly, S. (1995). *Rethinking media literacy: A critical pedagogy of representation.* New York, NY: Peter Lang.

Nations, C. (2001). How long do our children have to wait? Understanding the children of the twenty-first century. Retrieved from http://pt3.nmsu.edu/edu621/cynthia 2001.html

Nelson, C., Treichler, P., & Grossberg, L. (1992). (Eds.), *Cultural studies.* New York, NY: Routledge.

Ottosen, M. (2003). *Children as social actors: A critical comment.* Paper presented at the Danish Sociology Conference, Aalborg, Denmark.

Polakow, V. (1992). *The erosion of childhood.* Chicago, IL: University of Chicago Press.

Postman, N. (1994). *The disappearance of childhood.* New York, NY: Vintage Books.

Scott, D. (2002). What are Beanie Babies teaching our children? In G. Cannella & J. L. Kincheloe (Eds.), *Kidworld: Childhood studies, global perspectives, and education.* New York, NY: Peter Lang.

Spigel, L. (1998). Seducing the innocent: Childhood and television in postwar America. In H. Jenkins (Ed.), *The children's culture reader.* New York, NY: New York University Press.

Steinberg, S. R. (2001). *Multi/intercultural conversations.* New York, NY: Peter Lang.

Steinberg, S. R. (2007a). Introduction. In D. Macedo & S. R. Steinberg (Eds.), *Media literacy: A reader.* New York, NY: Peter Lang.

Steinberg, S. R. (2007b). Reading media critically. In D. Macedo & S. R. Steinberg (Eds.), *Media literacy: A reader.* New York, NY: Peter Lang.

Steinberg, S. R. (2010a). *19 urban questions: Teaching in the city.* New York, NY: Peter Lang.

Steinberg, S. R. (2010b). Not the real thing: A history of Hollywood's TV families. In M. Marsh & T. Turner-Vorbeck (Eds.), *Learning to listen to families in schools.* New York, NY: Teachers College Press.

Steinberg, S. R. (2011). (Ed.). *Kinderculture: The corporate construction of childhood, 3rd edition.* Boulder, CO: Westview Press.

Steinberg, S. R., &. Kincheloe, J. (1997). *Kinderculture: The corporate construction of childhood.* Boulder, CO: Westview Press.

Steinberg, S. R., & Kincheloe, J. L. (2004). *Kinderculture: The corporate construction of childhood 2nd Edition.* Boulder, CO: Westview Press.

Warde, A. (1994). Consumers, identity, and belonging: Reflections on some theses of Zygmunt Bauman. In R. Keat, N. Whiteley, & N. Abercrombie (Eds.), *The authority of the consumer.* New York, NY: Routledge.

Wartenberg, T. (1992). Situated social power. In T. Wartenberg (Ed.), *Rethinking power.* Albany, NY: State University of New York Press.

· 2 ·

CIPHER5 AS METHOD

Aesthetic Education, Critical Youth Studies Research, and Emancipation

Michael B. MacDonald

Aesthetic education, wrote Gayatri Spivak (2012), is the preparation of imagination for epistemological work. I understand this as a potentially limitless archeology and genealogy (Foucault, 1994) of singularities (Rancière, 1991) formed at the crossroads of perception, signification, art technique, power (culture, institutions, politics), creativity/innovation, self, subject, and community. This very dense knot provides a one-sentence manifesto for arts educators willing to take up the epistemological and pedagogical challenges of aesthetic systems. And nowhere is this more necessary than in schools.

For complex historical reasons aesthetic engagement—engagement with sensuous knowledge—does not appear on most teaching and learning agendas. Pioneering critical aesthetics educator Maxine Greene (1988) complained that:

> I did not see this kind of passion in looking at young people from my adult vantage point. What I observed among adolescents was a pervasive sense of not-caring ... I could find little enthusiasm for motivating students to engage in academic studies with little more relevance than the game of trivial pursuit. (p. 25)

Arts educators are not alone in this, but if *we* cannot get engagement in sensory knowledge figured out—in disciplines with aesthetics at the center—why should we expect success anywhere else?

Aesthetic experience is not limited to artistic practice. It is a facet of general knowledge about the world and has been afforded a place of philosophical importance since ancient times. Epicurus, for instance, placed sensory experience at the center of epistemology (Gordon & Suits, 2003; Klein, 2012). But as Foucault (2005) pointed out, this lineage has been overshadowed by Platonic and idealist notions of aesthetics as *concepts* and *ideas*. The sensory/empirical/material is almost always played down for the spiritual/metaphysical/idealist or since Kant, Descartes, and Bacon, in the name of *Reason* (Kincheloe, 2005). Building upon the Epicurean line I wish to take another starting point, one that places the study of sensory knowledge at the center of a critical pedagogy of aesthetics. This move returns *aesthetic education* to its ancient place as foundational knowledge (with literacy and numeracy). A critical pedagogy of aesthetics is the study of the production and transmission of oral, aural, and visual sign systems and the role they play in complex knowledge production that informs all registers of the human experience. As Greene (cited in Stinson, 1998) noted:

> Of course we need to introduce students to the symbol systems associated with the various arts, but we want to do so (or so I believe) to enhance their capacity to see, to hear, to read, and to imagine—not simply to conceptualize, or to join the great conversation going on over time. (p. 227)

Aesthetic education is distinct from the study of the history of specific arts practices and training in those expressive practices. It is "to help people to attend, to notice, to enter the particular state of consciousness that is aesthetic perception" (Greene, cited in Stinson, 1998, p. 224), to support the development of a rich and increasingly complex awareness of self. Aesthetic education is conscientization of both the sensory experiences and their attendant processes of signification that form systems of meaning and value I call *aesthetic systems* (MacDonald, 2014b).

But there is little space for students to engage in this type of learning. Aesthetic education is often reduced to arts training and aesthetics equated with art appreciation (Blumenfeld-Jones, 2012, p. 42; MacDonald, 2012; 2014a). Most alarming is that the consciousness that Greene and others worry after, what Michel Foucault called "the self," is left unattended. Perhaps it is unsurprising that students are disassociated from classrooms that "anesthetize learning,"[1] their bodies numbed by learning that excludes sense experience. Students are disciplined by a discourse of knowledge that ignores the development of techniques of body/sense attention. The consequence is a missed opportunity for youth to learn to understand the role of sensuous knowledge in their physical, affective, emotional, and intellectual development and to evaluate the impact of complex processes of signification that connect sensations to meanings, and meaning to value(s). Youth and teachers alike are instructed to silence their bodies (hooks, 1994, p. 113). Should it then surprise educators that students, after being implicitly or explicitly told to ignore the most obvious knowledge tool, wonder why they are attending school at all?

Anesthetized learning is education numbed to sensuous knowledge. It is learning that ignores affect in any form, be it excitement, tension, passion, frustration, or libidinal energies, let alone recognize the senses and sensory signification as a form of knowledge. Learning numbed to sensuous knowledge ignores a full spectrum of lived experience and misses an opportunity to engage with a range of theories of knowledge formation. But recognizing a current state of numbness is not the same as un-numbing. We need to find methods to undo the pervasive educational anesthetic being injected into student's imaginations at epidemic levels. Aesthetic education is the best way to resist an-aesthetic learning; learning that attends to the body-in-community as a central location for knowledge creation.

This chapter introduces Cipher5 as one method for researching aesthetic learning developed as part of an ongoing community research project on Hip Hop Kulture in Edmonton, Alberta, Canada. In other publications on Cipher5 I have discussed the content of Hip Hop learning (MacDonald, 2012), a microhistories approach to Hip Hop history (MacDonald, 2014c), as an example of aesthetic systems theory (MacDonald 2014b), and more generally as a cultural studies of aesthetics for critical youth studies (MacDonald, 2014a). In this chapter I will illustrate how Cipher5 expanded from an action research method for aesthetic research to an experimental community classroom.

Cultural Studies of Aesthetic Systems

So far I have used definitions of aesthetics focused on the Greek notion "sense perception or sensation" (Blumenfeld-Jones, 2012, p. 43). But this is not the only game in town. In fact, as Theodor Adorno (1984) and more recently Jacques Rancière have pointed out, the discourse of aesthetics is a political terrain. *Aesthetics*—not the study of signification but the word itself—becomes signified as a set of characteristics of expressive practices, the possession of decorous objects, and a branch of philosophy that studies art. Cultural studies of aesthetics (MacDonald, 2012; 2014a; 2014b; 2014c) must therefore begin with a meta-analysis or deconstruction of the term aesthetics, not to illustrate its lack of meaning but its excess of meanings that leads to confusion.

In popular usage the phrase "the aesthetic characteristics of" is so common that it seems unnecessary or perhaps unnatural to think deeply about it. It is as if art possessed a set of characteristics that the aesthetic philosopher, often simply called the critic, can enumerate. It is the surface of things except when unlocked by the magical gaze of the critic. The critic is the traditional authority over aesthetics, the individual endowed with the capacity to "see," account for, or at least make visible the aesthetic criteria that make a piece of art meaningful and valuable. It is this special skill that the aesthetic educator "performs" in the front of a classroom that so often leaves mystified students feeling distanced and alienated from aesthetic practice and analysis. In a discussion of the tension between *Aesthetics* and *Cultural Studies* Winfried Fluck (2002) noted that:

> It [cultural studies] breaks down the barrier between high culture and popular or mass culture and says that both—that all cultural practices—are worth studying. What distinguished post-World War II literary studies from philology was that it was based on certain aesthetics norms. Not all works qualified for serious professional consideration, and a crucial, if not *the* crucial, task of the critic was to determine what works were legitimate objects of study. (p. 83)

Aesthetics is tied to hierarchies and value(s) in both cultural and economic senses of the term. Aesthetic education has been used for the establishment and maintenance of cultural hierarchies under the auspices of *arts appreciation*. With the rise of popular music the critic has been replaced by the marketplace. Valuation has shifted from a supposed disinterested determination by an expert critic to valuation determined almost completely on an arts marketplace. Critics in the lineage of Adorno have argued that this shift to the culture industries has had profoundly negative effects. While I am not as willing as many in the Frankfurt School to demonize art business there are some obvious downsides to marketplace history. History of Popular Music textbooks are a catalogue, a collection of successfully marketed products with a historic value determined by their economic success either at the point of creation/release or (as is often the case) by later market valorization as a historically significant product.

The role of the critic and the marketplace are two expressions of the institutional mechanics for the creation of *aesthetic value*. But aesthetic value is not the only social process; people do not engage in aesthetics only as an exchange of value. To use Marxist political economic language there is not only *exchange value* but also *use value*. The use value of aesthetics is its *aesthetic function*.

Aesthetic function is an experience often mistakenly situated inside the work of art:

> The capacity of any system of signification to *draw attention to itself* [emphasis added] as a form of expression and *refers to itself* [emphasis added] as a sign, thus drawing our attention to the organization and patterning principles by which the object is constituted. For this purpose, the object is temporarily depragmatized and dereferentialized ... this temporary bracketing of reference is useful and often gives pleasure, not because it allows us to escape, if only temporarily, from reality but because it opens up the possibility of a new perspective on the object which we have missed in our exclusive concentration on the referential function. (Fluck, 2002, pp. 87–88)

But there are no systems of signification that draw "attention to itself"; there is instead always an aesthetic system composed of dynamic flows of aesthetic resources, aesthetic production, aesthetic labor, and aesthetic value which emerges as a singularity (Foucault; Rancière). The singularity is the *aesthetic experience* (Berleant; Dewey). Unfortunately, Fluck (2002) avoided recognizing the existence of aesthetic knowledge and yet couldn't ignore that "something" occurs. So instead of researching the complexity of aesthetic systems some writers prefer an idealist explanation that the work of art is endowed with special powers that allow "it" to produce affect and in the process of doing "it" establish a special substance (aesthetic) that only critics can make visible. This approach needs to be resisted. The aesthetic function is aesthetic knowledge emerging from the subject-of-aesthetic system relationship. Following Joe Kincheloe's (2005) explanation of Blues aesthetic-knowledge as Blues Epistemology, I suggest that what is required is not a reductivist or reified approach to aesthetic function but instead a more complex critical investigation of aesthetic systems. The result of this approach is the need for a cultural studies of aesthetics framed by aesthetic systems theory. Aesthetic education therefore is not just learning about art but is learning about, and developing an awareness of, the role of the senses and their signification in the production of knowledge as it emerges from flows of aesthetic resources, industrial processes of aesthetic production, the enactment of aesthetic labor, and the creation of aesthetic value.

Aesthetic education takes two roads. Either it is a pedagogy of liberating knowledge production by inviting students to take their place as joint producers of aesthetic knowledge, or, alternatively, and all too regularly, aesthetic education is used to dominate and discipline students' bodies, affect, imaginations and minds by instructing students on how they should, or ought to, understand/signify aesthetic experience.

Aesthetic Systems and the Culture Circle

As bell hooks (1990) noted in *Yearning*, thinking deeply about aesthetics is not limited to philosophers and critics. I was recently reminded of this in conversation with a senior ethnomusicologist at an academic conference. Trying to articulate my interest in aesthetic epistemology I used an example that I thought would be meaningful to him. Drawing from a geographical area he had been studying for more than two decades I asked where I might find a written discussion of a term found in the discourse of culture members. He admitted that although there is plenty written about how the music is made, little to nothing has been written about the system of knowledge that supports the expressive practices. I understand this as an exclusion of aesthetic epistemology that occurs when aesthetic research remains at surface descriptions of practices without attention to knowledge that guides these techniques. The physical motion of dancers, the notes sounded, the paint scratched or spread on medium silences, often unintentionally, a self that is busily carving out a new territory. This new space is *subject-of-aesthetic system*. While the same analytical discussion might suggest that agency is being enacted in the expressive practice, agency is cut down by surface descriptions. Aesthetic research methodology that does not include, in various registers, the voices of creative subjects limits and greatly simplifies knowledge contribution. Of course it is much easier to move towards knowledge reduction; to watch a performance, make a video document of it, make notes about it (even reflexive notes), and pose surface questions of participants. In fact you might resist what I am saying about the silencing of subjects by correctly pointing out that interviews provide an opportunity for creative subjects to voice their epistemological positions. But critical researchers have long been aware that discourse, because of its appearance as the common and the everyday, makes its functioning resistant to easy description *even by participants*. Aesthetic epistemology therefore requires the development of a method of research that provides a space for critical awareness, what might be called the development of cultural meta-analysis. For this I turn to Paulo Freire's (2010) *Culture Circle*.

In *Education for Critical Consciousness* Paulo Freire (2010) discussed the economic changes brought about in Brazil by the forces of rapid industrialization.

Brazilian educators were tasked with bringing literacy to illiterate communities to facilitate participation in industrialization. Freire realized that teaching Portuguese to indigenous communities was not absent of politics, indeed it was a continuation of colonization. Freire overturned the deficit of illiteracy by recognizing the powerful epistemologies embedded in non-literate cultures connected to complex cosmologies and grounded in environmental knowledge, now termed traditional ecological knowledge (TEK). Freire's method, the culture circle, brought community members together to discuss and make community knowledge explicit. To do this he worked with a visual artist to create visual *situations* that would provide a context for conversation. A facilitator brought the situation to the circle and worked with the participants to articulate, to make visible, knowledge of each situation. At the end of these twelve situations, members of the circle began to see that literacy in Portuguese is a social technology used to do work. Instead of being disciplined by a colonial language, formerly non-literate community members became critically multicultural in that they could function within both non-literate and literate epistemological contexts. One might be reminded that according to discourse theory, "discourses fix meaning by excluding all other meaning potentials. Two discourses can collide in an antagonistic relationship to one another when they try to define the same terrain in conflicting ways" (Jorgensen, 2002, p. 190). Freire saw another way. He used the situation of conflicting discourse as a way of making knowable both community and colonial discourse. Instead of one discourse dominating the other, two discourses could be held together in a tension that contributes to developing critical consciousness. Drawing from this awareness, I, along with Andre Hamilton, used a formation from Hip Hop Kulture, the cypher, to see if we could create a Hip Hop culture circle.

Cipher5: Creating a Framework to Make Hip Hop Knowledge Visible

A cypher is a Hip Hop circle in which hiphoppas freestyle or drop writtens (deliver prewritten rhymes) one after the other. Cypher also refers to a circle that forms to share other substances, sometimes marijuana. But cypher can also refer to an engagement with the subconscious in a stream-of consciousness delivery in rhyme. This kind of freestyle flow is often taken as a sign of mastery of the Hip Hop element of emceeing, something I have previously called epistemological flow (MacDonald, 2012). *Cipher*, spelled with an *i*, refers to cryptography and processes of encryption and decryption. In this sense cipher is recognition of the processes of signification and deconstruction that take place. Related to the cryptographic spelling of cipher is our use of the number five, Cipher5. Five refers to knowledge as the fifth element of Hip Hop Kulture after emceeing, graffiti, b-boying/b-girling, and DJing. Cipher5 is a cypher that brings together hiphoppas with students and professional researchers to produce and share knowledge about Hip Hop Kulture. Cipher5 takes place every Tuesday night at 7 p.m. at a local café. We have an arrangement with the café owner where we can organize chairs in a circle and make use of the sound system, projector, and computer for sharing videos, songs, and other online content related to Hip Hop Kulture.

As implied by the name and built on Freire's use of "situations" in the culture circle, Cipher5 works to make Hip Hop knowledge visible to members. I am using visibility in the sense that Cipher5 is a critical method for making explicit the often-subjugated knowledge of Hip Hop Kulture. This is aesthetic systems theory at work, a practice of publicly illuminating aesthetic epistemology. But Freire's situations required a translation process. While the purpose of Cipher5 is indeed *conscientização*, conscientizing, or the raising of critical consciousness, our situations had to make sense to us. Taking what may seem like a rather traditional approach we formed Cipher5 as a reading group in the basement of a local independent bookstore. It was an opportunity for local hiphoppas to gather to read *The Gospel of Hip Hop*, "presented by" KRS-ONE (2009).

An Emancipatory Book Club

My passion for a reading group did not spring from my experiences in grad school (as you may at first suppose), but from my first book club, a 3 am independent sci-fi circle at a now long-closed Tim Horton's coffee shop in Sydney, Cape Breton, Canada. This requires a bit of a story to illustrate the two lessons I learned from the experience: First, youth need only an opportunity for critical engagement and rarely need to be introduced to the passion of learning (they simply need a space to unleash what they possess), and second, as Gramsci long ago noted, the critical revolutionary intellectual is not always found in a university classroom, but in the make-shift classrooms of the community.

I was a teenager working summer back-shift at a grocery store. Sometime in the middle of the summer my sleeping pattern had become flipped backwards, so that on my days off I had a hard time getting back to a daytime schedule. So instead of trying very hard I would often take a book and find an open coffee shop. I had no plan. I was not trying to read enough to get into graduate school. In fact no one in my family had attended graduate school so I did not yet know what the domestic practice of scholarship looked like, what the scholar does in their spare time. I have what I now recognize to be a long-term passion for knowledge, and this passion is a vital component of knowledge: "For Foucault, as for Plato after the symposium, knowledge must be seen as a genre of desire" (Steigler, 2010, p. 172). But at that point I had no words for this. All I knew was the pleasure of late-night reading.

On one of these early morning adventures I walked into a coffee shop I had not yet visited. I purchased my coffee and, as was my habit, I headed for the corner where I would not be distracted by the activity at the counter. It was not long before I was interrupted by an increase in volume in the little shop. As was the case in all Tim Horton's of the time, there was a large square counter surrounded by stools that was called "the island." The island was full and was presided over by the very large security guard I passed when I walked into the shop. Now, however, he was transfigured. A large smile spread across his wide face softening the hard features of his large shaved head. He verbally poked the members of the group, pushing them to talk, coaxing them into debate. I guess I started to stare because it was not long before he was looking straight at me. I tried to break his gaze but he would have none of it. It was too late for me. He asked me what I was reading and shook his head with displeasure at my response. He called me over.

I was the youngest person at the table by at least fifteen years and I was not the focus of the conversation. I had unwittingly discovered an early-morning book club—it was the Fight Club of book clubs, really, but long before anyone would have that reference. Over that summer I was introduced to ideas and to Nova Scotia sci-fi authors I had never heard of, and, most importantly, I learned in that circle what culture circle members likely learned with Freire, that the world of the mind is not out of reach, that knowledge is not owned or managed by an exclusive class of people. I also learned there is knowledge-of-self that can be gained in this rough community classroom, the one that you choose as the place to take a stand against a world constructed for you. It was in this coffee shop where I learned that making knowledge is an emancipatory act.

I now have more than twenty years' distance on that classroom. Having had my first career in the music industry (and all of the classrooms that come with that life), and having also had the joys and pains of university seminars along the way on my journey to a PhD, I have gained perspective. There is no one single classroom that can teach all of the lessons that we will learn. And it seems that certain lessons come along with certain classrooms. With this in mind I partnered with Andre Hamilton to create a reading circle as situation or singularity that we call Cipher5.

Hamilton and I followed the lessons I learned at that coffee shop, and the ones he learned in a lifetime of Hip Hop Kulture, and we understood them through the lens of critical pedagogy and my newer teachers: hooks, Steinberg, Kincheloe, Freire, McLaren, and Giroux. The situation is the reading circle and the subject is often, but not always, *The Gospel of Hip Hop*. After the ritual introduction, necessary so everyone in the circle hears their own voice and is heard by the subjects that form the circle, we may only read two lines. Where the conversation goes after these lines are spoken is unknown. We have no curriculum and no timeline. We have been meeting for eighteen months as of April 2014 and have yet to read the entire book. Some sections, such as "The Hip Hop Declaration of Peace," have been read more than a dozen times because it is a collection of eighteen principles that hiphoppas are encouraged to live by. "The Fifth Overstanding: The Inner City," and the "Thirteenth Overstanding: The Hip Hop Activist," have also been read a number of times. But even these sections have not been completely read within the circle. Sections are recited, sometimes cypher style, each paragraph read by a different member of the circle, with books getting passed around.

And sometimes *The Gospel of Hip Hop* does not even get opened. Someone may come with a video or a section of lyrics for discussion. Perhaps a documentary, such as *The United States of Africa*, or Ice T's *The Art of Rap*, will be the focus. But whatever the focus, the process is the same; we come together to articulate our questions, forward our ideas, practice our critical thinking and leave Cipher5 excited and engaged with a more fully realized passion for knowledge.

Cipher5: Method for Research *and* Teaching

The practice of Cipher5 provides a way of practicing critical pedagogy as a model for critical research. At the root is a dismissal or a denial of the two-sidedness of the project, or, put another way, a denial of the distance between research and education. Research *is* learning. Arne De Boever (2011) took the denial a step further by denying a distance between research and philosophy. It comes down to the statement "philosophy is education: that it *was* and *has always been* education, since its beginning in Ancient Greece" (p. 34).

The practice of generating knowledge in Cipher5 is philosophy practiced by hiphoppas; it is the work of articulating the practices/art of living that Michel Foucault identified as culture. Philosophy, in this view, is the articulation and evaluation of a mode of life, not the professional practice of an intellectual elite. Cipher5 started as a way of generating research about Hip Hop, Hip Hop as the manifestation of Hip Hop Kulture, and became the practice of articulating the practices of Kulture, and therefore a form of philosophy classroom. Through Cipher5 we rediscovered a practical philosophy, or, at least, a renegade philosophy that occurs in the street, the kind of philosophy that Rancière (2011) called *political* because it creates an opportunity for those without voice to learn to speak:

> My vision of philosophy is first of all a vision of thought as a power of declassification, of the redistribution of territorial divisions among disciplines and competences. Philosophy says that thought belongs to all. It says this, though, at the very moment that it states division and exclusions. (p. 23)

Cipher5 calls our process the creation of knowledge but stops just short of naming ourselves philosophers or a philosophical community. Perhaps this is an expression of power that must still be undone.

But we also do not call Cipher5 a classroom even though it does the work of education. Gert Biesta in *Toward a New "Logic" of Emancipation: Foucault and Rancière* wrote that:

> The idea of emancipation plays a central role in modern education. To the extent that education is about more than the transmission of content and culture but involves an interest in fostering independence and autonomy, education can be said to be a process that aims at the emancipation of the child or the student. (p. 169)

If education is defined this way and not defined by the institutionalization of learning then we are free to study organized learning or the practice of community philosophy in any environment equally. Cipher5—as my research assistants maintain in autoethnographic works I will draw from below—is a practice of philosophy and complex practice of self-knowledge and care-of-the-self that points towards emancipation. It seems that cultural research-as-education works because it generates community knowledge of the forces of power that are experienced by members of the circle, who are free and encouraged by peers to speak their narratives. As Biesta noted: "The key idea is that emancipation can be brought about if people gain adequate insight into the power relations that constitute their situation—which is why the notion of demystification plays such a central role in critical pedagogies" (p. 171). But as Freire pointed out, if the pedagogue arrives to be savior then his very presence assures the learner will never be emancipated, but will fall under the authority of the teacher/critic, the one endowed with the magic power to de-mystify. But this practice leads to the emergence of another ideo- logical power evident in Marxist notions of "false consciousness" that has remained present in critical theory that Biesta called the "predicament of ideology":

> The "predicament of ideology" lies in the suggestion that it is precisely because of the way in which power works upon our consciousness, that we are unable to see how the power works upon our consciousness. This not only implies that in order to free ourselves from the working of power we need to expose how power works upon our consciousness. It also means that in order for us to achieve emancipation, someone else, whose consciousness is not subjected to the workings of power, needs to provide us with an account of our objective condition. (p. 171)

But the critical consciousness in the Freirean mode calls forth something alto- gether different. It relies on community-produced knowledge, or, more pre- cisely, on the effect of community-produced knowledge. In our formulation the collective act of philosophy-of-culture that we practice in Cipher5 places the development of consciousness in the center of an increasingly critical discussion. The effectiveness of this, as Freire also showed, is the simultaneous articulation of community knowledge and individual emancipation. Rancière (1991), in *The Ignorant Schoolmaster: Five Lessons in Intellectual Emancipation*, explained this process in another context.

Rancière (1991) told the incredible story of a quiet teacher and former French revolutionary deputy forced to flee to the Netherlands on the return of the monarchy, and the pedagogical adventure he unexpectedly undertook. The adventure begins with the fact that Joseph Jacotot could not speak any Flemish and the students he was tasked to work with spoke no French. So instead of giving educational lessons he provided a book with a translation and let the students do the work. He expected little, "he had believed what all conscientious professors believe: that the important business of the master is to transmit his knowledge to his students so as to bring them, by degrees, to his own level of expertise" (p. 3). So it was with great surprise that the students learned to read and write French and "the logic of the explicative system had to be overturned. Explication is not necessary to remedy an inca- pacity to understand" (p. 6), and in fact

before being the act of the pedagogue, explication is the myth of pedagogy, the para-
ble of a world divided into knowing minds and ignorant ones, ripe minds and immature ones, the capable and the incapable, the intelligent and the stupid. (p. 6)

Explication is not without power; according to Rancière (1991) (and Jacotot), explication is not only the stultifying weapon of pedagogues but the very bond of the social
order. Whoever says order says distribution into ranks. Putting into ranks presupposes
explication, the distributory, justificatory fiction of an inequality that has no other
reason for being. (p. 117)

Cipher5 is not, however, built on Jacotot's or Rancière's blueprint. It developed
from my book club adventure, from Andre Hamilton's basement where hiphoppas would gather to learn, from our practice of Hip Hop Kulture (MacDonald,
2012; 2014b). It was the impact of the socially produced knowledge at Cipher5
that left me looking for answers and explications that led me to question the
process of intellectual emancipation, and to Foucault, Rancière, and Jacotot.
And while I resisted drawing from these sources to explain my experience at
Cipher5, it occurred to me that enforcing this separation maintained the divisions between philosophy (including aesthetics), education, and cultural practice. This chapter is an act of tearing down these walls and confirming that
living Hip Hop Kulture is the act of living aesthetically.

Cipher5 as Learning Model in Students' Own Words

One of the joys of running a participatory action research circle is that you
have a constant engagement in knowledge production. This year I began a
new position as an assistant professor at a new university in a faculty of fine
arts with no legacy of social science research. This was the first time that
students from this department worked as research assistants (RAs) and I was
very interested in what kind of impact their participation would have on their
intellectual and scholarly development. I was cautious to choose RAs, knowing that their level of engagement would, in some ways, lay the foundation for
the near future. I decided to wait to see which students would attend the Hip
Hop Kulture symposium I organized in the first semester. As it turned out, two
students volunteered and showed up for everything. They made the decision
easy. Soon after the symposium I began the process of hiring them as research
assistants to support Cipher5. Their assignment was to attend Cipher5 over
the semester and to take notes. At the end of the semester they were asked to

provide an autoethnography of their experience. Once the autoethnography was written and submitted the three of us sat down and discussed their experience. I only then mentioned that I was interested in exploring Cipher5 as a form of classroom and that they, in fact, were the first students. I asked them to go back over their autoethnographies to produce another layer of analysis, this time identifying the connection between events and their own learning. What follows is a series of examples of their work. It is necessary to include their voice because it provides the evidence of the functioning of Cipher5 as both a research circle and as a form of emancipatory pedagogy.

Student 1:

- The open nature (circle) of the Cipher works to break down the idea that there is one all-knowing teacher who speaks to students who are inferior. I love this learning model, because what I'm experiencing is that good communication is a great tool for more thorough learning.
- I feel the circle has helped build my own confidence. I don't feel it gives me an ego boost; rather, exploring abstract topics that have many sides (spirituality, sexuality, religion, mainstream music) or points of view is a great opportunity to allow yourself to be scared and state your opinion anyway. I think it's important for members of the circle to remain open-minded, to be patient as listeners and not always feel the need to be right.
- The circle really gives its members a chance to share their own personal history and experience, which may be essential to the healthy development of our identities. It seems to be a therapeutic place where there is compassion for everyone's stories, which I think allows for healing.
- I had some really positive feelings tonight. For me, the community/ welcoming aspect of the Cypher keeps developing. It's starting to feel like a soccer team you join half-heartedly simply because your friend invited you and you committed to the first game. Before you know it you wouldn't even dream of missing a practice, let alone a game. This is the feeling of community. I don't necessarily yet know my role or the extent of my contribution to the Cipher, but I feel like my role and contribution not only exists, but is a stepping stone to further awareness and education around social issues. I have a place and when I look around the circle, everyone has a place. We are working towards a common vision, and there are so many facets to that vision (so many different backgrounds, motives, experiences that blend together beautifully).

Each time I take part in the Cipher, I think more and more about identity—both of others and my own. The sense of direction (or misdirection) an identity brings impacts our lives every day. Who we think we are, the kinds of things we believe in or don't believe in, the habits we form, etc., I feel like maybe my sense of identity hasn't been true to what I actually WANT and aspire to have in my life. This circle (through reflection) is helping me to form a more solid identity of myself. I don't know yet know what that identity consists of.

- Tonight a First Nations hiphoppa told us that when he was growing up as a First Nations youth, he felt society already looked upon him as scum so he felt like being poor and dealing drugs was of no further shame to him or his identity, whereas with middle-class (white) society they would never want to be caught dead selling drugs. But once Hip Hop glamorized it, suddenly it became "cool" and "badass" to do drugs. I think this argument and image of drug use has been around for years, if not centuries. That was a sad story for me to hear. I feel angry hearing about the racist mindset towards First Nations people (and any race). Often when a First Nations Canadian tells me a story about the injustice of their struggles, I am filled with rage and want to pursue this story of furthered colonialism. This thought brought me to the appreciation of our path in life. Six months ago, I never would have guessed I'd be attending weekly Hip Hop community circles discussing social and political and racial issues. This is amazing. My mother told me that going to school is never a waste of money. I was questioning whether that was true, but in this moment I am not necessarily thankful that I study music every day. I am thankful that I'm in the position where I am becoming exposed to higher levels of thinking, philosophy, and desire for social change. That's what I want to be a part of my life.

Student 2:

- Each time I attend, I always feel like I have so much to learn but instead of being discouraged with how much information there is in the world (which I often do at school/in a classroom environment), I feel inspired to continue listening to peoples' stories and to absorb as much as I can through this community.
- Through this reflection process I have developed a deeper understanding of myself: my social, political, musical, and religious positions, as well

as a critical evaluation of these beliefs. This has been both a learning opportunity and a challenge as I am dissecting my preconceived ideas of identity and challenging certain aspects that I do not like, such as those beliefs that do not fit into this new cultural group, or those that I no longer value and am struggling to let go of. There is a personal identity crisis going on: I am evaluating who I have become, what environmental elements have contributed to that formulation of self and whether or not that is somebody I want to continue to be. These questions and concerns are a direct result of the unique personal, transformative qualities of engaging in this method. This ties into the challenge and conflict of racial identity and prejudice. A huge challenge for me has been confronting prejudices I was not previously aware of, that were in my subconscious mind affecting my conscious behavior.

- Through this process, my ignorance of the cultural, political and social history of a marginalized group of people has been exposed. A unique element of this method is the development of relationship-based learning to generate this knowledge and awareness.
- This is a completely different model of education. It is an exchange and sharing of personal stories where the self is not divorced from the learning; it is an integral component. This brings up a unique set of challenges in the learning environment: trust between participants, a willingness and openness to share, express vulnerability, to be challenged, and potentially exposed in one's lack of knowledge and/or difference of opinion. The relationships formed provide the opportunity for the creation of a deeper level of understanding, acknowledging the emotional, physical, spiritual, social, and economic ingredients that make up a community and a culture.

Conclusions

So while there are a variety of levels of success in this method, there are some challenges presenting themselves as well. The realization of Cipher5 as youth activism, research, and pedagogical space requires a more thorough investigation of my practices. What role have I played in preparing the research assistants for their participation, and how might I fit this role into the model? The RAs were certainly not left alone to deal with their process; in fact, the research practice required, or at least provided a context for, the development of strong ties between RAs and myself as principal investigator. Further elaboration of these dynamics is required before too much more can be said about the value of Cipher5 as a teaching environment. Relatedly, it is necessary to evaluate how the rest of the community members of Cipher5 feel about contributing to student learning; what is the reciprocal contribution to the community? In my opening example of the security guard at the Tim Horton's coffee shop, it seemed like he was making community by sharing knowledge and sharing the creation of knowledge. But of course he was also getting paid to be there, and the draw of the reading circle made certain that there were bodies in the coffee shop late at night keeping him company. Likely, the mechanics of community are much more complex than we have yet addressed. Therefore, and in these directions, the research will continue. We will continue to publish articles about Hip Hop Kulture in our city, but we will now also publish about alternative learning environments, new approaches to community philosophy, and emancipation.

Note

1. The idea of anesthetized learning comes from the work of Sir Ken Robinson, in a number of widely available lectures online about the need for educational reform. See for instance his very famous TED Talk, *How Schools Kill Creativity*, retrieved from http://www.ted.com/talks/ken_robinson_says_schools_kill_creativity

References

Adorno, T. W. (1984). *Aesthetic theory* (C. Lenhardt, Trans.). New York, NY: Routledge & Kegan Paul.

Adorno, T. W. (1991). *The culture industry: Selected essays on a mass culture*. New York, NY: Routledge.

Arribas-Ayllon, M., & Walkerdine, V. (2008). *Foucauldian discourse analysis*. In C. Willig & W. Stainton-Rogers (Eds.), *The SAGE handbook of qualitative research in psychology* (pp. 91–108). Los Angeles, CA; London, England: Sage.

Battiste, M. (2013). *Decolonizing education: Nourishing the learning spirit*. Saskatoon, Canada: Purich.

Becker, H. S. (1984). *Art worlds*. Berkeley, CA: University of California Press.

Benjamin, W. (1968). The work of art in the age of mechanical reproduction (H. Zohn, Trans.). In A. Hannah (Ed.), *Illuminations* (pp. 219–253). New York, NY: Harcourt Brace & World.

Benjamin, W., Bloch, E., Brecht, B., Lukacs, G. (1977). *Aesthetics and politics*. New York, NY: Verso.

Berleant, A. (1991). *Art and engagement*. Philadelphia, PA: Temple University Press.

Berleant, A. (1992). *The aesthetics of environment*. Philadelphia, PA: Temple University Press.

Berleant, A. (1999). Getting along beautifully: Ideas for a social aesthetics. In P. Von Bons-dorff & A. Haapala (Eds.), *Aesthetics in the human environment* (Vol. 6, pp. 12–29). Lahti, Finland: International Institute for Applied Aesthetics.

Berleant, A. (2000). *The aesthetic field.* New York, NY: Cybereditions.

Berleant, A. (2004). *Re-thinking aesthetics: Rogue essays on aesthetics and the arts.* Aldershot, England: Ashgate.

Berleant, A. (2010). *Sensibility and sense: The aesthetic transformation of the human world.* Char-lottesville, VA: Imprint Academic.

Besley, T., & Peters, M. A. (2007). *Subjectivity and truth: Foucault, education, and the culture of Self.* New York, NY: Peter Lang.

Beynon, C. A., & Veblen, K. K. (2012). *Critical perspectives in Canadian music education.* Waterloo, Canada: Wilfred Laurier University Press.

Blumenfeld-Jones, D. S. (2012). *Curriculum and the aesthetic life: Hermeneutics, body, democracy, and ethics in curriculum theory and practice.* New York, NY: Peter Lang.

Bourriaud, N. (2002). *Relational aesthetics* (S. a. F. W. Pleasance, Trans.). Dijon, France: le press du reel.

Carr, W., & Kemmis, S. (1986). *Becoming critical: Education, knowledge and action research.* London, England: Falmer.

De Boever, A. (2011). The philosophy of (aesthetic) education. In J. E. Smith & A. Weisser (Eds.), *Everything is in everything: Jacques Rancière between intellectual emancipation and aesthetic education* (pp. 34–48). New York, NY: Art Center Graduate Press.

Dewey, J. (1916). *Democracy and education.* New York, NY: The Free Press.

Dewey, J. (1934). *Art as experience.* New York, NY: Capricorn Books.

Dewey, J. (1938). *Experience and education.* New York, NY: Macmillan.

Elliott, E., Caton, L. F., & Rhyne, J. (2002). *Aesthetics in a multicultural age.* New York, NY: Oxford University Press.

Foucault, M. (1972). *The archaeology of knowledge: And the discourse on language.* New York, NY: Vintage Books.

Foucault, M. (1977). *Discipline and punish: The birth of the prison.* New York, NY: Vintage Books.

Foucault, M. (1980). *Power/knowledge: Selected interviews and other writings 1972–1977.* New York, NY: Vintage Books.

Foucault, M. (1994). *The order of things: An archaeology of the human sciences.* New York, NY: Vintage Books.

Foucault, M. (2004). *The hermeneutics of the subject: Lectures at the College de France 1981–1982.* New York, NY: Picador.

Foucault, M. (2010). *The government of self and others: Lectures at the College De France 1982–1983.* New York, NY: Palgrave Macmillan.

Freire, P. (2001). *Pedagogy of freedom: Ethics, democracy, and civic courage.* Lanham, MA: Rowman & Littlefield.

Freire, P. (2010). *Education for a critical consciousness.* New York, NY: Continuum.

Giroux, H. A. (2004). Public pedagogy and the politics of neo-liberalism: Making the political more pedagogical. *Policy Futures in Education, 2*(3–4), 494–503.

Giroux, H. A. (2009). *Youth in a suspect society: Democracy or disposability?* New York, NY: Palgrave Macmillan.

Gordon, D. R., & Suits, D. B. (2003). *Epicurus: His continuing influence and contemporary relevance*. Rochester, NY: Rochester Institute of Technology Press.

hooks, b. (1990). *Yearning: Race, gender, and cultural politics*. Boston, MA: South End Press.

hooks, b. (1994). *Teaching to transgress: Education as the practice of freedom*. New York, NY: Routledge.

hooks, b. (2003). *Teaching community: A pedagogy of hope*. New York, NY: Routledge.

hooks, b. (2004). *The will to change: Men, masculinity, and love*. New York, NY: Atria Books.

hooks, b. (2008). *Belonging: A culture of place*. New York, NY: Routledge.

hooks, b. (2010). *Teaching critical thinking: Practical wisdom*. New York, NY: Routledge.

hooks, b. (2013). *Writing beyond race: Living theory and practice*. New York, NY: Routledge.

Ibrahim, A., & Steinberg, S. R. (2014). *Critical youth studies reader*. New York, NY: Peter Lang.

Kendall, G., & Wickham, G. (1999). *Using Foucault's methods: Producing qualitative methods*. Thousand Oaks, CA: Sage.

Kincheloe, J. L. (2005). *Critical constructivism*. New York, NY: Peter Lang.

Kincheloe, J. L. (2010). *Knowledge and critical pedagogy*. New York, NY: Springer.

Klein, D. (2012). The art of happiness introduction. In Epicurus, *The art of happiness*. New York, NY: Penguin Books.

KRS-ONE. (2009). *The gospel of Hip Hop: First instrument presented by KRS ONE for the temple of Hip Hop*. Brooklyn, NY: Powerhouse Books.

Lentin A., & Titley, G. (2011). *The crises of multiculturalism: Racism in a neoliberal age*. New York, NY: Zed Books.

MacDonald, M. B. (2012). Hip Hop citizens: Local Hip Hop and the production of democratic grassroots change in Alberta. In B. Porfilio & M. Viola (Eds.), *Hip Hop(e): The cultural practice and critical pedagogy of international Hip Hop* (pp. 95–109). New York, NY. Peter Lang.

MacDonald, M. B. (2014a). Cultural studies of youth culture aesthetics as critical aesthetic education. In A. Ibrahim & S. R. Steinberg (Eds.), *Critical youth studies reader* (pp. 434–433). New York, NY: Peter Lang.

MacDonald, M. B. (2014b). Aesthetic Systems Theory: Doing Hip Hop Kulture research together at Cipher5. *MusiCultures, 41*(2), 34–53.

MacDonald, M. B. (2014c). A pedagogy of cultural sustainability: YEGH3 (Edmonton Hip Hop History) as a decentralized model for Hip Hop's global microhistories. In B. Porfilio, D. Roychoudhury, & L. Gardner (Eds.), *See you at the crossroads: Hip Hop scholarship at the intersections* (pp. 29–44). Rotterdam, The Netherlands: Sense Publishers.

Macleod, C., & Sunil, B. (2008). *Postcolonialism and psychology*. In C. Willig & W. Stainton-Rogers (Eds.), *The Sage handbook of qualitative research in psychology* (pp. 576–589). Los Angeles, CA; London, England: Sage.

Mignolo, W. D. (2000). *Local histories/Global designs: Coloniality, subaltern knowledges, and border thinking*. Princeton, NJ: Princeton University Press.

Mignolo, W. D. (2011). *The darker side of western modernity: Global futures, decolonial options*. Durham, NC: Duke University Press.

Rancière, J. (1991). *The ignorant schoolmaster: Five lessons in intellectual emancipation.* Stanford, CA: Stanford University Press.

Rancière, J. (2000). What aesthetics can mean (B. Holmes, Trans.). In P. Osborne (Ed.), *From an aesthetic point of view: Philosophy, art, and the senses.* London, England: Serpent's Tail.

Rancière, J. (2005). From politics to aesthetics? *Paragraph, 28*(1), 13–25.

Rancière, J. (2007). *The politics of aesthetics: The distribution of the sensible* (G. Rockhill, Trans.). London, England: Continuum.

Rancière, J. (2010). *Dissensus: On politics and aesthetics.* New York, NY: Continuum.

Robson, M. (2005). Jacques Rancière aesthetic communities. *Paragraph, 28*(1), 77–95.

Spivak, G. C. (2012). *An aesthetic education in the era of globalization.* Cambridge, MA: Harvard University Press.

Steigler, B. (2010). *Taking care of youth and the generations.* Stanford, CA: Stanford University Press.

Steinberg, S. R. (2001). *Multi/Intercultural conversations: A reader.* New York, NY: Peter Lang.

Steinberg, S. R. (2009). *Diversity and multiculturalism: A reader.* New York, NY: Peter Lang.

Stinson, S. W. (1998). Maxine Greene and arts education. In W. F. Pinar (Ed.), *The passionate mind of Maxine Greene* (pp. 221–228). New York, NY: Routledge.

Swonger, M. (2006). *Foucault and the Hupomnemata: Self writing as an art of life.* Retrieved from http://digitalcommons.uri.edu/cgi/viewcontent.cgi?article=1017&context=srhonorsprog

Tuhiwai Smith, L. (2012). *Decolonizing methodologies: Research and indigenous peoples.* New York, NY: Zed Books.

Wright, H. K. (2003). Cultural studies as praxis: (Making) an autobiographical case. *Cultural Studies, 17*(6), 805–822.

PART II

ECONOMICS AND YOUTH RESEARCH

· 3 ·

TRAPPED INSIDE A POISONED MAZE

Mapping Young People's Geographies of Disposability in Neoliberal Times of School Disinvestment

Patricia Krueger-Henney

> Young people—as a concrete embodiment and symptomatic reflection of the abstract forces that govern the social sphere—are one of the most significant modalities through which to understand and launch an effective resistance to neoliberalism as a political, economic, and social movement.
>
> — Giroux, 2010 (p. 145)

A Word About Maps

Maps tell stories about the state of the world, and simultaneously connect the personal here and now with social structures and their ideological work. Maps tell stories about how people perceive, conceive, and experience spaces and places. In other words, maps are representative of people's spatial temporal experiences and knowledges. Hence, maps are always subjective and reflective of someone's points of view.

Maps and map-making are also tied to the history of white settler colonialism around the world. Maps created by cartographers have served European empires to document global economic expansions through land appropriations. Maps exhibit stories about accumulations of wealth (land, labor, and natural resources) but maintain invisible the power structures of settler colonialism reinforced by the ideology of white supremacy that erased and destroyed peoples and captured and enslaved others for labor. Indigenous peoples have always been at the frontlines of white settler colonialism's violent systematic appropriation by dispossessing people of their lands and resources (Harvey, 2003). The colonization and militarization of Indigenous Americans, the trans-Atlantic slave trade, and Manifest Destiny have all been visually documented in the form of maps; these visual narratives conveyed imaginations and physical trajectories of settler colonial nation-states' materialized visions and desires of world domination (Mignolo, 2000; Willinsky, 1998). Maps as visual narratives of settler colonialism have naturalized the systematic violence by "white supremacy, heteropatriarchy, and heteropaternalism … as components of civil society" in today's neoliberal world order (Tuck & Guishard, 2013). Further, the visual documentation of settler colonialism's ideology has proven not only longevity to dictate content knowledge about world histories taught in schools today; as master narrative it also continues to position the "academic researcher as expert" during knowledge productions that apply mapping methodologies to appropriate details about people, their social interactions, and physical surroundings.

That said, maps as both an outcome and a methodology for documenting people's lived experiences throughout time and space tend to follow a surviving colonizing mode of knowledge production in that the "God's Eye View" prevails over creating and reading maps from the distant outsider and top-down perspective. Today's street maps and subway maps are representative of this point as these make invisible the mobilization of resources and the uprooting of people and their communities necessary to build cities and networks of transportations (Mogel & Bhagat, 2008). Like stagnant stale air, the socio-historical contexts of systems of violence, ideologies of supremacy, and unequal relations in production linger between the given visually documented topography and the viewer's perception. Consequently, these same maps continue to leave unquestioned the geo-political borders of how people and land are divided into those who are free and those who are subjugated; between savages and civilized; majorities and minorities, citizens and undocumented, the "us" and "them;" centers and peripheries; the rich and the dispossessed; the private and the public; the world's hottest real-estate areas according to the Global House Price Index and the rural locations of maximum security facilities; and the sought-after consumers and those who are shunned as socially disposable. These spatialized hegemonizing binaries maintain the global graveyards of the human collateral damage created and maintained by the colonial origins of profiteering modes of production.

In this chapter I position map-making as a decolonizing research methodology (Smith, 1999) to privilege young people's expert knowledges with the working grounds of neoliberal ideology and dispossessing social structures in public education. Further, this chapter frames urban defunded and thus under-performing public schools in the United States as re-configured landscapes that systematically reserve academic opportunities and attainment for students from higher-income families. Under the spell of neoliberal education policies, centralized mayoral control over urban public school districts, intensified police presence and surveillance technology, systematic closure of failing schools, rapid expansion of charter schooling, corporatized high-stakes testing economy, and educational initiatives of philanthropic foundations decide on the expiration dates of local community schools (Buras, Randels, & ya Salaam, 2010; Fabricant & Fine, 2012; Lipman, 2004, 2013; Nolan, 2011; Pappas, 2012).

Additionally, the current infatuation of education authorities with advocating for intensified criminal-justice-centered discipline practices in "bad" schools (i.e., use of school suspensions to discipline students for non-criminal misbehavior such as bringing a cellular phone to school or arriving at school not wearing school uniform) and replacing them with smaller charter schools controlled by private businesses as seen in Philadelphia, Detroit, Chicago, New York City, New Orleans, Boston, Baltimore, and Philadelphia, disproportionately impacts Black, Latino, immigrant, and low-income students who predominantly attend public schools in urban areas (Duke, 2013). Charter schools have become known for applying rigorous sorting admissions practices to recruit students with greater social and economic capital; young people and their families from local and economically deprived communities tend to be sorted out and no longer have access to their neighborhood schools, as seen as in the documentary *Waiting for Superman* (Birtel & Chilcott, 2010).

Systematically dispossessing young people from educational opportunities and in-school learning time is based on social markers of race, class, language, gender, and nationality. Moreover, the current privatization of public education is an extension of the aforementioned settler colonialism in that low-income and non-white youth are disproportionately indexed as educationally disposable while private interests are appropriating the land of closed-down schools and turning them into profit-driven sites of educational production. Community organizers who are relentlessly fighting for the survival of their local schools have coined the current massive school closure "the land grab" because "the property occupied by the school could be turned into a pricey development" (Holliday, 2013), as witnessed in the creations of luxury and mixed-income housing developments in New York and Chicago (Naison, 2013; Smith & Stovall, 2008), and the recent announcement of a prison construction in Philadelphia (Gwynne, 2013).

In this chapter I offer high school students' perspectives of the policed and securitized spaces inside their schools. Their lived experiences with criminal-justice-based school safety and discipline practices (metal detectors, surveillance cameras, and overuse of school suspensions for non-criminal behavior) join the geographies of disposability found in some of New York City's (hereafter NYC) high schools. The selected schools represented some of the most scrutinized public learning spaces at the time of data collection and were located in some of NYC's most under-resourced neighborhoods. Criminal-justice-based school safety and discipline practices, widely known as the school-to-prison pipeline (Wald & Losen, 2003), are just one manifestation of the "slow violence" of neoliberal education reform. Labeled as "turnaround" schools, principals have a predetermined number of years to improve their cumulative student test scores before their schools are closed down or replaced with another (charter school). Schools placed under this probational status further marginalize the bodies of those already thought to be racially and economically disposable (Aggarwal, Mayorga, & Nevel, 2012). With their mental maps that exhibit the spatialization of dispossessing practices, the youth co-researchers of this participatory action research project illustrated how defunded schools are operating with intensified surveillance that socially controls and physically contains young people who are eager to complete their high school education.

With the data I present here I argue the two following points: the current neoliberal regime of high-stakes schooling exists simultaneously to the space production of abandonment and disinvestment in schools for non-white, immigrant, gender-non-conforming, and low-income youth. I especially focus on the spatialization of social disinvestment and disposability in public schools as outcomes of the school-to-prison pipeline. The framing of the social character of space production is pivotal for critically rethinking the "failing school" within an economic mode of production that eagerly disposes of young people whose bodies are indexed as socially undesirable for a consumer-driven society. This said, and reconnecting with the opening words of Henry Giroux, a space-driven epistemology analysis would remain "anti-youth" and hence regressive if we continue to ground research in and for youth studies within the pathologizing units of individual behavior (i.e., "it's their own fault they are poor") or specific geographic locations (i.e., "the ongoing violence in their Brooklyn neighborhood explains their acting out in school") that have constructed and strengthened a persisting conservative narrative of the "achievement gap" (Coleman, 1966). Instead, school failures are unequally spatialized and their embodied processes are determined by accumulations of wealth and economic opportunity; hence the unit of analysis here is a public education system that is increasingly controlled by private interests who profit from young people's social disposability. Through the systematic disposal of young people, these "circuits of dispossession" (Fine & Ruglis, 2009) make transparent that young people's survivance is a national public concern of utmost degree. Henry Giroux (2010) poignantly wrote,

> For those marginalized others considered useless and superfluous, progress is no longer about getting ahead or improving the quality of their lives: it is about the struggle to survive and not to succumb to the status of the walking dead. (p. 38)

I dedicate this chapter to the resilience of my co-researchers as well as to all the determined young people in this country who refuse and resist a racist ideology of disposability.

About the Study

The research findings discussed here were collected through a mixed-method youth participatory action research (YPAR) project based in NYC between 2007 and 2009 that gathered youth-centered perspectives and analyses of the school-to-prison pipeline as one of the most salient manifestations of the current privatization trends of public education in the United States. Ten high school students from five different public high schools located in three of the five city boroughs joined the research collective as youth co-researchers; six females and five males attended grades nine through 12 at the time of the study. Youth researchers composed the following descriptive statement to inform audiences about their backgrounds: "We are a research team consisting of multilingual and globally schooled, working class, South Asian, Black American, Caribbean, African, Latino, Native American, LGBTQ, immigrant youth, spoken-word artists, community activists and youth organizers." I was a doctoral student during the time of our study, and the documentation of our YPAR grew into my dissertation. Throughout this chapter I use "I," "we," "us," and "our" interchangeably to signify that youth co-researchers entrusted me to speak on behalf of our research collective (Krueger, 2009).

Prior to all weekly research meetings, youth co-researchers had indicated that each of their schools operated under increased safety measures (i.e., surveillance cameras, metal detectors, search tables, armed police officers). Youth co-researchers played a double role throughout the duration of the project: they were both researchers and participants. As researchers they collected data via the administration of a citywide youth survey (n = 117), established coding systems for analyzing its quantitative and qualitative data on how other high schools' students experienced and perceived punitive school safety practices, and presented some of the findings at regional and local media and academic conferences. As project participants, youth co-researchers created individual mental maps (n = 10) of their surveilled and securitized school spaces, joined weekly workshop discussions, and participated in individual semi-structured interviews (n = 10) to document both their understanding and lived experiences with spatialized practices of school safety and security (Krueger, 2011).

This double role of researcher-participant exemplified YPAR as a youth-centered and youth-guided epistemology in that young people were in charge of examining data validity and legitimacy (Cammarota & Fine, 2008). Moreover, while the young people produced and owned the data, they were also positioned as experts about the encounters they have had with structures of disinvestment (Krueger-Henney, 2012). Co-researchers both inquired and were inquired; they were objects and subjects of the inquiry process; they gathered and disseminated all data. Unlike more traditional research projects that maintain colonizing researcher-researched dichotomies (Chilisa, 2011), members of this research collective grounded their subjectivities within the national and international working grounds of neoliberal policies. Further, youth co-researchers added their own knowledge and skill-sets to the triangulation of the data.

The remaining pages of this chapter are filled with the presentation and discussion of the mental maps that two youth co-researchers created of their surveilled lifeworlds at school (Horton & Kraftl, 2006), or the real and imagined social worlds that include their individual race, class, and gender-specific journeys through the physical and materialized landscapes of their everyday student lives. The proceeding excerpt from one of the research collective's reflective discussions about the purposes of the securitization of their schools reveals that young people understand criminal-justice-based education practices as mechanisms that turn their schools into sites that contain and manage young people away from higher education and employment opportunities. Further, youth co-researchers show a profound awareness of their disposability in that "their futures—except as contained—are of little moment to the neoliberal formations in which they come of age" (Katz, 2011, p. 52). Together, co-researchers' mental maps and their excerpted conversation trace the contours of the geographies of disposability found inside their disinvested schools.

Mapped Geographies of Disposability

Mental mapping as a research methodology invites both the mental mapper and the viewer into naming often under-acknowledged mundane spaces, including school. Unlike colonial and colonizing traditions of cartography that are anchored in calculations of scales, precision, and "individualized, colorblind, Western, and white-privileged conceptualizations" of power relationships (Tuck & Guishard, 2013) that fix "people to a given place in the world" (Willinsky, 1998, p. 147), mental maps do not position the mapmaker as outsider to the documented lifeworld. Neither do mental maps frame the spaces under investigation as stagnant or homogenized. Instead, mental maps are extremely personal, subjective, and intimate, and hold "promise for understanding how space and place are internalized, interpreted, embodied and revised within individual-level experiences" (Futch & Fine, 2012). Further, mental maps show how the physical, remembered, and imagined spaces intersect in production of place and thus trace "a narrative or history of an individual or group via the discussion and/or portrayal of materialities such as spaces, bodies, or life events" (Gieseking, 2008). Most noteworthy, mental maps work from the scale of the body and move beyond location to levels of meaning of the intimate (i.e., "disposable"). Hence the numerous details on mental maps reflect the high level of meaning and personal connections the mapmaker has with his or her depicted lifeworld. As a result, the focus of mental maps "is not on people or things, but the spaces between people or things" (Tuck & Guishard, 2013), which is a central characteristic to the space production of disposability.

Youth co-researchers decided on the following map keys that guided their process of visualizing, identifying, and organizing the interaction between the type of security measure and the use values they attached to specific places inside school:

Security and Surveillance	Spaces and Places
Unarmed School Safety Agents (SSAs) = orange or purple dot	Places where I feel the safest = dotted green line
Police officers (armed) = black around orange dots	Places I do not use/access = dotted red line
Permanent SSAs = purple square	Most trafficked areas = dotted blue line
Metal detectors = outlined in green	Least trafficked areas = dotted orange line
Surveillance cameras = yellow dot	Places where I hang out with friends = dotted purple line
Police office/security office = outlined in red	Bright areas = highlight yellow/large circle
	Dark areas = highlight green/large circle

By creating a kaleidoscopic view of students' experiences with materializations of the school-to-prison pipeline, space production that creates and maintains learning environments of social control and containment, and the ideological structures of neoliberalism within which all social (hence spatial) production takes place, it was the collective's task to investigate to what extent youth co-researchers' daily journeys in school absorbed manifestations of systemic dispossessions and to document how they explained the purposes of their reconfigured lifeworlds at school. What follows is my reading of their mental maps.

Geography One

Dimples, a Latina senior from a high school in the Bronx, created this first mental map of her surveilled school.

The red solid line represents her daily movement that looped around the spaces on the first floor of her school. Upon entering her school building, she walked into the central area of the first floor, which is occupied by the main desk of SSAs. When we analyzed her map we noticed that the SSA desk was strategically placed in this centralized entrance area because it physically blocked anybody from either accessing or advancing to other parts of the building. From this position, SSAs were able to overlook and supervise most parts of the first floor. She added a red dotted line around the main security desk to indicate that this is a place she did not use or access. She also circled the desk with a purple dotted line to inform that this is an area where she hung out with her friends. Co-researchers asked her if she socialized with any of the SSAs there and she explained that most of them knew and talked to her. This might have been the reason why she considered the security desk a place for social interaction.

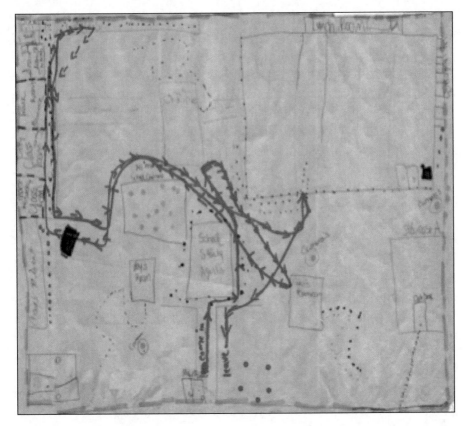

Figure 1. Surveillance map drawn by youth researcher Dimples, a Latina senior from a high school in the Bronx.

The first floor is also filled with numerous surveillance cameras. Immediately to the left of the SSA desk, Dimples filled a box with multiple yellow dots to show that this part of the first floor operated under multiple surveillance cameras. She identified an additional camera that is installed in the far right space of her map between staircase A and the two doors that lead to the lunchroom next to the permanently stationed SSA (darkened box). We noticed two surveillance cameras; one mounted near the boys' bathroom, the other right by the girls' bathroom. During the presentation of her map, Dimples detailed that unlike the boys' bathroom, the camera by the girls' bathroom was installed immediately above the door. From the standpoint of security staff, the installation of both surveillance cameras might have been explained by the school's need to prevent students from physically or verbally fighting within these two busy locations (see blue lines). Dimples shared with the research team how upset she was with the installation of this camera. Moreover, she was very angered by it and told us that the camera was invading a very private and intimate space for girls. According to her, the placement of this camera was inappropriate because "nobody got to know when I take care of my business." Consequently, she decided to no longer use the bathroom. Her surveillance map does not provide insight to any additional bathroom she might have been able to access while in school. She filled the area immediately in front of the girls' bathroom with a purple line to inform us that this is an area where she hung out with friends.

Her daily movement included also the hallway in the top left corner on her map where all of her classrooms were located. The science and history classrooms are outlined with a green line to represent two places where she felt safe. She explained to her co-researchers that she really liked her teachers there, because "they treated me right" and "showed me respect." To reach that hallway she had to bypass a seating area in front of the permanently stationed SSA (darkened box), which she did not use (red line). Filled again with blue and purple lines, this hallway was an area that was trafficked the most and it was a space where she hung out with friends (purple and blue lines). On top of the exit door in the top left corner on the map, or at the end of the hallway, she placed a surveillance camera that looked right down the classroom hallway as well as over the student locker area where she had some interaction with her friends (purple line). A yellow line to indicate that her first floor was a bright area frames her entire mental map of her school lifeworld.

Geography Two

Ja, a South Asian senior who attended a small high school in Brooklyn, created this second mental map. His school shared the building with three other small schools. Students from two of these schools used the same entrance and exit as students from Ja's school. Even though he designed a map for each of the four different floors that he used during the school day, I decided to only show his mental map of the first floor map because it contains a number of different types of safety and discipline measures.

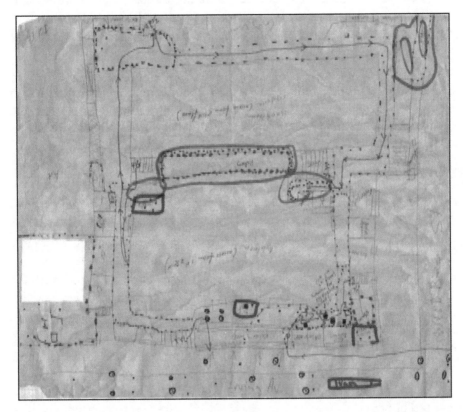

Figure 2. Surveillance map of Ja, a South Asian senior from a small high school in Brooklyn.

Of all schools that youth co-researchers attended, Ja's was probably the most policed and surveilled. Thirteen armed New York Police Department (NYPD) officers (orange dot circled in black) and 12 SSAs (purple dots) were stationed in front of the school building on a daily basis. In addition, a NYPD van, or "a precinct on wheels" as youth researchers called it, was parked there. The arrowed blue line symbolizes Ja's daily movement. Upon entering the building through the main entrance, he passed the main security desk that was operated by two SSAs. He then turned left to walk through a series of safety measures consisting of two metal detectors and two search tables (outlined in green). Four SSAs were permanently stationed within the space of this area (purple box) as well as one surveillance camera (yellow dot) in front of the security office (red box). Ja explained to his co-researchers that at each of these "safety stops" (the metal detectors, permanently stationed SSAs and search table), he strategically greeted safety personnel (indicated by "hi" on the map) to become a "familiar face" to them in order to avoid unnecessary questioning and interrogations. Overall, his daily schedule did not require him to use many of the places on the first floor because all of his classrooms were located on the following floors. Once he cleared the securitized entrance area he proceeded to a nearby staircase to move upstairs.

A few noteworthy points about the first floor remain to be mentioned: after moving our eyes across the hallway to the right side of the map, we acknowledged another long hallway that horizontally stretches across the mid-section of the mapped first floor. Ja circled this hallway in green to inform us that this dark area is part of a space that is not used very much by students (orange line). To the left of this hallway there is a security office (red box), which he filled with purple dots to categorize it as a place where SSAs are regularly located (purple dots). On the right side of the hallway, there is a narrower area that he filled with a purple and blue line to show that this is a busy area and also a space where he hung out with friends. In addition, he regularly accessed the elevator from this space. Ja explained that he had become friends with the elevator operator, who had granted him permission to ride the elevator (access to the elevator is usually restricted to visitors, teachers, administrators, and those who are physically unable to walk the stairs). Unlike most of his peers, Ja had gained privilege to ride the elevator and identified the elevator as one of the places and spaces at school where he felt safe (green dotted line).

In the far back, or on top of his map, another hallway stretches in front of his school's gym. The boys' locker room is located on the left side. Ja filled the area directly in front of it with purple and blue lines because it is an area that was most trafficked as well as a space where he hung out with friends. On the opposite end of the hallway is the girls' locker room. He also placed dark green circles within this space because he considered this corner a darker area in school. There is a surveillance camera installed in front of the girls' and boys' locker rooms (yellow dot). He speculated that this camera was positioned there to surveille the entire length of the hallway that fills the space between both locker room areas.

Naming the Poisoned Maze

Our analyses of the security technology's effects on the production of school space and the purposes that students attach to them often started with identifying images that co-researchers connected with to make their experiences with schools space more accessible to each other. Searching for metaphors facilitated an analytical process of relating their personal journeys in schools to the collectively shared encounters with the socio-political structures and ideologies that support disinvesting practices in schools. The following is an excerpt of one of these conversations (note: youth narratives from our data sets appear unaltered and in their original content. In addition, students' names have been changed, except for the name of the university researcher, also the author of this chapter, who received the collective's permission to report on the collective's research proceedings and outcomes):

Piper:	I am thinking of it [the pipeline] like more of a maze, with an initially prize inside of it. I don't know if there is an ending prize you can reach for, but with the pipeline, I don't know what you are looking for exactly. Like we are the rat, we are the students, or whatever, whether or not, we are pressuring through. We have the metal detectors, the SSAs or whatever, like that, we are still in the field of being influenced to go to prison. So I guess we are in this maze to find our ways out, that's why I thought of it as a maze.
MS:	A maze with obstacles.
Piper:	The thing is though with the pipeline, it seems hard to actually find the ending point. You don't know if there is a prize when you actually get there. Or if you are ever gonna get there.
MS:	A lot of students eat the poison that is put in there. To slow down the rat.
Patricia:	What's the poison?
KD:	The influence is the poison.
MS:	Yeah, it's the influence.
KD:	It's the neighborhood.
MS:	No, it's the people in the neighborhood, it's the students, cuz somebody can only choose what they want or what they go for.
Patricia:	Can you think of any other influences?
MS:	If you see somebody who is vulnerable, they just like hurting us, they think that just because we live in these neighborhoods and those kind of things go down in the neighborhood, that they might as well, just throw them in there.
Patricia:	Who is the "they?"
Vileta:	"They" is many people. You can't just say white people. We cannot just say cops.
Allemand:	But we can say rich people, because they can afford—
Vileta:	(jumps in)—so "they" is many.
Patricia:	Maybe it's more about an issue of power and where power is located.
Vileta:	But as far as power goes, everybody at city hall, it's white people. Seriously!

Youth co-researchers' equation of NYC schools with the grounds of a maze, a space designed to be puzzling and disorienting and throughout which the traveler is left to his or her own determination and resourcefulness to reach its uncertain ending point, is unsettling. Equally, if not more, concerning is Piper's metaphor of "a rat" to refer to herself and other young people who are working hard and "pressuring through" toward high school completion. The rat is an animal that evokes public imaginations of disgust, fear, repulsion, and urban uncleanliness. Less audible is the admiration of the rat's ability to survive a living environment that outwardly ignores or even rejects its existence. This toxic coupling of hostility and admiration may be applicable to the reality of surveilled youth in urban public learning institutions. The so-called prize after surviving their K–12 educational journey (i.e., high school diploma, employment, admissions to higher education) appears to be intentionally false and cruel: while instilling obedience and discipline in urban youth through intensified safety practices, students are also subjugated to ideological lessons about their "placelessness" in the current racist and neoliberal social order. Worse, the prized exit out of the physical and ideological mazes at school does not guarantee stability and social security during their adult lives.

On the contrary, surveilled youth are in consistent transit between different institutional spaces that warehouse "bad students," including prisons, detention centers, schools in low-income communities, and the foster-care system. Social disposability, then, as an outcome of systematic containment, denies surveilled youth access to a public status of social desirability and protection that are fundamental to their social survival. Indigenous scholar Jodi Byrd (2011) wrote, "what it means to be in transit, then, is to be in motion, to exist liminally in the ungrievable spaces of suspicion and unintelligibility" (p. xv). In other words, being trapped at the threshold of high visibility through institutionalized surveillance and the dead-end roads of disposability marks the geographies of dispossession of disinvested, under-resourced schools. As a result, young people are increasingly positioned within the deadly crossfire of "relational movements and countermovements" (pg. xvi), or between the ideological stunting of state-sanctioned surveillance and the social mobility acquired through a successful performance on state exit exams (i.e., Regents Exams).

In final analysis of the implications of this conversation, co-researchers not only brought to light the interconnections between the structural, ideological, social scaffoldings that silently weave together racialized, class- and gender-based inequalities in education, but they also underscore a dominant narrative that indulges in dismissing low-income and non-white students in

urban schools from the social grid of educational worth and public acknowledgment ("they just like hurting us"). This deliberate and poisonous disinvestment in both their learning spaces and collective social body makes a
successful maze completion for all of its travelers nearly impossible. Further,
co-researchers are clear about the ideological constructions of their social
status of economic vulnerability that is intimately connected to public perceptions of their neighborhoods ("they think that just because we live in these
neighborhoods and those kind of things go down in the neighborhood, that
they might as well, just throw them in there"). So-called "bad neighborhoods"
do not deserve the investment and support by those in power and who have
access to capital flow and wealth. Youth co-researchers' questioning of local
educational leadership signaled their truth-seeking around to what extent
authorities permit the deliberate poisoning of their public schools and the
legitimization of their economic abandonment.

When youth co-researchers first presented their mental maps to the collective, all of us immediately recognized the similar safety practices under
which represented schools operated, including metal detectors, surveillance
cameras, armed police officers, and an enormous presence of SSAs. But
co-researchers also exposed each other to the particularities of space production at their individual schools. Through Dimples' identification of surveillance cameras installed in front of the girls' bathroom we learned about the
gendered inscriptions of visibility and scrutinization onto school space and
the bodies of students. Ja's experiences with encountering temporary safety
inside the limited space of his school's moving elevator suggested the few
available places that young people under surveillance can access to find distance from the cacophony of policing authorities. Nevertheless, these details
suggest that a youth population placed in constant transit does not need or
deserve the presence of permanent support and assistance.

We struggled with identifying the directionality of individual movements
(arrowed lines); all we saw were looping lines confined predominantly to the
central hallways of any of the given floors without being defined by a specific
starting or ending point. The repeatedly appearing direction-less and circular
journeys of each youth researcher through school spaces immediately took
us back to our discussion of the physical setting of the poisoned maze. In
addition, as we familiarized ourselves with everyone's mentally mapped school
lifeworlds we frequently questioned our inability to recognize destinations or
stops along individual journeys. All the while the arrows on the thick lines
clearly define a directionality of students' journeys and pathways, they do

not indicate young people entering specific places to represent face-to-face encounters with teachers, school staff, other students, or computers inside classrooms, offices, or lunchrooms.

However, there was not one arrowed line to imply any interruptions in individual journeys, or any physical halts or stops during the school day. We concluded that youth researchers' journeys throughout the spaces of their schools are restricted to only a few places that students accessed on a daily basis. While all 10 youth researchers' maps included specific school entry and exit points (i.e., main entrance doors and side exits), only two of the youth researchers drew an arrowed line that moved to the exterior spaces off school grounds. The other eight mental maps do not show any beginning or ending points outside the spaces of their schools. Hence, Piper's words seemed terrifyingly real: "The thing is though with the pipeline, it seems hard to actually find the ending point. You don't know if there is a prize when you actually get there. Or if you are ever gonna get there."

Conclusion

As thoughtfully documented by Kenneth Saltman (2000) and Henry Giroux (2003), low-income and non-white youth are positioned as the next casualty of state-sanctioned domestic violence, given the intensified presence of repressive and punitive neoliberal schooling practices. Given the insights from this study it seems that underperforming public schools are positioned as sites that warehouse and reproduce the underclass; a socially unwanted, superfluous population that is undesired in the current high-technology economy. Through increased awareness and understanding of the inter-institutional circuits of dispossessions, in this case the alignment of public education with the criminal justice system, it is also possible to conclude that securitized public schools provide spaces to set up a social-control process for systematically depriving youth from acquiring the needed technical skills to survive in this fast-paced consumer society. In remembering schooling during the Reconstruction Era as a process that deliberately mis-educated and thus underdeveloped Black people (Anderson, 2010; Butchart, 1980; Woodson, 1998), I am afraid that the racist ideology among today's corporate leaders of public education is extending the colonial mode of production by using school safety and discipline practices as a means to divert wealth, power, and resources from already economically deprived communities to the profit-hungry privatization projects of neoliberalism.

The human collateral casualties of the school-to-prison pipeline are high and visible. Since the emergence of zero-tolerance-based educational policies in the early 1980s, scholars and activists have produced rich and urgent layers of quantitative and qualitative documentation of the disproportionate impact that criminal-justice-driven school safety and discipline practices have had on the lives of non-white students, immigrant youth, low-income adolescents, and gender non-conforming teens (Alexander, 2012; Himmelstein & Brückner, 2011; Hunt & Moodie-Mills, 2012; Meiners, 2007; Sullivan, 2007). Further, the thorough documentation of racialized and gendered school suspension and expulsion rates argues that criminalizing discipline practices have not been able to provide evidence for how law-enforcement-driven school safety practices are creating safer learning environments at schools (Brown, 2005; Gregory, Skiba, & Noguera, 2010; Mukherjee, 2007).

Fiscal figures provide additional insights to an unmistakable prioritization in the disinvestment in public learning institutions over the expansion of the prison system. For example, in 2005 the United States spent $213 billion on the criminal justice system, including police, corrections, and the judiciary, compared to $42 billion on housing and $56 billion on higher education (Petteruti & Walsh, 2008). During the same time the U.S. prison industrial complex exploded into a business that has incarcerated over two million people in the U.S. today, who are no longer able to regain full levels of civic participation, legal protection, and access to the benefits of human relations in production (Mauer, 2006). Similarly, urban public schools that have been issued the ticket to being next on the hit list of privatizing school reform are increasingly producing a social underclass. Neoliberal education policy-makers push for more highly standardized and test-driven literacy and science curricula to punish those who are not able to keep up with expected performances on test scores as measurable units to predict their productivity as working adults. One of the most visible consequences includes many economically marginalized urban schools not being able to move beyond equipping students with skills for manual labor or the service sector. Tragically, under such conditions of mis-education, schools produce none other than a highly under-skilled population that will have to accept the social roles of an unwanted, feared, superfluous, exploitable, and increasingly disposable labor force. In other words, and in light of this discussion of the geographies of disposability found inside the disinvested spaces of public education, highly surveilled public schools are producing a reserved cadre needed to occupy the transitional spaces of a cheap and exploitable labor force. The following point remains nebulous: the current neoliberal(ized) and racist social order rewards producers and productivity, and systematically abandons "flawed consumers" (Bauman, 2011) into quarantined sites (prisons, mental health institutions, detention centers, and underperforming schools) for being unable to participate in the economics of a profit-oriented consumer industry. However, with an outsourced manufacture industry, it is unclear exactly what future economic roles socially disinvested youth will be filling domestically.

Finally, when reframing social disposability as a collateral casualty of educational inequalities and as long-term inscriptions on the collective social body of young people, it becomes evident how public schools have a direct impact on what kind of society this country produces, what kind of schooling habits and behaviors are rewarded, and the kinds of lives students are allowed to live while in school. In other words, securitized and policed schools have become "spaces of no one," or the learning sites to which no producing and consuming parent wants to send his or her child. Yet these undesirable school grounds are simultaneously being shaped into sites for a growing number of disposable youth. Given this reality, I raise the following unanswered questions: How do young people bear to be in this world when their lives are endangered by their systemic erasure? Who deserves to live? Who is indexed to die? Whose bodies count?

As identified by critical pedagogue James Baldwin (1970) more than 4 decades ago, and as reincarnated in the work by contemporary PAR intellectuals (Patel, 2012; Ruglis, 2011), the goal of critical youth studies has to unravel the deeply racialized and racist biopolitics of our current neoliberal world. Identifying and unraveling the purposes of education, and, hence, the lives that young people are allowed to live, is intimately connected to: what does it mean to survive a racist capitalist system that is engineered to destroy minoritized youth? Diversifying methodologies for knowledge productions that are committed to not only outlining but also mobilizing academic communities to decreasing the mortalities in our current public education's geography means to disclose them fearlessly and to bear witness to young people's ongoing struggle for survival. It is yet to be determined what future role and commitment the interdisciplinary field of critical youth studies will assume within these growing deadly spaces for our young people.

References

Aggarwal, U., Mayorga, E., & Nevel, D. (2012). Slow violence and neoliberal education reform: Reflections on a school closure. *Peace and Conflict: Journal of Peace Psychology, 18*(2), 156.

Alexander, M. (2012). *The new Jim Crow: Mass incarceration in the age of colorblindness.* New York, NY: The New Press.

Anderson, J. D. (2010). *The education of Blacks in the South, 1860–1935.* Chapel Hill, NC: University of North Carolina Press.

Baldwin, J. (1970). My dungeon shook—Letter to my nephew on the one hundredth anniversary of emancipation. In J. Baldwin (Ed.), *The fire next time* (pp. 28–30). New York, NY: Vintage Press.

Bauman, Z. (2011). *Wasted lives.* Malden, MA: Polity Press.

Birtel, M., & Chilcott, L. (Producers), & Guggenheim, D. (Director). (2010). *Waiting for superman* [Motion picture]. United States: Paramount.

Brown, J. (2005). Education on lockdown: The schoolhouse to jailhouse track. *Advancement Project.* Retrieved from http://www.advancementproject.org/resources/entry/education-on-lockdown-the-schoolhouse-to-jailhouse-track

Buras, K. L., Randels, J., & ya Salaam, K. (2010). *Pedagogy, policy, and the privatized city: Stories of dispossession and defiance from New Orleans.* New York, NY: Teachers College Press.

Butchart, R. E. (1980). *Northern schools, southern Blacks, and reconstruction: Freedmen's education, 1862–1875.* Westport, CT: Praeger.

Byrd, J. A. (2011). *The transit of Empire: Indigenous critiques of colonialism.* Minneapolis, MN: University of Minnesota Press.

Cammarota, J., & Fine, M. (2008). *Revolutionizing education: Youth participatory action research in motion.* New York, NY: Routledge.

Chilisa, B. (2011). *Indigenous research methodologies.* Thousand Oaks, CA: Sage.

Coleman, J. S. (1966). *The Coleman Report: Equality of educational opportunity.* WGBH-TV.

Duke. (2013, March 22). Jersey Jazzman: School closings: The new apartheid [Blog post]. Retrieved from http://jerseyjazzman.blogspot.com/2013/03/school-closings-new-apartheid.html

Fabricant, M., & Fine, M. (2012). *Charter schools and the corporate makeover of public education: What's at stake?* New York, NY: Teachers College Press.

Fine, M., & Ruglis, J. (2009). Circuits and consequences of dispossession: The racialized realignment of the public sphere for US youth. *Transforming Anthropology, 17*(1), 20–33.

Futch, V. A., & Fine, M. (2012). Mapping as a method: History and theoretical commitments. *Qualitative Research in Psychology, 11*(1), 45–59. Retrieved from http://www.tandfonline.com/doi/abs/10.1080/14780887.2012.719070

Gieseking, J. (2008). *Mental mapping as a methodology: Its evolution, its usefulness, and the ways in which they may be analyzed.* Paper presented at the Royal Geographical Society with the Institute of British Geographers, London, England.

Giroux, H. A. (2003). Zero tolerance, domestic militarization, and the war against youth. *Social Justice, 30*(2)(92), 59–65.

Giroux, H. A. (2010). *Youth in a suspect society: Democracy or disposability?* New York, NY: Palgrave Macmillan.

Gregory, A., Skiba, R. J., & Noguera, P. A. (2010). The achievement gap and the discipline gap: Two sides of the same coin? *Educational Researcher, 39*(1), 59–68.

Gwynne, K. (2013, June 7). Philly closes 23 public schools, generously builds $400 million prison where kids can hang instead. *AlterNet*. Retrieved from http://www.alternet.org/education/philly-closes-23-public-schools-generously-builds-400-million-prison-where-kids-can-hang

Harvey, D. (2003). *The new imperialism.* Oxford, England: Oxford University Press.

Himmelstein, K. E., & Brückner, H. (2011). Criminal-justice and school sanctions against non-heterosexual youth: A national longitudinal study. *Pediatrics, 127*(1), 49–57. Retrieved from http://pediatrics.aappublications.org/content/127/1/49.short

Holliday, D. (2013, April 28). Organizers say Stewart school closure another word for "land grab." *DNAinfo Chicago.* Retrieved July 11, 2013, from http://www.dnainfo.com/chicago/20130428/uptown/organizers-say-stewart-school-closure-another-word-for-land-grab

Horton, J., & Kraftl, P. (2006). Not just growing up, but going on: Materials, spacings, bodies, situations. *Children's Geographies, 4*(3), 259–276.

Hunt, J., & Moodie-Mills, A. (2012, June 29). The unfair criminalization of gay and transgender youth. *Center for American Progress.* Retrieved August 12, 2013, from http://www.americanprogress.org/issues/lgbt/report/2012/06/29/11730/the-unfair-criminalization-of-gay-and-transgender-youth/

Katz, C. (2011). Accumulation, excess, childhood: Toward a Countertopography of risk and waste. *Documents d'Anàlisi Geogràfica, 57*(1), 47–60.

Krueger, P. (2009). *Navigating the gaze: Young people's intimate knowledge with surveilled spaces at school* (Doctoral dissertation). City University of New York, New York.

Krueger, P. (2011). Activating memories of endurance. *International Review of Qualitative Research, 3*(4), 411–432.

Krueger-Henney, P. (2012). It's not just a method! The epistemic and political work of young people's lifeworlds at the school-prison nexus. In E. R. Meiners & M. T. Winn (Eds.), *Education and incarceration* (pp. 108–133). New York, NY: Routledge.

Lipman, P. (2004). *High stakes education: Inequality, globalization, and urban school reform.* New York, NY: Routledge.

Lipman, P. (2013). *The new political economy of urban education: Neoliberalism, race, and the right to the city.* New York, NY: Routledge.

Mauer, M. (2006). *Race to incarcerate.* New York, NY: The New Press.

Meiners, E. R. (2007). *Right to be hostile: Schools, prisons, and the making of public enemies.* New York, NY: Routledge.

Mignolo, W. D. (2000). *Local histories/global designs: Coloniality, subaltern knowledges, and border thinking.* Princeton, NJ: Princeton University Press.

Mogel, L., & Bhagat, A. (Eds.). (2008). *An atlas of radical cartography.* Los Angeles, CA: Journal of Aesthetics & Protest Press.

Mukherjee, E. (2007). *Criminalizing the classroom: The over-policing of New York City schools.* Retrieved from the New York Civil Liberties Union Website: http://www.nyclu.org/pdfs/criminalizing_the_classroom_report.pdf

Naison, M. (2013, June 3). With a Brooklyn accent: Why I protest closing schools to build luxury housing near Lincoln Center [Blog post]. Retrieved from http://withabrooklynaccent.blogspot.com/2013/06/why-i-protest-closing-schools-to-build.html

Nolan, K. (2011). *Police in the hallways: Discipline in an urban high school.* Minneapolis, MN: University of Minnesota Press.

Pappas, L. N. (2012). School closings and parent engagement. *Peace and Conflict: Journal of Peace Psychology, 18*(2), 165.

Patel, L. (2012). Contact zones, problem posing and critical consciousness. *Pedagogies: An International Journal, 7*(4), 333–346.

Petteruti, A., & Walsh, N. (2008). *Moving target: A decade of resistance to the prison industrial complex* (p. 44). Washington, DC: Justice Policy Institute. Retrieved from http://www.justicepolicy.org/images/upload/08-09_REP_MovingTargetCR10_AC-PS.pdf

Ruglis, J. (2011). Mapping the biopolitics of school dropout and youth resistance. *International Journal of Qualitative Studies in Education, 24*(5), 627–637.

Saltman, K. J. (2000). *Collateral damage: Corporatizing public schools–a threat to democracy.* Lanham, MD: Rowman & Littlefield.

Smith, J. J., & Stovall, D. (2008). "Coming home" to new homes and new schools: Critical race theory and the new politics of containment. *Journal of Education Policy, 23*(2), 135–152.

Smith, L. T. (1999). *Decolonizing methodologies: Research and indigenous peoples.* New York, NY: Zed Books.

Sullivan, E. (2007). *Deprived of dignity: Degrading treatment and abusive discipline in New York City & Los Angeles public schools.* Retrieved from the National Economic and Social Rights Initiative Website: http://www.nesri.org/resources/deprived-of-dignity-degrading-treatment-and-abusive-discipline-in-new-york-city-and-los-angeles-public-schools

Tuck, E., & Guishard, M. (2013). Scientifically based research and settler coloniality: An ethical framework of decolonial participatory action research. In T. M. Kress, C. Malott, & B. Portfilio (Eds.), *Challenging status quo retrenchment: New directions in critical qualitative research* (pp. 3–27). Charlotte, NC: Information Age.

Wald, J., & Losen, D. J. (2003). Defining and redirecting a school-to-prison pipeline. *New Directions for Youth Development, 2003*(99), 9–15.

Willinsky, J. (1998). *Learning to divide the world: Education at empire's end.* Minneapolis, MN: University of Minnesota Press.

Woodson, C. G. (1998). *The mis-education of the Negro.* Trenton, NJ: Africa World Press.

· 4 ·

RESISTING MARGINALIZATION

Students' Conversations About Life in University

Carl E. James

Today's university campuses increasingly reflect the diversity of Canada's population. Among those attending in growing numbers are second-generation and generation-and-a-half (or 1.5-generation) Canadian youth whose immigrant parents often do not have the financial means to support them in university. But finances seem not to operate as a deterrent; for their immigrant parents have socialized them to accept that education is what will afford them access to the opportunities they seek in order to succeed in this society (see James, 2012; James & Haig-Brown, 2001; Kazis, Vargas, & Hoffman, 2004; Lopez, 2002; Nicholas, Stepick, & Dutton Stepick, 2008). To this end, many of these Canadian youth aspire to attend university, rather than college, believing that with a university education they will be best positioned to attain the needed capital resources that are necessary for social and economic mobility in any society (Adamuti-Trache, Anisef, Sweet, & Walters, 2013; Fuligni, 1998; James & Taylor, 2008; Wood, 2007).

This chapter provides a glimpse into the world of two cohorts of second- and 1.5-generation youth who attended university between 2001 and 2005 through an access program that provided financial, mentoring, and administrative support for the first 3 years of study. The 18 participants selected for the program had demonstrated that social, economic, familial, and cultural difficulties prevented them from attending university without financial support. While the participants still needed to meet the university's academic entrance requirements, once admitted, they were able to enroll in the program and courses of their choice. As part of the initiative (which recognized the particular needs students had in relation to their racialized, classed, and immigrant status), the students were required to participate in weekly meetings referred to as "the Common Hour." In these sessions, students discussed their experiences, shared concerns, and interacted with each other. My interest here is to use the conversations from the Common Hour to discuss how these second- and 1.5-generation Canadian university students experienced and negotiated university, understood and framed their marginalization, constructed their identities, and pursued their postsecondary aspirations.

The Common Hour

The weekly Common Hour sessions provided data[1] that was supplemented by individual life history interviews, application statements, and personal journals that participants kept during their time in the program. The Common Hour provided participants a space to interact with each other; build relationships; initiate and maintain contact with mentors, advisors, faculty and administrators; as well as share their ongoing and shifting identities and experiences in university—particularly difficulties related to their transition from high school to university. Sessions were also used to discuss courses including selection, instructors, and requirements, as well as administrative matters. At the request of participants, workshops were provided on study skills, essay writing, and time-management techniques as well as resume writing and job search (an indication to us that participants were thinking beyond their university years and making connections between their educational program and employment possibilities).

The Common Hour also gave participants a chance to identify their commonalities, bridge their differences, bond with each other, negotiate among themselves their divergent, and at times contradictory, views, and foster a sense of belonging in the university space. The sessions provided valuable insights into the students' ideas about themselves, about their experiences, and how they supported each other. In this regard, the Common Hour proved to be a very significant reference and data source, as well as a way to enable the development of trust among all of us involved in the sessions. In fact, while over time the Common Hour became a safe and comfortable space for participants, they initially expressed reservations about the sessions and understandably were hesitant to discuss certain details about their lives in the group. Seth explained that at first there were "certain topics you don't want to deal with," and Amy admitted, "I thought that my privacy was going to be compromised because I am in this program." The participants' initial hesitancy was not surprising since it was indicative of the suspicions marginalized young people tend to have of mainstream institutions, and accordingly they were cautious about exposing their personal lives and "histories to people they did not know" (Amy). Furthermore, their reservations about participating in the group sessions and relating their stories about barriers to university were likely attempts to resist participating in a risky process that they felt would re-inscribe their marginalization and racialization.

However, over time, the Common Hour became a comfortable space—a space where, as critical race and feminist scholars assert, they were able to "find their voice" in multi-vocal dialogue with similar others who validated their experiences (Ladson-Billings, 2000; Madriz 2000). Moreover, as Yosso (2005) contended, "hearing their own stories and the stories of others, listening to how the arguments against them are framed and learning to make the arguments to defend themselves" can help marginalized individuals "become empowered participants" (p. 75). The Common Hour, then, became more than an obligatory session, or a weekly "escape" from the challenges they faced in university, but as we will see in their conversations, it was also a "consciousness-raising" tool (Madriz, 2000) that participants used to help them negotiate the university structure and their challenges within it.

A Brief Profile of the Participants

Almost all of the participants were born in Canada. They were of different racial and ethnic backgrounds—African, Portuguese, South Asian, and Aboriginal—which also meant that while all of them were fluent in English, many of them spoke and were fluent in a second language that they used with their parents and in their communities. They resided in different communities (mostly low-income) in Toronto; and except for Amanda, Melanie, Luke, Amy, Seth, and Nadia, who grew up with both parents, the others were raised by, and lived with, their single mothers. All of them acknowledged that their own and their family's financial circumstances made it difficult, if not impossible, for them to attend university without assistance; but this did not seem to have limited their educational ambitions to pursue careers in law, medicine, business, teaching, and human resources. Most of the participants entered the program directly after high school; however, a few of them deferred their acceptance, or waited a year to apply in order to earn money or deal with family responsibilities. Many of them referred to university as a "coming of age" experience, signaling that being in university was a means of achieving independence from their families.

Participants revealed that family obligation, under-valuing of their potential and possibilities, racial and ethnic discrimination, personal depression, physical abuse, their arranged marriage and divorce at a young age, and family violence were some of the things that operated as obstacles to them accessing educational and career opportunities. Nevertheless, whatever their situation, they resisted framing themselves—or allowing others to frame them, their families, or their respective ethnic/racial communities—as "deprived" or "deficient," because they believed that their families or communities were not solely responsible for their deficient educational and social situation. They seemed to understand that accepting the deficit discourse would have meant having to admit that they did not have "the normative cultural knowledge and skills" for university and that their parents did not value or support their educational ambitions (see Yosso, 2005, p. 75). In fact, these students approached their university careers with a determination and confidence that somehow the social and cultural capital that they possessed would carry them to successful completion of their university programs (see also Nicholas et al.'s 2008 work with students of Haitian parents in Miami whose "sense of familial obligation" motivated them to succeed educationally "against all odds," p. 238). Yosso's (2005) framework of "Community Cultural Wealth" (CCW) is a useful reference for our examination of how these youths' identities, experiences, and aspirations operated in their refusal to engage with deficit models of marginalization and racialization.

Community Cultural Wealth

Yosso (2005) posited that racialized students are often assumed not to have the required knowledge, values, and language deemed necessary to perform productively in their schooling, and that their under-performance is a result of "deficiency" in those communities where they do not get to learn the language and behavior of success (see also Ibrahim, 2011; he shows that the "symbolic capital" and highly valued French spoken by African Canadian high-school students were seen to be deficient by their Franco-Ontarian French teachers, who treated them accordingly). Using the concept of community cultural wealth, Yosso argued that students of color possess "an array of knowledge, skills, abilities and contacts" that are nurtured in families and in communities, and which they utilize "to survive and resist macro and micro-forms of oppression" (p. 77). While Yosso's primary reference is to elementary and secondary education, her discussion is applicable in helping us understand the fact that students enter university equipped with a wide range of capital and community support.

Yosso (2005) outlined six "dynamic" and overlapping forms of capital or wealth that Communities of Color provide their youth. They are: aspirational, navigational, social, linguistic, familial, and resistant capital. Going beyond Bourdieu's conceptual offering of social and cultural capital, Yosso suggested that these forms of capital are in part responsible for the interests, ambitions, knowledge, and needs that marginalized students bring to their schooling; these are things that educational institutions tend to undervalue and ignore. In terms of university, the consequence of negating the racialized experiences of "the new insiders" can serve to "re-inscribe them as outsiders" and maintain the status quo or "cultural mold" into which they are expected to fit (James, 2002, p. 141). Therefore, if marginalized students are to productively engage in their educational process, their multiple sources of inspiration and "forms of cultural capital" must be recognized and valued (Yosso, 2005, p. 77).

Of particular significance to this discussion is what Yosso (2005) described as aspirational, navigational, and resistant capital. Aspirational capital refers the "resiliency" of group members, in terms of their "ability to maintain hopes and dreams for the future, even in the face of real and perceived barriers." This is evident in the ways parents themselves strive and encourage their children to do the same to achieve goals "beyond their present circumstances" (p. 78). This capital is often nurtured through what is perceived to be the promise of education. Ample research tells of immigrant parents' strong belief in the possibilities that education affords, and as a pathway toward social mobility and full participation in society (Adamuti-Trache et al., 2013; Nicholas et al., 2008).

Navigational capital denotes the ability of individuals "to maneuver through institutions not created with Communities of Color in mind" (Yosso, 2005, p. 80). And in their exercise of agency "within institutional constraints," as Yosso (2005) explained, individuals draw on their various social networks, and their social and psychological skills "to maneuver through structures of inequality permeated by racism" (p. 80). In so doing, individuals work to challenge the structures of racism that shape their own and others' lives. Yosso referred to "the knowledges and skills" that individuals demonstrate in this instance as "resistant capital"—a cultural wealth that is "fostered through oppositional behavior that challenges inequality" (p. 80). The resistance, Yosso explained, is strengthened when individuals are able to draw on the other forms of capital (i.e., linguistic, familial, navigational, etc.), and when parents "consciously [instruct] their children to engage in behaviours and maintain attitudes that challenge the status quo" (p. 81). It is worth noting that resistance is not always about "oppositional behavior, such as self-defeating or conformist strategies that feed back into the system of sub-ordination." Rather, resistance can and does operate in "transformative" ways by individuals who are aware of and recognize "the structural nature of oppression" and are motivated "to work toward social and racial justice" (p. 81).

Putnam's (2000) concepts of "bonding" and "bridging" social capital are also instructive for our reading of students' experiences. Bonding refers to the important connections individuals use and rely on by choice and necessity for their existence and success in a community or society generally. Bridging refers to the set of connections between socially heterogeneous groups. Putnam suggested that "Bonding social capital" is good for "getting by," but that "bridging social capital" is crucial for "getting ahead." Bonding and bridging are not "either-or" categories into which networks can be neatly divided, but "more or less" dimensions along which we can compare different forms of social capital (p. 23).

In the remainder of the chapter, I draw on Yosso and Putnam's frameworks referencing the students' conversations about themselves and their experiences. First, I discuss the ways in which the students pragmatically re/framed and re/defined their difference in order to enable their participation in university. Second, I unpack the significant strategies or initiatives of the students—namely constructing and nurturing bonding relationships with their peers, and bridging connections with administrators and instructors in an attempt to bolster their opportunities. Essentially, the focus of the discussion is on how these students, refusing to be marginalized, challenged and resisted markers of difference (based on race, ethnicity, class and/or immigrant status) by which they were read as imposters.

Re/framing Identities, Re/conceptualizing Difference

Throughout their participation in the project, participants used a variety of descriptors, language, and terminology that accentuated their potential, their possibilities, and their perceptions of their capacity to succeed and achieve their aspirations. Much like Yosso (2005) suggested in her discussion of community cultural wealth, students drew on understandings of themselves that high-lighted what they felt were key social credentials that would foster successful participation in university. In other words, they rejected being referred to as different because they were students in an "access" program. They believed that such categorization could stigmatize and marginalize them. Hence they insisted that they were "regular" university students with "unique" qualities.

For instance, in one Common Hour session, playing with the word "differ-ence," Seth offered a positive reconceptualization that signaled his desire for them to think of their difference as presenting their uniqueness, rather than something that sets them apart from other university students.

Seth:	Difference is more a pessimistic thought, where I like to think of difference as unique or special. So it's more like, I'd rather not be dif-ferent, I'd rather be unique.
Facilitator:	What's the difference there then?
Seth:	Well, to me unique is difference, but in a more upbeat way. Optimis-tic! I'm proud to be different, but I'm not different I'm unique.
Facilitator:	So being unique is a matter of valuing difference?
Seth:	I guess. For me I would rather not be considered different. I'd rather be considered unique 'cause it sounds better. 'Cause for me, difference is like really pointing out that you are different ... in a negative way. Whereas if you say that person is unique instead of different, it's like saying that person is special and is part of a whole ... Yeah, 'cause if you think that person is different, like that person is alone type of thing—that attitude.

The differentiation Seth is making between "unique" and "different" is signif-icant. He seems to be engaging in a strategy of resistance to an identification that would alienate or exclude him and his peers from full participation in the institution and society generally. Interestingly, it is not that Seth is rejecting his difference—he is "proud" of his difference; it is that he wished to provide an optimistic reading of their difference, suggesting that the words "unique" and "special" are more representative—in fact they are characteristics to be found in any group. In substituting unique and special for difference, Seth was looking for more generalizable conceptualization that can be applied to many, if not all, of the students on campus. He asked:

With your belief in difference and your cultural difference, do you feel that you fit in? Is there a point where you think to yourself walking down the hallway: 'Wow these people are really different?' Like to me, they think one way, they look one way, and they practice things one way that are different than you. Do you ever think of that?

Amy responded by telling everyone that she felt that her "uniqueness" allowed her to feel like she belongs, particularly in the multicultural setting of Toronto.

> But don't you think the beauty of Toronto especially, is the fact that everyone is so multicultural—so much culture … There's always someone you can relate to. There's people; there's Portuguese people; there's Chinese people; there's Jewish people. Even on campus there's always a good thing you can fit with. I think that's the beauty of Toronto, because if you go anywhere else in the world that's not going to happen. You're going to feel alienated, and wow, I don't belong here; I'm different. But here I totally feel comfortable. There's no need for me to say I'm an outsider, I don't belong, you know because Toronto makes me feel that way.

For Seth and Amy, being unique is perceived as a way of valuing difference—specifically, cultural difference. As such, they are not anomalous, especially in a multicultural city such as Toronto, and by extension the multicultural campus of the university. The participants held that because of multiculturalism their uniqueness is accommodated, which for Amy provided "comfort"—something that, as she said, was not possible "anywhere else in the world."

Participants' sense of themselves as "unique" rather than "different" was also represented in their disavowal of themselves as "access" students. They referred to the access program as "a scholarship program," choosing to see the financial support they were receiving as a "scholarship." Saying that they were in a "scholarship program" was empowering, for it implied that they were hard-working, high-achieving, capable, successful, worthy, and legitimate students who earned their places in the university by merit. By positioning themselves as scholarship recipients who were receiving support because of their academic abilities, these university students sought to identify themselves in positive terms, propagating consistency between their marginalized or cultural identities and their identities as scholarship students (Brathwaite, 2003; Hurtado, 2013; James & Mannette, 2000).

Amy proffered that she did not think that the barriers she encountered in her educational career lessened her chances of becoming a scholarship student. She recalled that when she read the application for the program and noticed that it requested that she write about the social and educational barriers she faced, she asked herself: "Does mine qualify?" Stephanie also had reservations about whether her experiences deserved support and initially resisted applying for the program, believing that the program was "for weirdoes or something." In addition, Amy declared: "From the very beginning, I just thought: 'Well, I don't think my troubles are that huge because I had a pretty good [grade point] average.'" She went on to tell her peers that because "only a few people know about the program, I just tell them it's a scholarship and I got this because I had good marks and I fit the description of what they wanted." Seeing themselves as scholarship students meant that they were part of an elite or exclusive club through which they were able to gain respect and opportunities.

Moreover, how participants negotiated their economic marginalization helped to broaden and shift the definition of social class to include attitudes, aspirations, and social behavior, rather than simply monetary status. In one group conversation, Laura offered a detailed explanation of her perceptions of social class. Like the others, Laura was experiencing severe financial hardship and needed support to attend university. Despite this reality, she refused to consider herself as lower or working class and offered her own definition of what class meant to her. Laura conceived of herself as "classy" and applied this identity to her engagements with the university and her peers. Conceding that "we measure [class] on an attitude, [and] on acceptability," she went on to say class can be an individual characteristic that one can "learn," such as a particular way "of speaking and dressing," "the way you walk," or how you "behave" or "act." Therefore, for Laura, social class was not only related to economic or material resources, for, as she put it,

> Nowadays, there's the rich, there's the poor. Everyone in middle class is in debt. So, there's no middle class, everyone is on the same level. So your class is usually, right now, identified by, like, how you present yourself; and not necessarily your clothes. It's really your attitude, and your education.

Laura's claim that she was no different from all the other students attending university was to assert that like them, she was getting an education that would help her make "something" of her life and be "classy." Accordingly, in Laura's construction of middle class as something one can easily acquire, and as a status she already holds, with her university education, she is destined for social success and realization of her aspirations.

This notion of social class informed participants' perceptions of the university they wished to attend, which was not necessarily the university in which they enrolled. Interestingly, Laura admitted that she chose to attend the smaller campus of the university, which is located in an upper-middle class area of the city, rather than the main campus, which is adjacent to a neighborhood perceived to be impoverished and dangerous. Her expectation was that attending the smaller campus would enable her to associate with "higher-class" students. Other participants stated that if it were not for

the "scholarship" opportunity, they would have attended other more reputable universities that they believed would have been more of an asset in
terms of employment and career possibilities. Submitting that they would
likely have chosen to attend a different university if they had the means
to do so suggests that these youth understood very well the social and cultural capital that is provided by the university one attends; and in the case
of Laura, unable to attend another university, she wagered that being at
the supposed "better" campus compensated for not having attended a more
reputable university.

The language of uniqueness, scholarship, and class that students used in
their narrations of themselves and their experiences indicates their pragmatic
articulations of identities that "built them up," motivated them, encouraged
them, and created a sense of hope and possibility. By reframing their circumstances and articulating their identities in ways that seemed to challenge
perceptions of deficit, these students were attempting to reconcile many of
the contradictions they faced as racial and ethnic minorities. These are the
identities participants brought with them and were part of their "cultural
wealth." In fact, their constructions of themselves and their minimization of
their limitations were not attempts to deny their racial, ethnic and minority
backgrounds and communities. Rather, they chose to draw on and present
those aspects of themselves that contributed to their idea of what is necessary
to succeed in postsecondary institutions.

The students' insistence on their abilities to achieve their goals chiefly
through hard work and dedication correspond to the neoliberal ethos of
individualism, competition, choice, and responsibility, by which they have
come to think of themselves as autonomous individuals whose successes or
failures were based solely on their own initiatives. This reasoning was also
evident among the black Canadian university students in Gosine's (2012)
study, whose strategies of "role modeling, and building black networks of
support" were seen as necessary components for them to effectively "negotiate white-dominated structures" (p. 2). According to Gosine, the students'
strategies for attaining their educational and career goals were "informed by
the neoliberal, meritocratic, and individualistic ethos of the broader society,"
which for his "high achieving" study participants—they were studying medicine, law, sciences, and engineering—seemed consistent with their socialized belief that success is possible within the existing structures of society.
Such thinking, as Luxton (2010) wrote, serves "to obscure or even deny the
class, gender and racialized relations that are fundamental to contemporary

society" (p. 180; see also Sukarieh & Tannock, 2008, who argued against the neoliberal "culture of responsibilisation and entrepreneurship through education," p. 309).

Navigating University, Negotiating Ambivalence

That the students in the access program believed that they could and should succeed on the basis of merit, and that education provides a path to their future opportunities, is no different from most other Canadians (Lessard, 1995; Lopez, 2002; Portelli & Solomon, 2001). However, at the same time, they recognized that as marginalized individuals, opportunities would not always come easily, and that they were likely to face hurdles and challenges (Frenette 2007; Henry & Tator, 2006; Kazis et al., 2004). Nevertheless, they remained optimistic, yet ambivalent, knowing that education is not always a useable "ticket" on the train to success. The following exchange aptly describes the ambivalence that participants felt about their chances of attaining their educational goals:

Lewis:	While little education will get you near the station [i.e., high school], the more education you get, gets you to the platform. There might be a barrier that won't let you onto the actual train. But education can get you that far. But at least you're there— and you have the opportunity to jump onto the train. And sure there are roadblocks there, but at least you're on the platform; and you're equal to everyone else and you can get on the train.
Tristana:	I completely understand what you're saying. But if you think about the increase in education for minority kids—before, there was segregation in schools, so white and Black kids got different types of education. With desegregation you're seeing more minorities getting education. But do you see the balance in jobs? Do you see Black CEOs? Do you see women CEOs? Do you see a change in the demographics of who holds jobs?
Several participants remarked at once:	But that's changing though …
Tristana:	But it's not changing drastically in terms of education policy. I understand education can get you to the station … but you have no ticket.

The ambivalence in this dialogue between Lewis, Tristana, and the rest of the group reflects an awareness that in order to meet their goals, they must also engage with a system that is oppressive and discriminatory (see James &

Taylor, 2008; Law, Phillips, & Turney, 2004). There were students, such as Tristana, who rejected the notion of merit as articulated by Lewis, making the argument that inequity and racism are structural realities; hence the possibilities of social mobility through education for minorities is limited. But what can we make of Tristana's argument, when she, like everyone else at the time, was pursuing postsecondary education with the expectation that she will successfully complete her program of study? It seems that as racial minority university students, their understanding of the possibilities education afforded them cannot be separated from their marginalized experiences. Consequently, they constantly attempt to reconcile the complex series of tensions, challenges, and contradictions that were all part of living with the ideology of meritocracy—an ideology into which they have been well socialized. This belief and commitment to meritocracy (and to their education) were maintained even when it was apparent (like for Tristana) that the university structures were not always equitable, and that teachers, administrators, and peers were not always supportive of their potential. Hence their participation in university was an ongoing constant process of negotiation in a state of constant tension.

In attempts to reconcile the tensions, challenges, and barriers that they faced as raced, classed, and second-generation Canadians, attending an institution that did not always acknowledge their experiences and interests, participants engaged in a variety of practices that bolstered their refusal to be limited by their marginalized status. They actively participated in a culture of support created by their cohort, maintained a sense of entitlement, and drew on their navigational, aspirational, and resistant capital that proved useful to them.

Given that experiences of marginalization can erode confidence in oneself and in one's sense of his/her potential (Frenette, 2007; Fuligni, 1998), the group became an important source of validation, legitimization, and nurturance. They created a bond with each other that enabled them to both provide and receive support in the face of, at times, challenging circumstances. They used the Common Hour to support and encourage each other through which they developed close friendships. They validated their presence in the university, and reinforced their sense of purpose: reminding each other why they were there. In addition, participants drew on each other to address their frustration, their feelings of alienation and discouragement, and their experiences with discrimination on and off the university campus.

In a conversation during which participants lamented their grades (which were not as high as they had hoped), Amy offered encouragement to her peers, saying: "You've just got to believe in yourself ... If you know you're smart. You know you're smart." And with reference to the challenges they faced, Nadia re-assured her peers, observing: "Yeah that's one thing about university. We're all experiencing the same thing—we're all going through the same thing." Ewart followed with "We are all in this together and we should all support each other. It would be nice if all of us could get 90s." This sharing and verbalizing not only served to build community but was also instrumental in reinforcing the fact that they each had "what it takes" to complete their university programs and as such deserved to be there. This act of sharing their experiences became, over time, an expedient and practical strategy that helped each participant to deal with their current situation and, as Nadia put it, "similar situations in the future." She went on to remind her peers that they were "not the only ones" facing challenges and assured them that, with support, their aspirations were achievable.

Having faith in their potential also meant believing that they were equal to everyone else and were therefore entitled to equal respect and treatment as all other students, including receiving a similar level of acknowledgment and support from professors, teaching assistants, and administrators. In their conversations, participants would remind each other that they deserved, and were entitled to, the same treatment as "regular" students. Ewart, for example, felt that he was entitled to the mentorship and personal support he needed from professors to attain the qualification necessary for him to attend medical school. He attributed his sense of entitlement to the messages he received from his high school teachers, his mother, aunt, and coworkers at the factory where he worked part-time. The fact that his expectations were not met was a frustration for Ewart—something that he shared with the group.

Ewart: You see I know a handful of people in this school and everyone is doing their own thing so there's no one really to take the time. There's plenty of professors. But there's only one professor trying to help me ... He's a calculus professor for applied calculus and he has his PhD in physics. And I have some theories on quantum mechanics that I try to bring to him and try to explain to him and he's the only one that tries to sit down and understand and take the time to understand or talk to me about them and see if they are logical. And ... you will see like professors in their room or their private offices, and you try to go and talk to them, and they're all too busy. And they're always directing you somewhere else.

Facilitator: Where are they directing you?

Ewart:	Like, I would go to a professor and I would see he is doing nothing in his office and I said could you help me with something. He's like: "I'm economics or I'm this," et cetera.
Laura:	But professors usually want an appointment made.
Ewart:	Some of these guys are laying back in their chair. They aren't doing anything. I just want to find someone who I can share my ideas with. Someone I can interact with.
Laura:	To them it's a job, it's not their responsibility.
Ewart:	I just want to find someone who doesn't hate their job.
Laura:	They want to be approached in a professional manner, so they want their time to be by appointment.
Ewart:	If that's the person, or the kind of person they are, I don't want to be working with them. I want someone who actually takes the time, who actually takes the initiative of being there for students. I want to find someone spontaneously one day who I can just find a link with.

As the conversation continued, Amy and Stephanie asked Ewart if he had any success obtaining help from teaching assistants (TA). He replied that a TA could not help him because his "questions are specialized questions." But Laura felt that rather than leaving students to their devices, professors have a responsibility to "help you" by assigning teaching assistants to deal with questions that students such as Ewart had. "Isn't that the whole point of a TA?" she asked rhetorically.

While for some people Ewart's expectations might be interpreted as reflective of his sense of self-importance, interestingly, his peers did not see it that way. In fact, no one in the group challenged Ewart. Instead, they passionately engaged in the discussion, sharing their own questions and concerns, their knowledge of how the university worked, and what they too expected from professors. This "rallying" around each other was quite common, and they would advise each other on how best to work the university system as they understood it. They understood, as Laura suggested, that students were to "make an appointment" because professors want to be "approached in a professional manner."

Furthermore, Ewart's desire to find a mentor—someone with whom he could engage—revealed his expectation of university regardless of his minority status or the status of the access program in which he was engaged. Like many of the others, Ewart refused to link the support he needed or sought out to his racialized identity or the access program. Most of all, not thinking of their race, ethnicity, or class as restricting, participants framed their expectations in ways that were illustrative of their belief and knowledge of what they were entitled to as university students. Their conversations reflected the constant process of negotiation in which they engaged in order to "fit" into the system and affirm their sense of belonging in order to survive and succeed in it.

In addition to bonding with each other as one strategy of survival, these youth also recognized that who they knew (and to whom they had access, especially people in administrative or powerful positions) was significant to their journey through university. The following exchange is illustrative of how privileged participants felt knowing that that the access program afforded them connections to the dean of a faculty.

Nadia: [At first] I thought it was going to be such a big deal. I thought, I don't want to decrease the seriousness of the program; but I thought it was going to take up so much more time of my life. I thought research group. I thought it was going to be doing tests and be tested and things like that. But then I thought it was really cool when the dean, the fact that the dean was there. I also felt like, wow, I know the dean.

Seth: You felt up there, right?—more privileged, I guess

For these youth, meeting the dean, making connections, and developing networks with individuals in positions of prominence in the university and community, having access to the project researchers and facilitators to ask questions and offer advice was an important part of how they found their way through university. As demonstrated in the above exchange, Seth and Nadia recognized that who they knew, especially administrators, was a significant "bridge" to their success in navigating university. Despite not wanting to admit to their impediments, and distancing themselves from their marginalized status but aware that their involvement in the access program had its consequences, participants remained optimistic and pragmatic in their use of the program as reference. They did so when their involvement fostered networking advantages (such as meeting the dean). This also reflects their understanding of the system and how it functioned. While participants refused to be limited by their marginalization, they were by no means oblivious to their racial, ethnic, and class backgrounds, or to the added value they received from their participation in the program. They clearly understood the benefits of the capital they brought to their university life.

Conclusion: Being University Students

What ran through the conversations of these university students was how they tried to reconcile their marginalized positions, their sense of themselves as university students, while drawing on the social and cultural capital that they brought to their postsecondary educational process. In the face of challenges and contradictions they experienced as university students, they re-defined their difference, their social class status, and identities as university students in an access program. They conceived of their difference as reflective of their uniqueness, their social class as a matter of personal class, and the financial assistance they received through the access program as academic scholarship. While they were optimistic about their educational and social outcomes, they remained pragmatic and hopeful, exercising their agency in viable ways that ensured that their economic and social circumstances would not operate as limitations.

While participants were ostensibly sold on the idea that meritocracy exists, at the same time, most of them expressed ambivalence about the extent to which they will ultimately be able to surmount their marginalization given the entrenched policies and practices of the university that were enacted by its members (particularly professors). Obviously aware of their marginalization (even when re-defining it) and the social, educational, and cultural structures that sustain it, participants remained resolute in the fact that the community cultural wealth they brought with them, and the support they received from each other, were sufficient for them to deal with whatever obstacles they encountered. Moreover, their faith in their aspirational, navigational, and resistant capitals seemed to nurture their determination to persevere despite whatever difficulties they faced in their negotiation and navigation of university. They resisted being limited by the institutional and cultural structures that regulated their lives as racial and ethnic minorities, economically disadvantaged, and second-generation Canadians. Clearly, negotiating university is a complex enterprise that requires a fundamental understanding of the institutional structures gained through critical analysis and exercising agency developed from that analysis. How students interpret structure and agency depends considerably on the meanings they construct from their experiences.

Note

Acknowledgment—I am indebted to Leanne Taylor for her contribution to the research and to Selom Chapman-Nyaho for his research assistance.

1. Participants had signed consent forms giving us permission to audiotape the Common Hour conversations, so they were aware of the research aspect of the sessions. Over the 2 years, participants were interviewed three times (when they entered the program, after their first year, and just before entering their third year).

References

Adamuti-Trache, M., Anisef, P., Sweet, R., & Walters, D. (2013). Enriching foreign qualifications through Canadian post-secondary education: Who participates and why. *International Migration and Integration, 14*(139–156).

Brathwaite, K. S. (2003). *Access & equity in the university*. Toronto, Canada: Canadian Scholars' Press.

Frenette, M. (2007). *Why are youth from lower-income families less likely to attend university? Evidence from academic abilities, parental influences, and financial constraints* (Analytical Studies Branch Research Paper Series). Retrieved from http://economics.ca/2007/papers/0131.pdf

Fuligni, A. J. (1998). Adolescents from immigrant families. In V. C. McLoyd & L. Steinberg (Eds.), *Studying minority adolescents: Conceptual, methodological and theoretical issues* (pp. 127–143). Mahwah, NJ: Lawrence Erlbaum.

Gosine, K. (2012). Accomplished Black North Americans and antiracism education: Towards bridging a seeming divide. *Critical Sociology, 38*(5), 707–721.

Henry, F., & Tator, C. (2006). *The colour of democracy: Racism in Canadian society*. Toronto, Canada: ITP Nelson.

Hurtado, S. (2013, May). *Diversifying science: Understanding the student and institutional issues in improving degree attainment in STEM*. Keynote address at 26th Annual National Conference on Race and Ethnicity in American Higher Education (NCORE), New Orleans, United States.

Ibrahim, A. (2011). Will they ever speak with authority? Race, post-coloniality and the symbolic violence of language. *Educational Philosophy and Theory, 43*(6), 619–634.

James, C. E. (2002). Achieving desire: Narrative of a black male teacher. *International Journal of Qualitative Studies in Education, 15*(2), 171–186.

James, C. E. (2013). *Life at the intersection: Community, class and schooling*. Halifax, Canada: Fernwood.

James, C. E., & Mannette, J. (2000). Rethinking access: The challenge of living with difficult knowledge. In G. S. Dei & A. Calliste (Eds.), *Power, knowledge and anti-racism: A critical reader* (pp. 73–92). Halifax, Canada: Fernwood.

James, C., & Taylor, L. (2008). Education will get you to the station: Marginalized students' experiences and perceptions of merit in accessing university. *Canadian Journal of Education, 31*(3).

Kazis, K., Vargas, J., & Hoffman, N. (Eds.). (2004). *Double the numbers: Increasing postsecondary credentials for underrepresented youth*. Cambridge, MA: Harvard Education Press.

Ladson-Billings, G. (2000). Racialized discourses and ethnic epistemologies. In N. K. Denzin & Y. S. Lincoln (Eds.), *Handbook of qualitative research* (pp. 257–277). Thousand Oaks, CA: Sage.

Law, I., Phillips, D., & Turney, L. (Eds.). (2004). *Institutional racism in higher education*. Sterling, VA: Trentham Books.

Lessard, C. (1995). Equality and inequality in Canadian education. In R. Ghosh & D. Ray (Eds.), *Social change and education in Canada* (pp. 178–195). Toronto, Canada: Harcourt Brace.

Lopez, N. (2002). Race-gender experiences and schooling: Second-generation Dominican, West Indian, and Haitian youth in New York City. *Race, Ethnicity and Education, 5*(1), 67–89.

Luxton, M. (2010). Doing neoliberalism: Perverse individualism in personal life. In S. Braedley & M. Luxton (Eds.), *Neoliberalism and everyday life* (pp. 163–183). Montreal, Canada: McGill-Queen's University Press.

Madriz, E. (2000). Focus groups in feminist research. In N. K. Denzin & Y. S. Lincoln (Eds.), *Handbook of qualitative research* (pp. 835–850). Thousand Oaks, CA: Sage.

Nicholas, T., Stepick, A., & Dutton Stepick, C. (2008). "Here's your diploma, Mom!" Family obligation and multiple pathways to success. *Annals of the American Academy of Political and Social Science, 620*, 237–252.

Portelli, J. P., & Solomon, R. P. (Eds.). (2001). *The erosion of democracy in education: From critique to possibilities.* Calgary, Canada: Deselig Enterprises.

Putnam, R. D. (2000). *Bowling alone: The collapse and revival of American community.* New York, NY: Simon & Shuster.

Sukarieh, M., & Tannock, S. (2008). In the best interests of youth or neoliberalism? The World Bank and the new global youth empowerment project. *Journal of Youth Studies, 11*(3), 301–312.

Wood, M. (2007). *Black girls and schooling* (Unpublished doctoral dissertation). York University, Toronto, Canada.

Yosso, T. J. (2005). Whose culture has capital? A critical race theory discussion of community wealth. *Race, Ethnicity and Education, 8*(1), 69–91.

· 5 ·

THE STANDPOINT PROJECT

Practitioner Research and Action When Working With Young People From Low-Income Families

Tony Kruger, Jo Williams, and Marcelle Cacciattolo

Introduction

The Case of Lucky

Lucky was a gorgeous kid when he smiled. He started year 7 at the beginning of 2008, a Vietnamese student in a good-natured and well-mannered class. The trouble was that Lucky didn't smile very often. In fact, even over the first week it seemed that he grew more self-conscious and less willing to grin at anything!

Lucky constantly seemed to be a little behind the rest of the class, a little slower to get himself and his work organised, and as I write this case study partway into term 2 he has only just paid his school fees and got a diary.

The thing is I know that Lucky wanted to get a diary; whenever I asked him about it he looked increasingly embarrassed and promised to get one soon. Whenever a form or permission went home Lucky had trouble getting it back because his parents often worked out in the country and he didn't see them. I should have woken to the evidence and realised that money might be a problem in Lucky's family.

But despite my last enlightening case study I continued to apply pressure about getting the diary even after Lucky turned up with a cheap little notebook that was clearly intended to do the job of a diary. No, it was not until I saw Lucky's teeth that I realised what the problem might be. (First year out teacher case writing extract)

The recently published *Handbook of Social Justice in Education* (Ayers, Quinn, & Stovall, 2009) demonstrates a disturbing global trend in educational research and policy-making. While 20 or more years ago the impact of poverty on the lives and educational participation of the least advantaged was prominent in academic and government publications, it has now become, if the *Handbook* is evidence, a largely unasked and unanswered question. The *Handbook's* broad omission may be evidence of an acceptance that the question is unanswerable! Perhaps that is correct when viewed conventionally: from the dominant top-down policy-dependent regimes adopted in modern education systems.

But it was the possibility of finding an alternative to such top-down impotence that initiated the Standpoint Project reported in this chapter. The Project, intended to be an uncovering of the political content of schooling by teachers who work with students such as Lucky, emerged from a collaboration between the School of Education at Victoria University (Melbourne, Australia) and Good Shepherd Youth and Family Services Inc., an activist social welfare organisation. A Good Shepherd financial counsellor approached the School of Education and sought to open up a dialogue about the disabling impact that family poverty was having on access to education for the young people that she came into contact with in the area in which the University was located. For her, the pressing concern was the exclusion of students from high-value, and, frequently, high-cost learning activities and how schools could allow such socially divisive policies and practices. The dialogue enabled the Victoria University team to express its primary interest as making visible the political content of the caring and pedagogical responses committed teachers make to the circumstances of the least advantaged. Through discussions lasting about a year, the two groups agreed on an initiating question for a research project.

> In general terms, how do we as educators, health care providers, policy makers, leaders and youth workers come to a "place of knowing" or to use Connell's term to take the "standpoint of the least advantaged" (Connell, 1993) so as to see more clearly the impact of poverty on young people's life circumstances—in structural terms as well as in the practices which teachers adopt.

The genealogy expressed in Connell's standpoint argument should prompt practitioners and researchers towards identification with the interests of the least advantaged. Not an anodyne expression, taking a standpoint means a standing with the least advantaged; seeing the world from their point of view; and, in education, acting against the interests that cruelly constrain their access to elite knowledge (Freire, 1970/1996). In situations where teachers are asked to think through questions from the interests of the education system—just a proxy for the obsessions of the politicians whose interests have been tied directly to public perceptions of system success—taking the standpoint of the least advantaged is a move of considerable civic courage for teachers.

What the Good Shepherd and Victoria University researchers agreed was that wealth, poverty, and their socially dividing effects are enduring conditions of modern society. In the case of education, wealth-related social division appears to have an intractable character, and has been further entrenched through the neoliberal reforms and policies of the last 3 decades (Apple, 2006; Lipman, 2011). Connell has described the effects of the neoliberal agenda as being one of "a steady decline of interest in 'equity' issues in education, accompanied by an erosion of the 'idea of education as a common good'" (Connell, 2002, p. 324). In Australia, for example, the neoliberal educational discourses of successive governments have rendered the poverty and education nexus invisible behind a neoliberal concern with the reduction in what has come to be known in Australia as "the long trail of underperforming students from disadvantaged backgrounds" (Donnelly, 2008).

The intent of this chapter, which outlines the principal practices and some of the findings of the Standpoint Project, is to show how teachers can inform their civic courage and can prepare to undertake local social action with system significance. An essential impetus was given to the Project when the Good Shepherd team was able to provide informed political support for the University's application for research funding. The result was that the Victorian Department of Education approved the application for a collaborative research project with six schools in western Melbourne.

In encouraging the small teams of teachers who volunteered to participate in the research in each school, the combined research team emphasised that the practitioner understanding emerging from the Project was to initiate some limited change action. That is, the Project invited the teachers to understand and positively act upon the challenges that students and their families confront in everyday schooling (Connell, 1993; Hayes, Mills, Christie, & Lingard, 2006). For Connell—and thus for the Standpoint Project—the focus for change is not the young person who needs "fixing up"; it is the institution that disadvantages young people that is in need of radical reform.

In the first instance the following two questions prompted the Project's inquiry:

• What are the practices and structures within classrooms and schools that can best support and encourage the participation and successful engagement of students from low-income families in higher-order learning?
• Conversely, are there practices and structures that might deter or exclude some children and young people from full participation in education?

The outcomes of the Project are no more than partial. But they do point to ways in which teachers can take collective and socially significant action. What continues to be missing is an awareness of how teachers, separated in different schools, can appropriate sufficient power to act against bureaucratically applied domination that so constrains their commitment.

Social Justice and Teachers: What the Literature Says

While educational actions by teachers within schools cannot solve all of these societal problems by themselves, they can contribute their share to the building of more decent and just societies. The most important point is that neither teaching nor teacher professional development can be neutral. We, as teachers at whatever level, must act with greater political clarity about whose interests we are furthering in our daily actions, including our approach to professional development, because like it or not, and whether or not it is acknowledged, we are taking a stand through our actions and words. We should not, of course, reduce teaching only to its political elements, but we do need to make sure that this aspect of teaching does not get lost as it often does.

Zeichner (2009, p. 130) has expressed the political content of teachers' work. He emphasised the need to understand how the actions and inactions of teachers are in fact political acts; acts that serve to hinder or encourage young people from participating in, and achieving success in, education. Zeichner's insight is that teachers' interactions with young people and their families are fundamental to understanding how schooling might be transformed to act against the marginalisation, oppression, and disenchantment of the least advantaged young people. In keeping with socially committed arguments for teachers as researchers (Kincheloe, 2003), such an awareness can result only from collective inquiry by teachers into the barriers to participation and success confronting young people.

The practical barriers to educational participation encountered by families living in or close to poverty are an indictment of Australian education. By law, schooling in the compulsory years is meant to be free, and secular. It is none of these, not even in government schools; and especially it is not free. While government schools don't charge fees for tuition and the poorest one third (approximately) of families receive additional government support for education expenses such as books, art, and laboratory equipment and other "optional" items, the grants don't cover the entire cost, especially in the post-compulsory years. Students who take expensive subject areas, such as art, English literature, and the sciences, or who want to participate in field trips are confronted by substantial "optional" fee demands. As a result, many young people from low-income families are unable to gain access to elite knowledge fields. The work of Teese (Teese & Polesel, 2003) in Australia, researching within Bourdieu's theoretical framing, clearly shows the enduring and depressing connection between educational achievement and socioeconomic status.

Not only do young people from the wealthiest families and the most endowed schools do better at school, their achievement is also characterised by success in acquiring the high-status knowledge of the kind giving access to elite university courses and associated professions (Apple, 1979). Those knowledge fields, including advanced mathematics, the physical sciences, and the most formal of the humanities, are clearly associated with a distinction between the richest and poorest in society. Conversely, young people from the poorest families select to take knowledge areas at school that lead to substantially reduced opportunities to enter university and are constrained to the "hands-on" domains of technical work.[1] Connell's (1993) discussion of schooling and social justice, an outcome of many years of research (p. 19), including a substantial review of the Australian Disadvantaged Schools Program (White, Johnston, & Connell, 1991), argued for a re-thinking "of justice in education *around the issue of curriculum*" to complement the more commonly held definition of justice as one of the distribution of social goods. In this, Connell foreshadowed a more extensive philosophical discussion of social justice and education presented by Gewirtz (1998), who argued that socially just practices had three characteristics:

- They expressed a recognition of those who lived in unjust circumstances
- They were concerned with socioeconomic distribution
- They were also concerned with the power relations experienced by young people in classrooms.

That last quality of social justice in education, as defined by Gewirtz, is similar to Connell's discussion of what she termed "curricular justice." The search for relational curricular justice is what underpinned the Standpoint Project. For Connell, the consideration of the interests of the least advantaged means "concretely" taking "the standpoint of the least advantaged." Not only did the Standpoint Project seek to co-opt Connell's insight as the title of the Project, it also intended to generate a socially practical methodology by which educational practitioners could take the standpoint of the least advantaged in investigating and acting to change their own practices and those of their institutions.

Social Justice ... But Where Is There a Concern for Those Living in Poverty?

At the heart of this chapter is a conviction that what is missing from much thinking about poverty and education is means of discussing the effects of education that don't run into the social division brick wall. Social theory and sociological research, in the work of Bernstein and Bourdieu, for instance, present educational achievement as more or less related to the socioeconomic positions held by students. Whether termed "reproduction," following Bourdieu (Grenfell & James, 1998), or "correspondence," in the expression applied by Bowles and Gintis (1976), the disadvantaging effects of schooling on the poorest young people disturb all socially committed educators and researchers of education. The problem is that social theorising of this kind can lead to a conclusion that the least advantaged have almost no possibility—serendipity aside—of finding schooling to be advantaging.

In setting up the project we have named "Standpoint," we sought to confront what we saw as a disabling separation between the research activity within faculties of education in universities and the increasingly constrained possibilities that teachers in schools encounter in their work with the least advantaged students in schools. The Project recognises that the current epoch in education is dominated by an ethos of effectiveness in which the act of teaching has been reduced to technical specification: system-sponsored research establishes the nature of effective practices and the education authority then applies highly organised professional development, evaluation, and accountability strategies to induct, even coerce, teachers into the use of the practices. An example of such practices with currency in the Australian setting is the work of Hattie (2012), whose explicit instruction/"visible learning" model has emerged from a substantial meta-analysis of effectiveness research.

Ironically, the increased emphasis on quantification and standardisation at the centre of the neoliberal agenda for education (Apple, 2013) has shed further light on social inequity in education, despite the fact that, as Giroux (2003) argued, such accountability measures are always "divorced from broader considerations of social responsibility." As education systems become increasingly proficient at measuring student learning outcomes, the evidence of social division becomes even more compelling. The least advantaged students encounter obstacles in gaining access to, and becoming successful in acquiring, the high-status knowledge contained in the official curricula of schools and universities. White et al. (1991, p. 23) made clear the notion that "class inequalities in education … persist on a massive scale in contemporary Australian society," and as such, in the presence of unemployment, disability, homelessness, low levels of literacy and language, the least advantaged groups are marginalised even further. Arguably from this perspective, enacting inclusive learning pathways can only evolve when teachers and school leaders are actively engaged in the struggles of young people from the poorest communities to make sense of formal education. This engagement is not just an exercise in empathy. It requires educators to recognise how schools and school systems fail to take account of the economic circumstances of students from low income families; to signpost how school decisions inhibit young people from fully participating; and to open up safe spaces for them to inquire into the curriculum structures and pedagogical practices that limit young people's opportunities to learn.

Such an approach requires a rejection of the current top-down, corporate-driven policy agenda in education that simultaneously silences and blames teachers for educational dilemmas, and evokes "reductionist ways of seeing, teaching and learning" that undermine rather than support democratic and inclusive education practices (Kincheloe, 2003, p. 9). Teachers and students are relegated to the roles of functionaries and consumers respectively, with critical local knowledge ignored. By contrast, here, we are informed by a Freirean-inspired approach that consciously privileges grassroots experience and understanding and repositions teachers in the research process as agents of change.

A disturbing feature of effectiveness ideology and policy in schooling is the extent to which school authorities have been able to deflect teachers' attention from the objective conditions of schooling faced by the least advantaged young people; and therefore from the impact those conditions have on teaching, learning, and educational participation and success. Socially critical research (Zeichner, 2009), on the other hand, regards the socioeconomic circumstances faced by young people as the starting point for understanding how schooling discriminates against their interests. Schooling in the language of Teese and Polesel (2003) is "undemocratic" and acts to entrench the power of the most advantaged economic, cultural, and social-capital-owning minority.

Confronted by the modernising "juggernaut" that is the effective education system, there is little wonder that teachers have resorted to what can only be interpreted as contemporary and more intellectually developed versions of "deficit" explanations and programs of action. The declaration, by consultants such as Ruby Payne (2005) and programs such as AVID (Biddle, 2001), that the least advantaged young person lacks the cultural skills to participate successfully in schooling, may be an advance on earlier, crude psychological prejudices. If the anecdotal evidence is to be believed, Payne's work and AVID certainly have struck a chord among the teachers who work in some of the least advantaged schools in parts of Australia. Perhaps they are popular because they provide teachers with an organised, if simplistic, approach in dealing with the least advantaged students. Education systems have provided little in the way of moral, intellectual, or practical support in their dealings with the difficult circumstances in schools serving the least advantaged communities. We should not be surprised that teachers take a line of least resistance and apply strategies that proclaim effectiveness even if they locate the problems in the perceived deficiencies of their students.

Depressingly, in its own way, socially critical educational research has also failed to come to terms with the structural location of teachers. Advancing highly theorised explanations for social division in education may satisfy the criteria for publication in learned journals but it does little to provide tangible support to the teachers whose struggle is to apply practices that are in keeping with their morally based democratic principles. In many ways, the academy has been derelict in its resort to critique in dealing with the effectiveness turn in education. If the least advantaged young people are the "collateral damage" (Bauman, 2011) of education systems managed to enact neoliberal strategies, then teachers are little more than "cannon fodder" in a struggle that privileges the interests of the already advantaged few.

The Standpoint Project intended to inscribe into and privilege an explicit social content in the inquiry of teachers into their classroom practices. If the rationale for the Standpoint Project was intended to be socially grounded, then the challenge for the research team was to generate a research methodology that was just as socially connected and that, as much as possible, sought a democratic inclusion of teachers who are the principal agents in both socially critical and effectiveness conceptions of education. In fact, the practical contribution the Standpoint Project sought was the formation of tools to enable practitioners to work critically and effectively. In the words of Bauman (2000),

> If the old objective of critical theory—human emancipation—means anything today, it means to reconnect the two edges of the abyss which has opened up between the reality of the individual de jure and the prospects of the individual de facto. And individuals who relearned forgotten citizenship skills and reappropriated lost citizen tools are the only builders up to the task of this particular bridge building. (p. 41)

Taking the Standpoint of the Least Advantaged: Toward a Socially Committed Research Methodology

In her discussion of schooling and social justice, Connell (1993) argued that teachers should seek a "counter hegemonic" curriculum that produces for the least advantaged what she called the "hegemonic curriculum" constructed for the wealthiest: access to the highest-status knowledge. Taking the standpoint of the least advantaged, the essential requirement for curricular justice, "is not easy" Connell (p. 44) argued. Its challenge to educators is to adopt a practice of thinking "through economic conditions from the standpoint of the poor not the rich"! The methodology adopted in the Project was to find a means by which the participating teachers could see their educational practices and the structural and cultural practices of the school and school system from the standpoint of the least advantaged. Taking the standpoint of the least advantaged is itself a socially practical "citizen tool," an approach to inquiry grounded in the teachers' interactions and understandings of their students. The methodology in the Project established two purposeful conditions for inquiry. The standpoint of the least advantaged was constructed through the:

1. use of a Low Income Awareness Checklist (Stafford & Stafford, 2004) as a reference marker for consideration of the material circumstances of the least advantaged students and their families and local communities (see the Appendix for an abridged version of the checklist);
2. participation in the research meetings by representatives of staff from Good Shepherd Youth and Family Services, with the intention of interposing their understandings of the impact of poverty on students and their families, through the provision of socioeconomic information

and also through the intimate knowledge of cases of family poverty and its effects on young people.

Both conditions set a practical, if discomforting, structure for discussion, the nature of the data collected and analysed in the project, and the generation of research findings. They were also powerful prompts for the teacher teams to plan some action in direct response to their inquiries.

Collaborative Practitioner Research

The Standpoint Project applied what the University research team termed collaborative practitioner research (CPR). Formed within the principles of Action Research (Reason & Bradbury, 2006), the Project expressed a commitment to collaborative, democratic, and participatory practices leading, the research team hoped, to the generation of shared practical understandings of use. Arguably, the CPR methodology employed here emphasised a process of self-empowerment and education as advocated by Freire. The collaborative and dialogical approach to knowledge generation placed the teams of teachers in positions to see beyond existing oppressive structures and blockers, and to imagine new, diverse, and critical practices.

> For apart from inquiry, apart from the praxis, individuals cannot be truly human. Knowledge emerges only through invention and re-invention, through the restless, impatient, continuing, hopeful inquiry human beings pursue in the world, with the world, and with each other. (Freire, 1970/1996, p. 53)

Throughout the project the participants reflected on their own and others' understanding of practices and possibilities. They contested perspectives and re-shaped ideas to clarify meaning, resulting in a set of research findings "owned" by the school-based research teams themselves. With reference to Bauman's citizen tools, such a process paves the way for a highly engaged and insightful involvement with the action outcomes of the project. Here is a crucial step, for, as Freire (1970/1996) explained, words that cannot realise constructive action—where educational actors are "deprived of their dimension of action" (p. 68)—are reduced to a benign *verbalism*.

Throughout the Project there was also a philosophical consistency to the application of the CPR methodological approach, from research intention to processes, and, finally, outcomes as informed by the literature review and theoretical framework. In responding to many of the problems of existing educational research and activity that leave teachers, students, and families largely disempowered, the Standpoint methodology does two critical things:

1. it privileges grassroots knowledge and experiences as vital elements in the construction of new social knowledge and as part of reclaiming voice in the development of policy and social action in education;
2. it repositions teachers in the research process, supporting them to engage with their practice so that they see themselves as agents of change.

In this sense, CPR reflects Paulo Freire's view of education as social praxis. Freire argued for an engagement with educational practices that explicitly seek to identify and explain existing structures and power relations that maintain the disempowerment of oppressed peoples, in order to change them. Through the following research procedure, the Standpoint team sought to express just such a commitment to action.

- The research team invited six schools serving communities with many low-income families to join the Project. A small number of teachers in each school volunteered to participate in the research.
- School-based research teams discussed their experiences in working with the least advantaged students and the associated social and educational insights that the teachers had formed. Each school team was composed of the participating teachers and one University and one Good Shepherd colleague.
- Each teacher selected an element of experience to be written as a case of practice (nominally 1000 words of practical description). Over the course of the project most teachers completed two or three cases.
- The school team discussed their impressions of the cases, which involved team members asking questions of clarification, the respectful presentation of commentaries related to personal practice and school and system structures, and, finally, the proposition of action possibilities.
- Following the discussion, each team member analysed the cases using the sketching and threading technique devised for use in Collaborative Practitioner Research.
- The team members then presented their analysis, which were composed of the threads of practice or related beliefs or key words, which were then "bundled" by the team into a set of concepts; in the process setting out what were the connections between the elements in a concept map—a theorising of the collected case writing and analysis.

- School teams then presented their collected cases and accompanying analysis in collaborative validation meetings.
- Following the initial case writing, analysis, and the first collaborative validation meeting, each team took time to explore the action possibilities arising from their inquiries.
- The Project culminated in a final validation discussion, which prepared a collective concept map theorising the findings of the research at that point.

After the first round of case writing and analysis and within the limited time and resources available for the Project, each school team planned a small-scale action designed in response to the team's analytically informed insights. The final round of case writing and analysis collected the school teams' understandings of the action and their impressions of its impacts with each school. Using the proceedings of the final collaborative validation meeting, the University and Good Shepherd research team was able to advance a set of standpoint propositions on which to construct the framework and tentative elements for a standpoint checklist with curriculum and pedagogical moments.

A Case of Practice Analysed

Here, we present a case of practice that exemplifies the application of the sketching, threading, and theorising used in collaborative practitioner analysis and research. The case, crafted by a secondary school teacher, describes how a student in the final year 12 of schooling was obstructed in her participation in a high-status knowledge field by her inability to purchase the expensive books needed for successful learning. Through the teachers' analysis of the case, important elements of the Project findings become evident.

From Case Analysis to Theorised Beliefs and the New Elements of a Standpoint Checklist

Jackie's case is telling because it shows how an important element of the Low Income Awareness Checklist—whether a school is sensitive enough to provide learning resources for students who can't afford them—helped the teachers to question an important component of school policy and organisation. But the case also introduces critically significant elements that refer to teachers' practices, their relationships with students, and their pedagogical

Account and Sketch	Thread (What are the key words, ideas?)	Theorising/Research Proposition (What I have learned, believe, realise from this case.)
Jackie		
Dad is a single parent of 11 children. Jackie is placed in the middle, she has five younger than herself. Mum left dad and the children just over 1 year ago. Jackie shares that Mum was having an affair before she left and has now moved in with her new boyfriend near Geelong.	Difficult family circumstances	Few teachers comprehend the circumstances of the least advantaged students. How would they know?
Jackie went to Geelong to be with her mother for a short time last year, but she was kicked out by the new boyfriend and quickly returned to dad.		
Mum has a mental illness—a bipolar disorder, she refuses to get help. We have tried says Jackie. Mum just wants to have babies now with the new boyfriend.		
At home Jackie is responsible for washing, ironing, and looking after younger kids. The older brother does the cooking.	Jackie is responsible for many parenting tasks at home.	Young people are resourceful.
Jackie reports being enthusiastic as she began her VCE this year. It had not been smooth during her year 10 but she had just managed to pass and progress to year 11. Jackie felt committed to having her best year at school, the VCE staff had motivated all the students in her year level and highlighted the importance of the next 2 years and how it will affect the future.	Jackie was enthusiastic and motivated as she began Year 12.	Despite the home and family difficulties, Jackie wants to do well in her VCE.

Account and Sketch	Thread (What are the key words, ideas?)	Theorising/Research Proposition (What I have learned, believe, realise from this case.)
A week before the school year started Jackie was not able to come up to the school and pick up her box of textbooks, like many of the other kids were doing, because she had never even placed the order at the end of last year.	Jackie was not able to pick up her books for next year.	The books for class participation are essential but very expensive and Jackie can't afford them. This gets in the way of her learning.
Unfortunately dad was unable to have her booklist filled out. The costs for Jackie doing the subjects she chose were well over $500. She loves reading and enrolled in English and Literature classes, along with others, these require many books. I guess it would have been nice to start reading at least one of the novels before starting the year.	Jackie could not do any reading before the start of the school year.	
As the year began, Jackie, along with many other students, did not have all the books they needed for class. This is normal for the start of a year as students wait for back orders of books to arrive.		
Staff and students are then sharing their books during class for this period. However, while the book orders arrive and students begin getting themselves into study patterns, others such as Jackie were still waiting for books. Of course, for Jackie, the books have not even been ordered yet. Jackie's father remained unable to afford the books.	Jackie's father remained unable to afford the books.	
In the beginning of the year Jackie's teachers were aware that some people were waiting for books, but as the weeks and then months passed by, teachers would simply assume that Jackie would have got her books.	Teachers assumed Jackie had her books.	Teachers weren't aware of the financial constraints faced by students such as Jackie.

Account and Sketch	Thread (What are the key words, ideas?)	Theorising/Research Proposition (What I have learned, believe, realise from this case.)
Jackie said it became harder and harder to keep up with the work. Pages and exercises were set for homework and she did not have a book to use at home. Jackie would make up some excuses in some classes about where her books were; maybe she'd say she left them in a locker or at home. She would just share with a friend or teachers would loan her a copy for that lesson.	Jackie made up excuses about her lack of books.	The teachers' assumptions result in Jackie becoming defensive and embarrassed because she feared the teachers thought she was disorganised.
Jackie felt embarrassed whenever she was asked about books. Her excuses were running out. It was really just looking like she was disorganised or lazy.	Jackie felt embarrassed because she looked disorganised or lazy.	
It was not just the books though. There was also the standard Internet fee the college charges and this was $85. There is an expectation that all students have this levy paid because so many classes require the Internet for research.		
In many classes at this level the Internet is vital. Jackie coped with having no Internet levy paid, by getting her friends to log on under their names, but that was not always possible. She missed out again.	Jackie couldn't access the Internet.	Young people have personal networks to support them. But the resources of those networks are limited.
Activities, research and access to the Internet are just an absolute necessity in classes.		
On top of this there would be a curriculum bases excursion that was compulsory to attend. She would scrounge together the money or borrow it. It is a senior curriculum excursion, the organisers don't necessarily stop to think that there may be students who can't get the funds for such an event. It may only be $10, but in a family of Jackie's size there is not always even that to spare.	Other compulsory activities which cost money Organisers don't necessarily think about students who can't get the funds.	Teachers assume that families can afford additional class expenses.

Account and Sketch	Thread (What are the key words, ideas?)	Theorising/Research Proposition (What I have learned, believe, realise from this case.)
In some classes Jackie felt more comfortable with her teacher and would ask if pages could be photo copied for her. This was kind of them but still very embarrassing to continually need to ask.	Jackie felt comfortable with some teachers … but it was embarrassing to ask.	Even with trusted teachers, a student in Jackie's situation can be embarrassed by having to ask favours.
With all the preparation the VCE leaders said we would need to cope with VCE, all the warnings about keeping up with work and that being organised was vital, all seemed increasing difficult as time went on through term 1.	Keeping up with the work was difficult.	
For Jackie personally, not having books and being that disorganised went against her natural flow. At home Jackie actually has a very tidy bedroom for a teenager. She reports having always been a neat person who likes things to be organised.	Being disorganised is her against her natural flow.	The problems in paying for resources result in students falling behind because they don't have access to essential learning resources.
Are there any surprises that Jackie began to miss some classes? Maybe she would be asked where her book was again or maybe they were going to the computer lab and her friend is absent, how would she log on? Jackie describes how quickly she seemed to fall behind. Although she worked during her classes, she did not do all the homework and after she'd missed a few classes per subject, she lost touch with current topics.	Jackie began to miss classes, fall behind and lose touch.	Students whose circumstances cause them to slip under teachers' radar may be assumed by teachers to be disorganised or lazy.
Jackie is a generally very quiet student who can slip under the radar. The embarrassment of not having enough money means speaking out, and asking for help is uncomfortable and almost unbearable.	Jackie is a quiet student who can slip under the radar.	Schools need a budget provision to ensure that lack of money is not a barrier to participation.
When Jackie's situation is discovered, the Standpoint budget was used to purchase her books. Jackie feels organised for the first time this year.		

choices, constrained as all of them are by system and school organisation, curriculum, and resourcing decisions. The case and its analysis, together with the other cases written by the school team, encouraged the teachers to develop and present professional development for teachers at the school, a task that involved challenge in the local politics of the school. Finding space in the school's professional development timetable was a considerable professional task in the face of the opposition from school management that had determined that "effectiveness" strategies were a higher priority than social critique and action.

Grounded in cases such as Jackie's, the Standpoint Project has advanced a set of six propositions that give a practical rendering to Connell's expression of "curricular justice" and Gewirtz's diagnosis that social justice possesses recognition, relational, and distributional content.

- The importance of teachers being aware and respectful of the family and social circumstances of the least advantaged students—not in any sense of surveillance but in an attempt to take their standpoint in educational decision-making, planning, and resourcing.
- The least advantaged students, such as Jackie, are resourceful and ready to learn but their resourcefulness is partial and needs informed support by the school, the most powerful institution in the students' lives.
- Socially just teachers actively connect the interests of the least advantaged to the official curriculum through their awareness of the circumstances of the students and families.
- Such a curriculum and pedagogical strategy can often require teachers to locate the contexts of their classroom programs in the sites that interest students—in the local community, for example.
- Teachers, in becoming aware of the circumstances and interests of the least advantaged, are in contact with and are able to learn from parents and significant community members in advancing student learning.
- In sustaining student engagement and a focus on learning, schools and their teachers can require the support of external agencies in meeting the direct welfare needs of the least advantaged students and in establishing programs with the social connectedness required for active student participation.

These characteristics point to an essential quality possessed by a school's teaching faculty professing to take the standpoint of the least advantaged students: it will be a communicative and a communicating institution. A communicative school will be one encouraging teachers to be the principal communicating actors within the school and between the school and the families and the educational, cultural, sporting, and other education organisations in its local community. In such a discursive environment, a commitment to curricular justice, to use Connell's expression, will impel a school to actively seek to clarify its teachers' understanding of the effects of poverty on students' participation and learning, and to search for ways to connect teachers' insights and imagination with the demands of the official curriculum.

Can such a school exist? And what would a whole school system that takes the standpoint of the least advantaged look like; one which urged schools to be as communicative as much as they are effective?

Note

1. We note here that some young people from the poorest fraction of society have always "made it" in education; and we count ourselves in that group! What we are arguing is that the emphatic tendency is for schooling, everywhere, to discriminate between young people on the basis of wealth or the lack of it.

References

Apple, M. (2006). Understanding and interrupting neoliberalism and neoconservatism in education. *Pedagogies: An International Journal*, 1(1), 21–26.

Apple, M. (2013). *Educating the "right" way: Markets, standards, God and inequality* (2nd ed.). New York, NY: Routledge.

Apple, M. W. (1979). *Ideology and curriculum*. London, England: Routledge.

Ayers, W., Quinn, T., & Stovall, D. (2009). *Handbook of social justice in education*. New York, NY; London, England: Routledge.

Bauman, Z. (2000). *Liquid modernity*. Cambridge, England: Polity Press.

Bauman, Z. (2011). *Collateral damage: Social inequalities in a global age*. Cambridge, England: Polity Press.

Biddle, B, J. (2001). *Social class, poverty, and education: Policy and practice*. New York, NY: RoutledgeFalmer.

Bowles, S., & Gintis, H. (1976). Schooling in capitalist America. New York, NY: Basic Books.

Connell, R. W. (1993). *Schools and social justice*. Philadelphia, PA: Temple University Press.

Connell, R. W. (2002). Making the difference, then and now. *Discourse: Studies in the Cultural Politics of Education*, 23(3), 319–327.

Donnelly, K. (2008). A "fair go" in schools. *Policy*, 24(2), Winter, 3–4.

Freire, P. (1996). *Pedagogy of the oppressed.* London, England: Penguin Books (Original work published 1970).

Gewirtz, S. (1998). Conceptualizing social justice: Mapping the territory. *Journal of Education Policy, 13*(4), 469–484.

Giroux, H. A. (2003). Selling out higher education. *Policy Futures in Education, 1*(1).

Grenfell, M., & James, D. (1998). *Bourdieu and education: Acts of practical theory.* London, England: Taylor & Francis.

Hattie, J. (2012). *Visible learning for teachers: Maximizing impact on learning.* New York, NY: Routledge.

Hayes, D., Mills, M., Christie, P., & Lingard, B. (2006). *Schools making a difference: Productive pedagogies, assessment and performance.* Crows Nest, Australia: Allen & Unwin.

Kincheloe, J. (2003). *Teachers as researchers: Qualitative inquiry as a path to empowerment* (2nd ed.). London, England: RoutledgeFalmer.

Lipman, P. (2011). *The new political economy of urban education: Neoliberalism, race, and the right to the city.* New York, NY: Routledge.

Payne, R. K. (2005). *A framework for understanding poverty.* Highlands, TX: aha!

Reason, P., & Bradbury, H. (Eds.). (2006). *Handbook of action research, concise paperback edn.* London, England: Sage.

Stafford, C., & Stafford, G. (2004). Low income awareness checklist. In *Poverty and education: A guide to action.* Melbourne, Australia: Melbourne Brimbank Emergency Relief Network.

Teese, R., & Polesel, J. (2003). *Undemocratic schooling: Equity and quality in mass secondary education in Australia.* Carlton, Australia: University.

White, V., Johnston, K., & Connell, R. W. (1991). *Running twice as hard: The disadvantaged schools program in Australia. Policy development and analysis.* Geelong, Australia: Deakin University Press.

Zeichner, K. M. (2009). *Teacher education and the struggle for social justice.* New York, NY: Routledge.

Appendix

The Low Income Awareness Checklist—Abridged (Stafford & Stafford, 2004)

These statements are indicators of areas where schools may need heightened awareness of the needs of low-income families and students. How many of these match your school's policies and practices?

1. Special Provision/Advocacy/Internal Policy Development

a. Special funds available to support the needs of low income students.

b. Special provision for students who are homeless or whose families are in crisis.

   c. Special grocery/necessities supply for students and families who are on a low income or homeless.

   d. Active support and advocacy on behalf of students who have received transit or other fines.

   e. Links with agencies in the local area so that specialist support can be provided for students/families in crisis.

   f. Mechanisms for researching and monitoring the impact of government social policies on low income families and students.

   g. Practices to ensure that staff are regularly reminded of the needs of low income families and students.

   h. Policies available in languages evident in the community.

   i. Access to or provides interpreters.

2. Booklists/Equipment

   a. Monitors booklists to ensure that unnecessary items are not added as "compulsory" purchase items.

   b. Monitors booklists to ensure that expensive items are not included without sound educational reasons being provided in a structured school forum.

   c. Monitors booklists to ensure that textbooks are not changed from year to year without sound reasons being explored in an appropriate forum.

   d. Procedures to ensure that second hand textbooks can be purchased by students.

3. Excursions/field trips

   a. Policies to ensure that excursion costs are kept to a minimum at each year level.

   b. Dignified and discreet provision for families who cannot afford even low-cost excursions.

   c. Ensure that excursions do not include lunch stopovers at fast food "restaurants" where students on low income could be embarrassed.

   d. Policy regarding trips and camps to ensure costs are kept as low as possible with provision made to subsidise costs of low income students.

4. Homework

   a. Approaches to information technology facilities which does not assume students have access in their own homes.

   b. An approach to the setting of homework that does not assume that every student has a quiet study space at home, or has made provision for a homework space/program at school for students.

5. Nutrition

   a. A canteen policy which enables the dignified provision of nutritious food supply to needy students when necessary.

   b. A "breakfast club" providing basic breakfast food for students at nominal cost on a daily basis.

PART III

YOUTH IDENTITY AND RESEARCH

· 6 ·

KINSHIP NARRATIVES

Beat Nation, Indigenous Peoples (Hip Hop), and the Politics of Unmasking Our Ignorance

Haidee Smith Lefebvre and Awad Ibrahim

Imagine a long-playing phonograph record, a black vinyl "LP" with its central spindle hole surrounded by a grooved area. Now switch vinyl for copper and duplicate the album 136 times. Picture a record collection totaling 136 reddish-brown albums with a bright metallic luster installed on the museum wall of the Vancouver Art Gallery. The records are loosely arranged into inverted disordered triangles. The museum piece, entitled *Ellipsis* (see Figure 1), was created by Sonny Assu (Ligwilda'xw (We Wai Kai) of the Kwakwaka'wakw nations, British Columbia, Canada). In his artist's statement, Assu (n. d.) explained that,

> the 136 copper LPs act as a conceptual "record" for the [as of 2012] 136 years of the Indian Act.[1] The act itself is a tool used to oppress, segregate or assimilate the indigenous people and is rarely understood or known by Canadians [...]. The upside down, abstracted equalizer pattern indicates the silence or the omission of the oppressive act from our collective Canadian consciousness.

Ellipsis is part of the exhibition *Beat Nation: Art, Hip Hop, and Aboriginal Culture*. Assu's artwork and the surrounding pieces by 28 Indigenous artists from Turtle Island (a term used by some to refer to North America) create a complex portrait of the intersectionality of Aboriginal *and* urban youth culture.

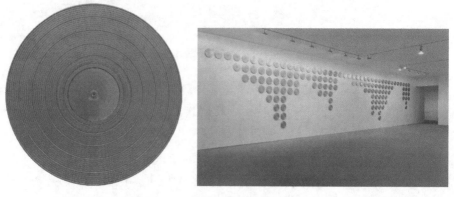

Figure 1. Sonny Assu, *Ellipsis*, 2012, copper LPs, 11–$\frac{3}{4}$ inches diameter each, installation of 136 series. Courtesy of the Artist and Equinox Gallery. Installation view and detail from the 2012 exhibition *Beat Nation* at the Vancouver Art Gallery. Photo credit: Rachel Topham, Vancouver Art Gallery, sonnyassu.com.

Adopting Hip Hop aesthetics, the artists use a variety of media: mixed media (e.g., *Anishnaabensag Biimskowebshkigewag [Native Kids Ride Bikes]*), graffiti (e.g., Corey Bulpitt and Gurl 23), photographs (e.g., Cheryl L'Hirondelle), cut 'n mixing electric powwow sound tracks with video imagery (e.g., Bear Witness). In its totality, *Beat Nation* underscores the ellipsis or the notion of omission. For our purpose, Assu's (n. d.) definition is significant: "Ellipsis, by definition, simply means an omission of something that would be commonly understood to be known."

The art collection showcased in the *Beat Nation* exhibit does not do away with traditions; rather it 'works through' them. For example, Assu took a modern commodity (a vinyl record) and reproduced it in copper, the most central symbol of wealth, power and prestige for the Kwakwaka'wakw nations (Jonaitis & American Museum of Natural History, 1991). The copper records also represent audio recordings of coastal First Nations songs taken during the early-twentieth century, a time when strict Canadian laws were written into the Indian Act that ensured anybody caught engaging in Indigenous cultural activities would be jailed and fined (Chen, 1995). The record collection is installed in a pattern that symbolizes our collective Canadian consciousness. The inverted motif, as we shall see, appoints this piece as a pedagogical space, where one learns about the repressed histories of injustices against Indigenous people, in particular the Indian Act. *Ellipsis* uses notions of kinship to transition viewers into a pedagogical moment within the space of Hip Hop;

a moment that unmasks North Americans' ignorance of/about Indigenous People culture, arts, and history. We follow Justice (2008) to define kinship not as "something that *is* in itself so much as something we *do*—actively, thoughtfully, respectfully" (p. 2). In this pedagogical space, which is contextually Canadian, viewers are challenged to explore questions such as "How do I read this artwork?" "Where do I place it?" "Who is the artist?" "What does this knowledge call into question?" Our chapter offers a modest methodological example of what could occur when we pursue this line of (ontological) questioning. Our intent here is not only to initiate a conversation with and scrutiny from critical readers, but more significantly to initiate a process-oriented discussion that works toward kinship as active, thoughtful, and respectful.

Our pedagogical pursuit is an ethical one. *Beat Nation* forced us to acknowledge four things, which became the four objectives we want to accomplish in this short chapter. First, initially when we saw *Ellipsis*, we were introduced to a new notion of "kinship." *This concept* purposefully works against binaries (Aboriginals vs. Non-Aboriginals; past vs. present; Hip Hop vs. traditional culture; etc.). Ultimately, we hope to emulate and embody this kinship. Second, however, this emulation and embodiment must be done with humility, within an "ethics of engagement" that inhibits us from superimposing our own cultural categories and meanings onto Indigenous categories and meanings. This ethics of engagement, third, is a work-in-progress, a working through the mess. Here, we mean a metaphorical and literal state of confusion and disorder on many levels. For example, the epistemological shift in our non-Indigenous thinking about kinship while reading *Beat Nation*, or the artistic process we presume *Beat Nation* artists undertook to produce their oeuvre and arts movement. Perhaps the biggest mess is the complex results originating from Canada's colonial and White supremacy history, a background that governs the contemporary relationship between the State and Indigenous nations. As Hip Hop scholars, our engagement with *Beat Nation*, fourth and finally, is a modest contribution showing (a) how Hip Hop has become a pedagogical space within the exhibition, (b) how this space created what we call 'Hip Hop sensibility' and (c) how this sensibility becomes a form of kinship. Specifically, we analyze *Ellipsis* as a kinship narrative that illuminates some of the ways the Assu family are always appearing in the midst of dominant society despite Canada's attempt to assimilate them into mainstream society. Kinship, we conclude, can be used as an interpretive tool and Hip Hop sensibilities are portable and both can be brought to kinship narratives.

We put kinship into practice by using it as a lens to interpret *Ellipsis* as a kinship narrative that circulates stories about Assu's personal life and political views. *Ellipsis* does more than expose the accumulating years that the Indian Act has been in effect. In a phone interview with Crystal Baxley (2011), Assu signaled that he has done his job to work through "the mess;" thus he produced his artwork. Now, through *Beat Nation*, he challenges viewers to educate themselves:

> What I like about my work is that if the viewer doesn't have an understanding of what I'm talking about, they're going to go out and educate themselves on the issue that I'm bringing to the table. That is where I feel my work is successful, it's not only aesthetically pleasing, but it challenges the viewer to take it upon themselves to educate themselves because they might not know the true history of the treatment of the First People's of North America. (n. p.)

Focusing on *Ellipsis*, our thought experiment is to discuss what we have learned by accepting Assu's challenge. *Ellipsis*, we argue, is a kinship narrative where viewers can unlearn aspects of Canadian history that have erased Kwakwaka'wakw cultural practices and worldviews from the public imagination. We conceptualize kinship as an action (Justice, 2008) that pivots around two axes that we refer to respectively as Genealogy Kinship (GK) and Cosmos Kinship (CK). We demonstrate, as well, that the *Beat Nation* exhibition invites scholars to broaden conceptualizations of Hip Hop to include artists who *do* what conventionally might be called Hip Hop without calling themselves Hip Hoppers. As we shall see, their artwork speaks to 'Hip Hop sensibility': the audacity of speaking out against oppression and passing ideas and politics on to others. We enact kinship, finally, by learning about the source of inspiration for *Ellipsis*.

Kinship: A Methodological Trope

Borrowing from Justice (2008), we already defined kinship as something we do—actively, thoughtfully, and respectfully. For this chapter, we acted on our emerging understanding of kinship in two ways. First, we educated ourselves about the issue that Assu brought to the table, namely the Indian Act, by featuring *Ellipsis* in the *Beat Nation* exhibit. Second, we read *Ellipsis* as a kinship narrative. Our reading necessitated adding another layer to Justice's definition: a way of doing, a methodology of sorts, that went beyond genetic explanations. For Kamboureli (2014), building off Emberley (2014), kinship as "a methodological and socio-political trope has the potential to suspend the Western privileging of blood as the single most important element of kin relations" (p. 19). Once we suspended the primacy of genetic explanations, we became interested in Markstrom's (2011) explanation that kinship pivots around two axes (see Figure 2). When viewed vertically, Cosmos Kinship (CK) connects to present day family, clan, and tribe, as well as animate and inanimate entities in all spheres of creation. Similarly, horizontally Genealogy Kinship (GK) includes genealogy or descent; it also runs through time—past, present, and future—such as ancestors, relations, and generations, respectively.

Our emergent understanding is that kinship is an action that revolves around two axes: CK and GK. CK involves connections to animate and non-animate beings and entities in the physical and spiritual realms (e.g., air, animal, deity, human, land, plant, water). In CK, individuals are embedded in a tribal web of kinship rights and responsibilities. Meanwhile, bound by time, GK ranges from an infinite past to the situational present to the infinite future symbolized by genealogical links to ancestors, contemporary relations, and future generations. In GK, individuals enact specific roles within a shared kinship network. Both CK and GK integrate physical, social, and spiritual realms; kinship recognizes that these realms contain concrete relations between and among people, the land, the elemental forces, and the cosmos.

Kinship roles contain expected behaviours and implied expectations for fulfilling kinship responsibilities "to the cosmology, to one another, and to

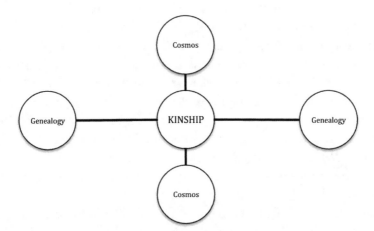

Figure 2. (Emergent) Kinship Model. This figure illustrates kinship as an action that rotates around two axes: genealogy bound by time and cosmos bound by space.

the broader environment where plants, animals, natural elements (e.g., air, water) and geographical sites (e.g., mountains) are endowed with certain forms of identity and power" (Markstrom, 2011, p. 523). Kinship communities can pinpoint a person within the kinship network. For example, an individual will have had a lengthy affiliation with a person and the person's family, including a temporal point in an ancestral lineage, with the expectation that the generational relationship will continue into the future (Allen, Mohatt, Markstrom, Byers, and Novins, 2012). Nelson, Kelley, and McPherson (1985) describe the Indigenous community as a network where interrelationships are both complex and high in number. Individuals are embedded "deeply and equally" (p. 233) in reciprocal relations that are not separated into politics, human relations, government, or religion. Indigenous communities tend to have a relationship with the entire social system all at once (DeMallie, 1998; Markstrom, 2008). Kinship people are interdependent and the dominant system boundary envelops the entire community, including individuals and family units. Thus, in the context of a tribal community, everyone has accepted duties and obligations to different people who may or may not be blood relations.

Beyond the Aesthetically Pleasing: Toward a Hip Hop Sensibility

Beat Nation began in 2008 as a website in collaboration with the *grunt gallery*, an artist-run centre in Vancouver, British Columbia. Over time the website generated live performances and an exhibition that toured Canada. The exhibit, *Beat Nation: Art, Hip Hop, and Aboriginal Culture*, explored the role and influence of Hip Hop on art making in Indigenous communities in the land we now call Canada. *Beat Nation* artists engage with the Hip Hop sensibility to expose the distinct patterns of systemic injustices[2] and to exchange ideas and politics among and between performers and spectators. Reading through the literature (Gorlewski & Porfilio, 2012; Recollet, 2010; Tabi & Hudson, 2015), it was not uncommon to read that many Indigenous youth relate to the way the Black community used Hip Hop to speak out against oppression and to declare their own identity. For example, in an interview with Leah Sandals (2013), co-curator Tania Willard (Secwepemc Nation) reflects on how Hip Hop is localized by Native youth as a cultural expression that speaks the language of local Native politics and struggle:

Much of the overlap has come from conscious Hip Hop coming out of marginalized black inner-city communities. Native youth were identifying with those politics, and that's where lots of those connections developed. When we were putting together the online gallery, Hip Hop definitely came across as a way people were expressing themselves and passing ideas and politics on to others in their communities. (n. p.)

Beat Nation artists work through a confusing troubling and state of affairs (i.e., the contemporary historical relationship between the Canadian government and Indigenous people); out of this mess they produce ideas and politics. Eventually, these insights find creative expression in the artwork they make available to the public. For example, within an ethics of engagement, audiences learn about the centrality of Indigenous knowledge to settler society's survival and eventual wealth that extends far beyond the fur trade (Krech, 1981) and the Seven Years War (Jennings, 1988). Accordingly, the artists deploy a Hip Hop sensibility to neutralize erased or negated Indigenous knowledge by dismantling colonial education. Simultaneously, however, they transform the stereotype that authentic Indians and Indian culture are relics of the past; possibly relaxing the grip the colonial imagination has on Canada's collective consciousness where authentic Indians are relegated to the past.

For example, in his interview with Baxley (2011), Assu explained that *Beat Nation* artists sit "outside the perceived notion of 'what is authentic aboriginal art?'" where authentic restricts them to "a craft from a perceived to be dying culture." Assu addressed the repressive nature of bearing witness to what it means to be an artist *and* Ligwilda'xw (We Wai Kai) of the Kwakwaka'wakw nations. The spectre of 'and' is haunting, it seems, because one is forced to straddle the hidden side of the colonial subconscious, where culture is frozen in time and space, and the visible side of the postcolonial, where arts is messy, contingent and forever becoming. *Beat Nation* artists who straddle the colonial and the postcolonial are often criticized by older community members who perceive the Hip Hop influence as breaking away from tradition toward assimilation into mainstream popular culture (Beat Nation, n. d.). By contrast, some art critics use the "worlds in conflict" metaphor to refer to the artists' break with traditional art. As Litt (2013) put it, *Beat Nation* "is where we sense the struggle, where we glimpse the inseparable, intertwined and yet conflicting worlds of aboriginal tradition and urban First Nations life" (n. p.). *Beat Nation* co-curators Kathleen Ritter and Tania Willard shed light on their philosophical approach to the exhibit in an interview with Elissa Barnard (2014). Willard in particular appeared to reject the "worlds in conflict" metaphor. As she put it, "We carry deep connections to ancestors and language and culture. I don't think traditional and contemporary have a meaning that makes sense." That is to say, it is a moment of cultural genocide and death if we see 'traditional' and 'contemporary' as mutually exclusive. To this, Ritter added:

> Aboriginal cultures are not in the past. They are here and now and present and thriving. That's what the exhibit is saying ... We want to get away from the idea there is a new generation of artists making work that's cool and fun. The work is deeply political. (n. p.)

Ritter and Willard reject the worlds in conflict metaphor and repudiate authentic aboriginal art as a by-product of a dying culture. In so doing they invoke the idea of kinship, where traditions are strength to draw upon and where history is not passé but a living entity. By calling upon kinship, they make it necessary for scholars to reimagine the Hip Hop culture and its adherents.

Typically, Osumare (2001) explained, local youth communities begin to adopt, adapt, localize and translate those Hip Hop elements that are available to them. Over time this adoption flips commercialized Hip Hop over its head, where local communities' own stories increasingly dominate their creative productivity of Hip Hop. When mimicry matures into originality then practitioners produce authentic Hip Hop that is deeply local. Most Hip Hop scholarship characterizes practitioners as local youth steeped in one or more of its iconic elements (graffiti, b-boying or breakdancing, deejaying, and emceeing) with little or no traditional (passed down by elders) and formal arts training (Gorlewski & Porfilio, 2012; Ignace & Ignace, 2005; Marsh 2009; Recollet, 2010). Hip Hop youth immersed in the culture tend to self-identify as *Hip Hop headz* and to weave Hip Hop practices into most areas of their lives (cf. Petchauer, 2012). In contrast, many *Beat Nation* artists have received training both from community elders and from Canadian art institutes such as the Emily Carr University of Art and Design. Additionally, their involvement with Hip Hop culture remains peripheral to their identities and lifestyles. We believe that by and large the *Beat Nation* exhibition summons Hip Hop pedagogical space because the artwork exemplifies what we termed Hip Hop sensibility and what Ritter and Willard (2012) identified as political:

> *Political* or *conscious* Hip Hop has been used as a tool of empowerment, as a means to speak from the margins, a way to give voice to struggle, a vehicle to inspire and mobilize and a catalyst to assert a continued, contested presence in our contemporary world. (p. 9)

As a catalyst, *Beat Nation* challenges audiences to question the origins of both Canada's wealth and the rights and benefits Canadians enjoy based on the dispossession and disenfranchisement of Indigenous peoples.[3] As a vehicle to inspire, *Beat Nation* demonstrates that Hip Hop sensibilities are portable because they comprise two crucial aspects: self-expression (better yet, self-determination) and the transmission of politicized knowledge bases. Possibly, these intangible aspects are immune to commodification in ways that most Hip Hop products cannot resist. When *Beat Nation* artists detach Hip Hop sensibilities from Hip Hop culture and attach it to artwork saturated in kinship narratives, we are galvanized to push our thinking beyond celebratory messages. A typical communication describes Indigenous youth as using the medium of Hip Hop to champion the survival of their people and worldviews. Though this is true and though there is much to celebrate, rather than characterize Assu as a Hip Hop artist, we recognize him as an artist who used two materials to create *Ellipsis*: copper *and* Hip Hop sensibility. This recognition opened up new sightlines, drawing our attention away from preconceived notions that distorted our understanding of *Ellipsis*.

It Isn't What It Seems: The Inspiration for *Ellipsis*

In *Mythologies*, Roland Barthes (1972) reflected that mythologies rid things of complexity and dialectics. Mythologies simplify them and efficiently organize a world purged of depth and history. *Ellipsis* consciously works against mythologies. Assu puts up a fierce fight against oppressive mythologies that work to obliterate Kwakwaka'wakw nations and their histories from the nation's imagination. The fight is to create a balanced space between the celebratory and the abject.

The first time we saw *Ellipsis* we assumed Assu referenced the vinyl record because he produced (or at one time had produced) Hip Hop music based on the practice of *sampling* (the process of incorporating a track from a recorded song into a brand new song). Schloss (2013) explained that sampling forms the foundation of Hip Hop production and requires source material. Typically, the source is a collection of vinyl records that are acquired by "digging in the crates." This term refers to a highly developed skill that leads to acquiring rare, usually out-of-print, vinyl records that serve as raw material for sample-based Hip Hop producers. Schloss explained:

Evoking images of a devoted collector spending hours sorting through milk crates full of records in used record stores, garages, and thrift shops, the term [digging in the crates] carries with it a sense of valour and symbolizes an unending quest for the next record. (p. 79)

Initially our assumption that Assu produced Hip Hop music was reinforced by a story about the source of inspiration for *Ellipsis*. The story as told by Kevin Griffin (2012) in the *Vancouver Sun* could be interpreted as Assu rescuing a record from the garbage that "turned out to be his great great grandfather (sic) Chief Billy Assu singing traditional songs at a potlatch[4] with Mungo Martin" (n. p.). At the time of the recording, strict laws were written into the Indian Act that ensured Chief Billy Assu and Mungo Martin would have been jailed and fined if they were caught singing traditional songs at a potlatch (both the singing and the potlatch were illegal). Assu (n. d.) explained in his artist's statement, "during that ban, my Great-Great-Grandfather was allowed to sing these songs for the sake of anthropological preservation, but he was unable to legally practice the culture outside of these recording sessions."

From a Hip Hop perspective, Griffin's (2012) story appears plausible. Assuming Assu was a devoted collector on a perpetual quest, he would constantly be on the alert for the next out-of-print record. The chance "discovery" of the rare recording of Chief Billy Assu singing traditional songs infuses the iconic Hip Hop record collection with the historical fact that the Indian Act has been in force for over a century; here, Chief Billy and the Indian Act represent recorded songs that create a brand new song, *Ellipsis*. The new song conjures the Canadian tradition of treating Indigenous knowledge as insignificant; the copper records symbolize the weight of time: 136 years and counting of colonization. In a casual conversation with the first author, when asked about his relationship to Hip Hop, Assu said he listens primarily to Hip Hop music but has no other connection to the culture. In other words, we were mistaken, Assu was not a Hip Hop music producer or deejay. Eventually, we located a video recording of a public lecture where Assu (2014) tells the origin story for *Ellipsis*. He recounted that one afternoon when his mother was working in their home community (Cape Mudge) as a receptionist for the now disbanded Treaty Nations she received a call that may have come from Langley, British Columbia. The caller said,

I was in a thrift store and there was a box of records that said, 'Free or Garbage.' This record was in there, this collection was in there, I did a quick Google search, you guys were the first thing to come up, I phoned you, these might be important to you. Do you want them? (35:19–36:13).

Assu's mother said yes. Eventually Assu had the collection digitized. For this portion of the lecture he presented a slide featuring Chief Billy Assu and the front and back of the record jacket *Indian Music of the Pacific Northwest Coast* (Folkways Records, 1967).

Certainly, it matters that we read *Ellipsis* as public outrage over Canada's aggressive assimilation policies, but confining Assu to the role of a Hip Hop artist limits our understandings of *Ellipsis* to Western interpretations and definitions that "locate Indigenous peoples outside the flow and influences of time" (Justice, 2008, p. 6). To do so would turn this chapter into another incident of erasure of Indigenous knowledge. That is to say, had we been satisfied with our initial assumption shored up by Griffin's article, we would have been complicit in erasing or marginalizing Indigenous knowledge. Our premise that Assu was a Hip Hop artist occurred because *Ellipsis* contests the Indian Act's validity and longevity. Here, Assu's contestation creates a pedagogical moment—something we are accustomed to in Hip Hop spaces (Ibrahim, 2014). We collapsed that pedagogical space when we leapt to our assumption that led to an incomplete understanding of *Ellipsis*. That is why we call for a kinship literacy, one that is mindful that "it isn't what it seems."

Although Griffin's version of the story contains accurate details, it also creates an urban myth where the hero rescues his vanishing culture from obscurity and extinction. The myth relies on stereotypes that portray Indians as dying off culturally and literally. Assu unsettles these common stereotypes and assumptions regarding Indigenous peoples, their history and traditional culture by the simple fact that he is an actual person who is not a relic of the past or a "romantic casualt[y] of a dying race" (Ritter & Willard, 2012, p. 48). From a colonist understanding, Indigenous traditional songs threatened cultural assimilation to such a degree the Indian Act outlawed them until eventually they became so worthless that giving them away was on par with throwing them away. In contrast, when we read *Ellipsis* as a kinship narrative we learn some of Assu's family history and a small bit about songs as kinship artifacts. *Ellipsis* circulates stories about Chief Billy Assu and his great-great grandson, Sonny Assu; their kinship narrative illuminates the unbroken circle and ever-presence of the Ligwilda'x̱w (We Wai Kai) of the Kwakwaka'wakw nations, their traditional songs and cultural practices in the nation known as Canada.

It is worth noting the record that inspired Assu, *Indian Music of the Pacific Northwest Coast* (Folkways Records, 1967), was recorded in 1967 by Ida Halpern, an ethnomusicologist. Halpern, like many of her contemporaries, believed Indians would soon vanish; she assumed the responsibility of saving whatever music and songs could be recorded, to collect as much information as possible on what many assumed to be the dying Kwakwaka'wakw culture. The assumption that the Kwakwaka'wakw nations were dying off was supported by depopulation and by Canadian legislation. The rapid population decline, according to Webster (1991), was due to the introduction of diseases and alcohol, while Canadian legislation created to save the Indians by civilizing them through cultural assimilation was "founded on the conscious intent to eliminate Indians and 'Indianness' from Canada" (Mathias & Yabsley, 1991, p. 35). The primary vehicle used to eliminate Indian identity and values was strict laws written into the Indian Act. For example, section 140(1)[5] ensured that anybody caught engaging in Indigenous cultural activities would be jailed and fined.

Against this background, *Ellipsis* deemphasizes Kwakwaka'wakw's authentic songs and traditional repertoires, neatly averting the "dying culture" debate. Instead, Assu emphasizes the meaning of the Indian Act, while praising the Kwakwaka'wakw nations' defiant resistance to circumvent its laws (cf. Cole, 1991). For Assu (2014), *Ellipsis* defines the Indian Act as apartheid. He asserted:

> [The piece explains] in the most simple way as possible the Indian Act. It's apartheid, that's exactly what it is: the separation of peoples from the state (36:49–36:58) … The 167 records are installed in an inverted equalizing pattern to indicate that even through this oppression and this segregation and the effect of colonial genocide, that we as a People, multiple peoples from across the country, have maintained the knowledge of our culture to make sure that we grow and develop as various cultures across this country. (38:37–38:53)

Assu acknowledged that although tribes from Indigenous nations were diminished, they did not vanish. Building from Justice (2008), in *Ellipsis* kinship transcends something that simply is to become something that is done. In this sense (being-doing), kinship remains in continuous motion. Justice asserted that the continuity of Indigenous nations originates from Indigenous peoples' relationships to other humans and the rest of creation. He explained that "such kinship isn't a static thing; it's dynamic, ever in motion" (p. 6). When Indigenous peoples assert their self-determination, they assert the presence of Indigenous nations in the face of erasure; freeing themselves from the "ghost-making rhetorics of colonization" (p. 6). In effect, kinship asserts an unbroken Native presence in the nation known as Canada, a nation "implicated in and indebted to Indigenous knowledges" (Emberley, 2014, p. 71). All this to say that kinship disrupts the colonial imagination, asserts Indigenous people as contemporary, thriving beings, and maintains traditional territory as inextricably bound to Indigenous culture and sovereignty.

Two points are drawn from our discussion above. First, Assu, through *Ellipsis*, calls upon a kinship literacy that requires familiarity with not only his ancestral Kwakwaka'wakw culture and heritage, but also with the Indian Act. Assu calls on viewers to educate themselves on both fronts. As someone with a strong sense of kinship, it is not Assu's responsibility to educate us about his art. It is our ethical and moral responsibility to educate ourselves. Here, two competing discourses are forged into *Indian Music of the Pacific Northwest Coast*: (1) Halpern who records the language and songs of a dying culture and (2) Assu who contests the Indian Act. In *Ellipsis*, we are not simply standing before a piece of art; we stand before the 136 cumulative years of the Indian Act.

To conclude, there is an element of mystique about how *Ellipsis* came into being, one that addresses the two axes of kinship. The cultural weight and significance of Chief Billy Assu's songs, along with the cultural proto-cols surrounding them, one may argue, raise the possibility that these objects connect to cosmological and genealogical kinship. For example, the songs were and still are governed by strict rules that regulate ownership, perfor-mance, and use. Also, they are forms of hereditary wealth that connote prestige and rank (Chen, 1995). Accordingly, from the CK perspective, the songs link the Ligwilda'xw (We Wai Kai) people to beings and entities appearing in various physical and spiritual realms. From the GK perspec-tive, the Assu songs extend into both the infinite past and future. They symbolize continuous hereditary wealth that was undoubtedly threatened for the 67 years that Section 140(1) of the Indian Act was in force. Simulta-neously, Chief Billy Assu can be located in the near past while Sonny Assu is located in the present. Far from being invisible, as told by his great-great grandson,

Chief Assu had an immense amount of status[6] along the entire Pacific Northwest coast, all the way from Washington State to the tip of Alaska. He was a very import-ant figure for the entire Indigenous people in the West Coast; but he was also recog-nized as being important to the Canadian government. When he passed away in the early 60s, the military did a fly-by over the reservation to pay respect to him, which is interesting and ironic considering. (Assu, 2014, 22:37–23:06)

The military gesture is ironic because the Canadian government paid hom-age to Chief Assu, yet at the same time it was adamant about implementing

Section 140(1) that forbade the songs recorded in the *Indian Music of the Pacific Northwest Coast*.

If Chief Assu represents the painful yet resistant past of Indigenous people, Sonny Assu represents the present and hopeful future. As a multidisciplinary artist, Sonny Assu's status has been steadily increasing over the past decade. According to his biography,[7] his work has been accepted into the National Gallery of Canada, the Seattle Art Museum, the Vancouver Art Gallery, the Museum of Anthropology at UBC, and in various other public and private collections across Canada and the United States. It is fair to say that though they may go unnoticed, at least in the larger popular culture sphere, both men are always appearing in the midst of dominant society. From the kinship continuum, Sonny's artwork samples Chief Assu's music to illuminate the urgent necessity for Canadians to educate themselves about the Indian Act. In many ways, *Ellipsis* forces viewers to acknowledge Chief Assu's capacity to resist colonization, for he always appears either as the man granting permission to Halpern to record him singing, as the song on a record album in a milk crate, as a story waiting to be told about the inspiration for his great-great grandson's creative work, or as a vocalized song that remains part of our soundscape regardless of whether or not it is heard.

By Way of Concluding: Toward a New Notion of Kinship (Literacy)

Unlike Canadians who relate to various categories within dominant society (e.g., government, human relations, politics, or religion), kinship roles and responsibilities involve having a relationship with an entire social system all at once (DeMallie, 1998). In other words, individuals are deeply and equally embedded in "an ongoing and dynamic system of mutually-affecting relationships" (Justice, 2008, p. 6). The dual nature of kinship (doing-being) invites us to understand kinship not only in its "traditionally overdetermined" (Emberley, 2014, p. 71) meaning, but also as a methodological trope that reflects how kinship "is produced by, is responsive to, and unsettles inherited technologies of knowledge" (Kamboureli, 2014, p. 18). Conversely, in settings where political or religious categories, for instance, construct social roles and responsibilities, inherited knowledge includes Eurowestern stereotypes and deficit narratives that are attributed to Indigenous people, along with historicized contexts that limit Indigenous knowledge to the fur trade (Krech,

1981), the Seven Years War (Jennings, 1988), and other stereotypes. Overall, these types of knowledge contribute to the eventual erasure of Indigenous communities and lifestyles from Canadian society. Returning our attention to *Ellipsis*, we reiterate that Sonny Assu does not identify as a *Hip Hop headz*; yet, by asserting his (and his nation's) continued, contested presence in our contemporary world he opens up the cipher—the informal, portable pedagogical space (Lefebvre, 2014)—crucial to the Hip Hop culture. However by privileging kinship narratives, Assu expect us to do the work, to make sense of his art, to learn how to carry out kinship. We hope we have done exactly that. In embodying the new (to us) kinship literacy, where the onus is on the viewer to teach her/himself, we discovered the need to go beyond given categories, such as "Hip Hop artist." Sonny Assu challenged us to bring together separate and disparate entities: ethics of engagement, Hip Hop sensibility, history, kinship literacy, time and tradition. These entities are a comprehensive system that we interact with and transform according to kinship rights and responsibilities. By working from the kinship continuum, a network of reciprocal relationships, we practice kinship. From here, we can acknowledge the mess and complexity of Sonny Assu's work. *Ellipsis*, we repeat, is not simply a work of art. When approached from an ethics of engagement bound to kinship literacy, we uphold a testifying space of 136 years of suffering, colonization and apartheid; yet also of resilience, resistance, persistence and hope. Sonny Assu illuminates a sightline where we catch glimpses of the possible; it is our ethical and moral duty to learn from this vantage point. Clearly, our best is here, but our absolute best is yet to come. We are obliged to engage with kinship—to put it into action—with the aspiration that kinship moves all Canadians beyond the mess of colonization into a more hopeful future. Nothing prepares us for how to carry kinship other than carrying out kinship itself.

Acknowledgments

Haidee Smith Lefebvre's research was supported by the Social Sciences and Humanities Research Council of Canada. Big up to Sonny Assu and Shirley Steinberg for supporting our work. Above all, we thank all Beat Nation artists. The learning curve is incredible, but it is high time we/non-Natives unmask our ignorance and teach ourselves. Yep, we hear you Sonny: ya-do-you'r-thang, we-do-ours!

Notes

1. Enacted in 1869, the Indian Act, an aggressive assimilationist policy, made possible the destruction of Indigenous communities, families, and cultures by controlling the "day-to-day lives of registered Indians and reserve communities" (Indigenous Foundations, n. d., n. p.) and curtailing the practice of Aboriginal culture and traditions. In force today, the Indian Act continues to define who qualifies as Indian, determine the land base of reservations, and impose structures of governance (band councils) on Aboriginal communities.
2. Examples of systemic injustice include the economic forces, government policies, and social programs that confine status Indians to substandard, overcrowded housing, where violence, substance abuse, and suicide become a means to cope with the dispossession and disenfranchisement of Indigenous peoples.
3. Canada ranks among the top-five countries on the UN Human Development index, while Canada's Indigenous population lags in 78th place (O'Neill, 2007).
4. According to Jonaitis (1991), the Kwakwaka'wakw potlatch was and continues to be a complex ceremonial during which the host family communicates its status by displaying inherited privileges in lavishly decorated artworks and dances as well as by making eloquent speeches detailing these privileges. The guests are treated to sumptuous cuisine and, at the end, receive gifts as payment for having witnessed these displays. (p. 12).
5. Every Indian or other person who engages in, assists in celebrating or encourages either directly or indirectly another to celebrate any Indian festival, dance or other ceremony … is guilty of an offence and is liable on summary conviction to imprisonment for a term not exceeding six months and not less than two months. (Indian Act, R. S. G. 1927, G. 98, s. 140)
6. See Haplern's liner notes for a biographical sketch of Chief Billy Assu that culminates in a quote by George Clutesi (Nootka), "Billy Assu was a big king, not a chief; what tore down his prestige among all Indians was that the white people considered him a chief. The chief was CHA MAN DA. He was a king" (p. 3). http://media.smithsonianfolkways.org/liner_notes/folkways/FW04523.pdf
7. http://sonnyassu.com/pages/biography

References

Allen, J., Mohatt, G., Markstrom, C., Byers, L., and Novins. D. K. (2012). "Oh no, we are just getting to know you": The relationship in research with children and youth in Indigenous communities. *Child Development Perspectives*, 6(1): 55–60. doi: 10.1111/j.1750-8606.2011.00199.x

Assu, S. (n. d.) *Ellipsis*. <http://sonnyassu.com/pages/ellipsis> accessed 16 February 2014.

Assu, S. (2014, February). Sonny Assu: Body of work. Lecture presented at the Le Programme ICI (Intervenants Culturels Internationaux), Montréal, Canada. <http://T.com/86739058> accessed 3 March 2014.

Barnard, E. (2014, March 28). At the galleries: Celebrating evolving Aboriginal art. *The Chronicle Herald*. <http://thechronicleherald.ca/thenovascotian/1196708-at-the-galleries-celebrating-evolving-aboriginal-art> accessed 29 April 2014.

Barthes, R. (1972). *Mythologies*. New York: Hill and Wang.

Baxley, C. (2011). Sonny Assu - Laich-kwil-tach (Kwakwaka'wakw): Phone Interview by Crystal Baxley. <http://contemporarynativeartists.tumblr.com/post/6030123932/sonny-assu-laich-kwil-tach-kwakwakawakw> accessed 10 February 2013.

Beat Nation. (n. d.). http://www.beatnation.org/

Chen, K. (1995). Ida Halpern: A post-colonial portrait of a Canadian pioneer ethnomusicologist. *Canadian University Music Review/Revue de musique des universités canadiennes*, 16(1): 41–59. doi: 10.7202/1014415ar

Cole, D. (1991). The history of the Kwakiutl potlatch. In A. Jonaiti, and American Museum of Natural History (Eds.), *Chiefly feasts: The enduring Kwakiutl potlatch*, pp. 135–176. Seattle: University of Washington Press.

DeMallie, R. J. (1998). Kinship: The foundation for Native American Society. In R. Thornton, (Ed.), *Studying native America: Problems and prospects*, pp. 306–356. Madison, WI: University of Wisconsin Press.

Emberley, J. (2014). The Accidental Witness: Indigenous Epistemologies and Spirituality as Resistance in Eden Robinson's Monkey Beach. In S. Kamboureli, and C. Verduyn (Eds.), *Critical collaborations: Indigeneity, diaspora, and ecology in Canadian literary studies* (pp. 69–82).

Folkways Records. (1967). *Indian Music of the Pacific Northwest Coast* [Double-LP, Album No FE 4523]. New York: Folkways Records. Available at http://www.folkways.si.edu/indian-music-of-the-pacific-northwest-coast/american-indian/album/smithsonian

Gorlewski, J., and Porfilio, J. (2012). Revolutionizing environmental education through Indigenous Hip Hop culture. *Canadian Journal of Environmental Education*, 17: 46–61.

Griffin, K. (2012, February 24). Beat Nation: Aboriginal art that breaks boundaries. *The Vancouver Sun*. <http://blogs.vancouversun.com/2012/02/24/beat-nation-aboriginal-art-that-breaks-boundaries/> accessed 15 November 2013.

Ibrahim, A. (2014). *The rhizome of blackness: A critical ethnography of Hip Hop culture, language, identity, and the politics of becoming*. New York: Peter Lang.

Ignace, Marianne, and Ignace, George. (2005). Tagging, rapping and the voices of the ancestors: Expressing Aboriginal identity between the small city and the rez. In W. Garrett-Petts (Ed.), *The small cities book* (pp. 2–28). Vancouver: New Star Book.

Indigenous Foundations. (n. d.). http://indigenousfoundations.arts.ubc.ca/home/government-policy/the-indian-act.html

Jennings, F. (1988). *Empire of fortune: Crowns, colonies, and tribes in the Seven Years War in America*. New York: Norton.

Jonaitis, A., and American Museum of Natural History. (1991). *Chiefly feasts: The enduring Kwakiutl potlatch*. Seattle: University of Washington Press.

Justice, D. H. (2008). 'Go away water!': Kinship Criticism and the Decolonization Imperative. In J. Acoose, C. S. Womack, D. H. Justice, and C. B. Teuton (Eds.), *Reasoning together: The native critics collective*. Norman, OK: University of Oklahoma Press.

Kamboureli, S. (2014). Introduction. In S. Kamboureli, and C. Verduyn (Eds.), *Critical collaborations: Indigeneity, diaspora, and ecology in Canadian literary studies* (pp. 1–28).

Krech, S. (1981). *Indians, animals, and the fur trade: A critique of keepers of the game*. Athens: University of Georgia Press.

Lefebvre, H. S. (2014). The breaking (street dance) cipher: A shared context for knowledge creation. In A. Ibrahim and S. Steinberg (Eds.), *Critical youth studies reader*, (pp. 407–417). New York: Peter Lang.

Litt, C. (2013). Art review: Beat Nation lures, captivates, educates. *The Kamloops Daily News*. http://license.icopyright.net/user/viewFreeUse.act?fuid=MTczMjIxMzk=

Markstrom, C. A. (June 01, 2011). Identity Formation of American Indian Adolescents: Local, National, and Global Considerations. *Journal of Research on Adolescence, 21*(2), 519–535.

Markstrom, C. A. (2008). *Empowerment of North American Indian girls: Ritual expressions at puberty*. Lincoln: University of Nebraska Press.

Marsh, C. (2009). "Don't call me Eskimo": Representation, mythology, and Hip Hop culture on Baffin Island. *MUSICultures: Canadian Society for Traditional Music, 36*: 110–129.

Mathias, J., and Yabsley, G. R. (1991). Conspiracy of legislation: The suppression of Indian rights in Canada. *BC Studies: The British Columbian Quarterly, 89*: 34–45. <http://ojs.library.ubc.ca/index.php/bcstudies/article/view/1383/1427> accessed 17 January 2015.

Nelson, C. H., Kelley, M. L, and McPherson, D. H. (1985). Rediscovering support in practice: Lessons from Indian Indigenous human service workers. *Canadian Social Work Review, 4*(2), 231–248.

O'Neill, B. (2007, February 1). Why we can no longer call Canada an advocate for Human Rights. *Huffington Post*. <http://www.huffingtonpost.ca/bernie-farber/canada-human-rights-record_b_2598003.html> accessed 15 January 2015.

Osumare, H. (2001). Beat streets in the global hood: Connective marginalities of the Hip Hop globe. *Journal of American & Comparative Cultures, 24*(1–2): 171–181. doi: 10.1111/j.1537-4726.2001.2401_171.x

Petchauer, E. (2012). *Hip Hop culture in college students' lives: Elements, embodiment, and higher edutainment*. New York: Taylor & Francis.

Recollet, K. (2010). *Aural Traditions: Indigenous Youth and the Hip Hop Movement in Canada*. (Unpublished doctoral dissertation). Trent University.

Ritter, K. V., and Willard, T. (2012). *Beat nation: Art, Hip Hop and Aboriginal culture*. Vancouver, BC Canada: Vancouver Art Gallery.

Sandals, L. (2013). Q&A: Tania Willard on Life Beyond Beat Nation. *Canadian Art*. <http://www.canadianart.ca/features/2013/06/28> accessed 12 April 2014.

Schloss, J. G. (2013). *Making beats: The art of sample-based Hip Hop*. Middletown, CT: Wesleyan University Press.

Tabi, E., and Hudson, A. (2015) Where We @? Blackness, Indigeneity and Hip Hop's Expression of Creativity. In S. Steinberg and A. Ibrahim, *Talkin Bout Their Generation: Critically Researching Youth*, New York: Peter Lang.

Webster, G. C. (1991). The contemporary potlatch. In A. Jonaitis American Museum of Natural History (Eds.), *Chiefly feasts: The enduring Kwakiutl potlatch*, pp. 227–250. Seattle: University of Washington Press.

· 7 ·

"TOO MUCH DRAMA"

The Effect of Smartphones on Teenagers' Live Theater Experience

John M. Richardson

While a trip to the theater is a familiar aspect of many high school English and drama programs, the presence of smartphones in the pockets of youth audience members has altered the experience of watching live plays in significant ways. Based on a qualitative study of students at the end of a four-play series, and building on earlier research that suggested eight new mindsets shape teen responses to live theater, this chapter looks into "the blue glow from the back row" to consider the effect of growing up in the participatory culture of Web 2.0. It finds that smartphones disrupt and complicate the relationship between viewer and performer, shifting power from the stage to the audience while enabling students to slip from one site of drama, the theater, to another, the social media website. It also explores students' positive and negative responses to live theater, and finds that theater has relevance for many young people, who are hopeful that they will be moved, provoked, and inspired by the stage. The chapter concludes by suggesting how educators might use this information to better prepare students raised in the digital world for the experience of live performance.

I teach senior English and drama at a co-educational independent school in Ottawa, Canada, and every year I attend a series of four plays at the National Arts Centre (NAC) and the Great Canadian Theater Company (GCTC) with my students. On the last day of school 5 years ago, my students and I were chatting about that year's series when I was asked if had seen "the blue glow from the back row." I had no idea what the student meant; along with my teacher colleagues, I had been too focused on the plays to pay much attention to the back row. Everyone laughed. So many young people had been texting and surfing the web, the students told me, the entire back row glowed blue. Looking back, I'm surprised at how shocked I was at this revelation, although that in itself is a reflection of how rapidly information and communication technology (ICTs) have transformed so many aspects of our lives—including the youth experience of live theater (Richardson, 2011, 2012, 2013). This led me to conduct a study to answer the question, "How do members of the wireless generation experience live theater?" (Richardson, 2010).

One of the study's key findings was that, in comparing the students' thoughts to my own—a middle-aged theater aficionado who has studied theater, acted, directed, written for the stage, and taught drama—eight new mindsets could be discerned around the high school student's experience of attending a live play (Richardson, 2010, 2013):

- Mindset 1: "I have to watch this play alone? Without speaking?"—I noticed in their attitudes a shift from individual to group consciousness (Zamaria & Fletcher, 2007). Students were accustomed to constant communication.
- Mindset 2: "I have to pay for this?"—the shift from a scarcity economy, in which supply and demand determine value, to an attention economy, in which getting noticed on the Web is the goal (Lankshear & Knobel, 2007).
- Mindset 3: "I have to sit still for 3 hours?"—the shift from slow to fast capitalism (The New London Group, 1996).
- Mindset 4: "Why is the usher looking at me?"—the shift from a hierarchical to flat world view (Friedman, 2007), with authority dispersed as opposed to ordered.
- Mindset 5: "What's so special about theater?"—the shift from reverence for high culture (Alvermann & Hagood, 2008) to a telescoping of high and low culture into instantly accessible play lists.
- Mindset 6: "I'm not supposed to text?"—the shift from theatrical to virtual space.
- Mindset 7: "Where's the screen?"—the shift from looking at people to screens (Kress, 2009).

• Mindset 8: "We're meant to believe THAT?"—the shift from the metaphor of the stage to the realism of the screen.

In this chapter, I would like to pick up on one of those mindsets—Mindset 6, the shift from the theatrical space to the virtual space—in light of new research I conducted at the conclusion of the 2012/2013 theater season. My research question remained "How do members of the wireless generation experience live theater?" but I sought to deepen my understanding of how growing up within the participatory culture (Jenkins, 2009) of the ever-connected world of Web 2.0 may shape student responses to live theater. How does the presence of smartphones, for example, affect the relationship between the audience member and the performer? Does theater have relevance to young people, or are kids just too digitized in their outlook to care about people in make-up and costumes on stage? We have been hearing about the death of theater for a long time—is the smartphone the final, digital nail in its coffin?

Literature Review

This exploration of youth theater-goers is based upon the belief that "learning in the arts is fundamental because the arts are an essential aspect of human knowing and being in the world" (Bucheli, Goldberg, & Phillips, 1991). However, it responds to the call from a number of scholars in the fields of media education, critical pedagogy, audience studies, and social media research to better understand what McCarthy, Giardina, Harewood, & Jin-Kyung Park (2003) called "the radical reconfiguration and cultural re-articulation now taking place in educational and social life" (p. 462) due to the rise of ICTs.

Clapp and Edwards (2013), for example, noted how "the onset of the information era, the spread of globalism, and the increased ubiquity of digital and visual culture have considerably changed the ways we engage with the world" (p. 6), while Buckingham and Kingdom (2003) argued that the "development of new media is resulting in a more heterogeneous environment, in which the boundaries between mass communication and interpersonal communication, and between producers and consumers, have become increasingly blurred" (p. 310). The student in the theater, updating her Facebook status, uploading material to the Web, sending a text, or surfing the Web is part of that newly complicated environment, both receiving and contributing content (Jenkins, 2009; Selwyn, 2009). There is a need to study the ways in which her actions "reproduce social relations and in whose interests they serve" (Selwyn, 2012, p. 219) so that the power relations surrounding new technologies can be better understood and teachers can be better prepared to work with their students.

Burwell (2010) cautioned against the celebratory script that accompanies many references to participatory culture, suggesting instead that a more "critical examination of the politics of digital participation" (p. 385) is required. Her comments echo Willis (2003), who wrote that "popular culture should be understood in relation to the strong urge of young people to make and maintain a viable informal cultural identity acknowledged by others, in shared social space" (p. 407). "Accepting popular culture," he added, "does not mean a lazy throwing open of the school doors to the latest fad, but rather committing to a principled understanding of the complexity of the contemporary cultural experience" (p. 411).

This study also responds to work done by Bennett (1990), who saw audience members as physically passive while mentally active in the decoding of theatrical sign systems, to audience researchers who explore and question the relationship of the audience member to the production (Barker, 2003; Gallagher & Riviere, 2007; Lee-Brown, 2002; Reason, 2006; Tulloch, 2000) and to Peggy Phelan (2010), who suggested that the real action during a play may have shifted from the stage to the audience members' cellphone screens.

It also speaks to the work of Internet researchers such as boyd and Marwick (2010), who wrote about how

> the idea of the "audience" as a stable entity that congregates around a media object has been displaced with the "interpretive community," "fandom," and "participatory culture," concepts that assume small, active, and highly engaged groups of people who don't just consume content but produce their own as well. (p. 16)

They described the "networked public" as one that is restructured by technology, "a highly accessible space where wide audiences can gather, and a collection of people who want to share what Sonia Livingstone describes as 'a common understanding of the world, a shared identity'" (boyd & Marwick, 2011, p. 7). Teens flock to networked publics "because they are some of the only spaces to which they have access. In trying to create a place for themselves in these places, they are not trying to be public, but rather, to be in a public" (boyd & Marwick, 2011, p. 26). Within these networked publics, students are "audience and performer at the same time" (Abercrombie & Longhurst, 1998, p. 73). They interact and adapt their behaviour based on who is in the actual audience, navigating "frontstage" and "backstage" areas of their lives in an active process of "impression management" (Goffman, 1959) akin to that used by celebrities to maintain their status (boyd & Marwick, 2011).

Within the blue glow of the back row, then, operates an active theater sub-culture: a networked youth public within a theater public; performers within the audience; people front of stage actively managing the entrances and exits from the "frontstage" and the "backstage" (Goffman, 1959) of their cyber-lives; audience members co-opting the celebrity management techniques of the rich and famous.

But what has my own research revealed about this public within a public, this audience within an audience, these performers before performers?

Methods

I accompanied students on a series of four productions that began with a filmed version of a live production of *The Last of the Haussmans*, a big, messy, family drama broadcast to cinemas around the world from London, England's National Theatre. Then came a Vancouver production at GCTC, *The Number 14*, a Commedia-dell'arte–inspired play set on a bus. *Metamorphoses*, a retell-ing of Greek myth set in a swimming pool, followed at the NAC. Our season concluded with *The Edward Curtis Project*, a multi-media-enhanced play at GCTC about the famous photographer of First Nations peoples. The number of students who attended each performance ranged from 100 to 140 students.

All of the grade 11 and 12 theater-going students were sent two anon-ymous surveys in the form of Google Docs forms, each with 12 questions, some of a factual nature but most requiring open-ended, text-box responses. The first survey focused on the students' responses to the plays we had seen together, their thoughts about the relevance of live theater, and comparisons between live theater, movies, and online activities. Seventy-five students chose to answer the survey. Picking up on some interesting student responses, the second survey 2 weeks later sought to examine more closely the effects of social media and to open up and explore the meaning of "Mindset Number 6," the shift from theatrical to virtual space. Sixty-one students responded. In total, the surveys generated 50,000 words of commentary. With the help of research assistants, and working within parameters established by the Univer-sity of Calgary ethics review board, I also conducted seven focus groups and interviews with the grade 11 and 12 theater-goers. These began with students creating a simple artwork in response to the prompt, "Draw a picture that communicates your experience of live theater." The students were asked to explain their artistic choices, and then the semi-structured interview began. Interviews and focus groups lasted between 45 minutes and 2 hours.

The survey data and interview transcripts were analyzed according to the qualitative research methods described by Miles, Huberman, & Saldaña (2014) and Saldaña (2013), a method that sees qualitative research as a process of data condensation, data display, and conclusion drawing/verification (Miles et al., 2014, p. 12). During First Cycle Coding, the Eclectic method— including In Vivo, Initial, Emotion, Value, and Judgment Coding (Saldaña, 2013)—was followed. During Second Cycle Coding, a Focused Coding approach was taken in order to consolidate First Cycle codes into broader themes. These were displayed in tables, expressed as analytic memos, and then as assertions. Images were analyzed in a similar manner, with codes applied to what was apparent in the picture, and that analysis combined with the speaker's own descriptive words in the transcript (Miles et al., 2014; Gee, 2010). In order to arrive at findings, assertions were triangulated between at least three data sources: images, focus groups, interviews, and both surveys (Miles et al., 2014, p. 293).

The combined research method of open-ended survey, focus groups, interviews and artworks was employed in order to provide a number of affordances. The online survey reached a large number of students, and by allowing students to write their responses anonymously, a broad range of frank, in-depth commentary emerged (Creswell, 2008, p. 228). The high quality of the writing suggested that students valued the opportunity to reflect as they wrote. The use of drawings provided an alternative avenue into students' experiences, as well as an engaging way to begin the discussions (Bagnoli, 2009; Feldman, 1973; Harper, 2005; Morawski, 2008; Reason, 2008). The use of focus groups and in-depth interviews has a long and established history in qualitative research, and in media and audience studies in particular (Creswell, 2007; Kamberelis & Dimitriadis, 2005; Morley, 2003; Radway, 1991), allowing students to share, articulate, and build upon their ideas and experiences.

One could argue that since the students in this study come from an independent school and economically privileged families, the results will be unhelpful in understanding how wireless teens experience live theater. However, the economic profile of most independent school parents tends to match that of North American theater goers (National Endowment for the Arts, 2008), which suggests that students in the study will tend to resemble many future theater goers. Besides, one should not assume that economic privilege necessarily brings pre-existing bias toward having attended live theater.

One of the interview subjects featured in this article, "Jane" (all names are pseudonyms), is highly accomplished academically and has lived all over the world, but had never been to the theater before this year's series. Although a detailed study of the interviewees' Internet usage patterns was not part of this study, the data suggest that students' digital proclivities are typical by North American standards (Ipsos, 2009; Lenhart, 2012; Lewin, 2010; Rideout, Foeher, & Roberts, 2010; Zamaria & Fletcher, 2007).

One could also argue that the plays that are featured in this study are overly traditional, and that students may have provided entirely different responses if they had been exposed to avant-garde theater that uses new media technologies in innovative ways (Dixon, 2007; Klich & Scheer, 2012; Kuksa & Childs, 2010; Murray, 2004; Salter, 2010; Wardrip-Fruin & Harrigan, 2004). However, this study is predicated on the notion that there is educational value in exposing students to traditional, live, literary theater. Besides, the teachers in this study, like educators everywhere, do the best they can with local resources. Every effort was made to select plays—including one set in a swimming pool, and another set on a bus— that would stand the best chance of appealing to teens.

Results

Three significant findings to emerge from this study are:

- Smartphones in the bags and pockets of youth audience members disrupt and complicate the relationship between the viewer and the performer in a variety of ways, shifting power from the stage to the audience.
- Students offer a variety of opinions on the ways in which social media can be seen as "the new theater," and agree that Web 2.0 sites provide venues for drama, performance, and role-play.
- Many students enjoy live theater, often because of the opportunity it provides for a break from their online lifestyles. They believe that it can be relevant to young people, particularly if they have been exposed to it at an early age.

In order to expand upon these findings, I will draw upon the results of in-depth interviews with Jane and then with Anna, supported by a representative sampling of written comments from the online, anonymous, written survey.

Cellphones as a Disruption to Live Theater

Jane is a student in the International Baccalaureate (IB) Diploma Program, and winner of a prestigious scholarship to one of Canada's top universities. Fast-talking, opinionated, curious, articulate, and scientifically minded, she had a lot to say, and the interview lasted well over an hour.

Jane began the interview by drawing the picture that communicated her experience of live theater (see Figure 1).

In the background are shapes that suggest excitement and wonder—an explosion, outlines that suggest newly open tulip heads or flames, fluffy clouds that evoke a summer sky, and the word "Wow!" with an explanation mark to accentuate the feeling of excitement and pleasure.

Figure 1. Jane's response to the prompt, "Draw a picture that communicates your experience of live theater."

Closer to the viewer, the clouds persist, but they are obscured by heavily drawn, vertical lines that suggest either the hands of a clock or the outline of an angry face. The reference to time is reinforced by a clock on the left, whose clear lines are in contrast to the softly effervescent outline in the background, the numbers, lines, and evenly spaced borders of its circular shape a mathematical intrusion on the softer background.

The seats in the foreground, black and regularly shaped like tombstones, are empty, and the stage itself is dominated by another, larger gravestone-like shape, as though the stage represents the end of something. The word "WHY?" written in darker pencil and in stronger lettering, with more emphatic punctuation, cuts across the seating. The drawing suggests the possibility of good things, but the intrusive reality of anger, frustration, and ennui.

"I started by drawing what it feels like to be in the seat when it comes to a good piece of live theater," said Jane. "It tends to be me and the actor, and no one else. I don't see or experience any other people in the audience. It's more of a co-operative experience. Whereas when I'm watching a piece of live theater that isn't great I tend to be increasingly aware of the audience and it ends up becoming the audience versus the actors."

"In live theater that I don't enjoy, I leave frustrated. I wrote 'WHY?' in capital letters because that tends to be the question I leave with if I don't enjoy the play. Also, during the play I tend to be increasingly aware of the time as it passes rather than really being stuck in the story."

"Hence you drew ...," said the interviewer.

"The clock. A big, angry clock."

This reference to the "big angry clock" points to one of the major themes in Jane's remarks. Although she is alive and open to the rich possibilities of live theater, and sees it as capable of more subtlety and intelligence than movies, running through her comments is a high degree of judgment about how she has spent time in the theater—often expressed in fabulously strong, teenage terms.

"I *despised* that play," she said of *The Metamorphosis*. "Absolutely *despised* it. I felt it was disorganized and the acting was forced and the story made no sense, and there was no time line. I also felt that the incest scene was really, really, really gross." Her disappointment and disapproval is clear. "I *was* really open, really excited to see it," she said, but "I was disgusted by the play and felt like leaving, and so I turned on my phone to try to distract myself because it was that bad."

"How long would you say you were on the phone for?" asked the interviewer.

"Well, the duration of the play after the incest scene."

"Okay, so from that point on?"

"We all sort of *gasped*. Then it was, like, immediately *out*."

"Everyone pulled out their phones?"

"Definitely. Just to try to get out (laughing) ... *Get me out of here!*"

At this moment in the production of *The Metamorphosis*, the cooperative relationship between the audience and the performers is over, and the adversarial relationship alluded to by Jane becomes visible. The spectators Rosen (2006) called "the people formerly known as the audience" turn to their cellphones as a means of escape, protest, and resistance. The cellphone becomes a means for the audience to take back some of the power in the relationship they have with the performers.

"Describe whether your daily, digital lifestyle affects your experience with theater," the interviewer continued.

"I would say the only thing would be I want to check my phone," Jane replied.

"Did you feel frustrated not checking your phone?"

"It depends on numerous factors," she said, "like who, or when, but most of the time no. I can put away my phone for, like, *ever*, if I have to. It just depends on whether said activity is more interesting to me than my phone. There's always that comparison."

"That comparison"—between the often gentle, cerebral pleasures of live theater and the quick hits of texting, social media sites, game-playing, and general web surfing—is another dominant theme in student responses to live theater. Looking at the cellphone to check the time and from there to look at messages and other content is a constant temptation unless the play succeeds in holding the student's attention. Even when the cellphone is turned off, just knowing that it is there, tucked in the backpack, purse, or pocket, alters the nature of the student's experience of the theater space, making immersion in the world of the play more difficult, less total.

Jane's relationship to her cellphone while watching a play is similar to that of Anna. Like Jane, Anna is bound for university in the fall. Unlike Jane, however, Anna has seen many productions and intends to study theater with the goal of becoming a performer. For her artwork, she drew a simple heart.

"I love live theater," she said by way of explanation. "Theater evokes emotions differently than seeing a movie. You make more of, like, a physical connection with the people on stage ... You're transported to wherever the people on stage are. You're, like, looking in on their lives."

Anna speaks in rapid bursts, her enthusiasm for theater evident in her strong voice and insistent tone as she seeks to explain the appeal of live theater over digital culture.

"It's there, it's live, and it's raw," she said. "It's not recorded, it's not edited ... You can't pause live theater. You can't put it on a different stream. You can't put headphones on ... It's more like an experience. It's an outing. It's a social event. It's like so many different things in one night."

The relationship between the audience member and the performer, together with the relative spontaneity inherent in a show, are part of what fuels her zeal. Like Jane, however, her cellphone is never far away, but for her, the feelings around the device are even more powerful.

"I have an anxiety problem and my cellphone's my trigger," she said. "If somebody takes my cellphone I'll have a panic attack. That's why it's always within arm's reach of me."

So how does she cope in the theater?

"I do have my phone with me in my pocket. I don't text during shows. It's always there in my pocket and it will be on. I can't turn it off ... When my phone dies, like, when the battery dies? It's like the end of the world."

Anna is able to watch the show, but only if she feels she has a constant connection with her friends and family.

"I can kind of tune it out," she said. "I'm so used to having it there that, like, when my phone buzzes, I'll kind of know in my head it's become so routine that I'll know if it's my boyfriend, if it's one of my friends, if it's Facebook, those sorts of things. There's different buzz tones for different notifications. The only thing that will throw me off is if I get a phone call because nobody phones me. ... I'd be, like, why am I getting a phone call? People usually don't *phone* people. Is something going on? Do I need to answer this? Or a bunch of text messages, like, buzz, buzz, buzz, and then my phone starts ringing. I'm, like, somebody really wants to get a hold of me. It will cut the connection, like, briefly, to the point where I have to glance in my pocket and look and see who it is."

For Jane, the cellphone is a means of escape from unpalatable productions. Not overly committed to live theater given her lack of history, the potential for her to mentally exchange the brick and mortar theater space for cyberspace is always there. Anna is a more committed theater-goer, but she has a much stronger attachment to her device. Watching live performances is important to her, but it can only be done with the reassuring presence of a cellphone intermittently buzzing against her leg.

The written responses from students support the ways in which the presence of cellphones complicates and disrupts the relationship between the audience member and the performer revealed by Jane and Anna's interviews. Some comments are blunt and direct, such as, "As soon as the audience becomes bored, they check their phone for missed calls, texts or the time," and "I've adapted myself to be stimulated. Theater does not stimulate me like the digital world does therefore I dread theater." Other comments reflect an ability to look beyond the student's particular needs to consider the phenomena of wireless teens and theater more broadly and to suggest some degree of difficulty inherent in the very act of going to a place where cellphone use is discouraged:

> It is inexplicably hard for one to part themselves from their technology such as their phones because the temptation is too great in trying to keep up with the latest gossip and to hear from their friends. The age of technology is definitely affecting the live theater experience, as chronicled by the constant LED screens I would see lighting up during the production.

Some comments relate most directly back to Jane's comments, and suggest that the most interesting drama is not on stage—it is in cyberspace:

> If the play is bad or dreadfully long there is that ever-present temptation to check my phone for any new messages or notifications … If something is happening in my life that is interesting to me at the time that I am viewing a live production, I find it very challenging to fully engage myself in the story because at the back of my mind I am wondering what will happen next with my current life drama.

So is Peggy Phelan (2010) correct? Is Facebook the new live theater?

Social Media as "The New Live Theater"

Students offered a variety of provocative opinions on the ways in which social media could be seen as "the new theater," with a strong consensus around the notion that social media sites are venues for drama. On the comparison between the two media, the opinions of theater skeptics can ring through with a certain tartness: "One is interactive, social and entertaining, the other is outdated and can often be boring," wrote one teen, "and you can guess which is which." Others are more willing to draw parallels in spite of the obvious differences between screen and stage: "In social media, everyone is an actor. Some like to take center-stage, others like to take supporting roles, and some prefer just watching the whole show." Many note that social media is more off-the-cuff and immediate, while theater is polished, intellectual, and intentional. "Social media is less intellectual and thought-out than live theater, yet it often provides a more realistic glimpse into people's lives," wrote one respondent. "Online, stories and tales, accounts and videos and comics will spread like wildfire, and really can't be stopped. Theater usually conveys a message, but online the original meaning of something can quickly become twisted and warped," wrote another. "There are certainly many people who use social media as their 'stage,' to become as interesting, funny, or beautiful as they want, even if it is not their reality."

Regarding the parallel that can be drawn between live theater and social media, student responses reflected the depth of their immersion in online theatrics, and the subtlety of their observations. "I think there is more drama online than in person nowadays because people aren't afraid of reactions, repercussions, etc.," wrote one person. "I do find that people try to seem like the center of attention on social media," wrote another. "They try to get people to sympathize, empathize, or be emotionally attached … since they enjoy the attention." Many try to take the high road when it comes to Facebook drama, noting that it exists but that they try to avoid it. "I tend to ignore this side of social media," wrote one teen. "I'm not one for rumors, gossip, or lies."

"There is TOO MUCH drama online," wrote another respondent. "It's extremely annoying." Many pointed out that there is an interplay between online action and real-life friendships. "There is a TON of drama on Facebook," wrote a student. "The posting of personal information can lead to the loss of friendships, and can cause problems between friends and family." "Often it's not actually drama that starts online more than it is drama that happens in real life that is taken to social sites," added another. "The way to navigate through this," advised another, "is to look at who is saying it and think of whether or not that person would truly say what they post online."

Continuing to develop the comparison offered by Peggy Phelan (2010), students overwhelming agreed that people "play roles" on social media sites such as Facebook and Twitter. Some play the person they wish to be; others, the person they wish to be seen to be. "On Facebook, you get to define yourself, and you get to choose what light you want to portray yourself in," wrote one student, taking a pragmatic stance toward the realities of self-presentation, while "in real life, other people make decisions about you." "All humans are flawed," wrote another, striking a more philosophical note. "If you have the opportunity to present yourself as an exceptional person, then I don't believe there is any reason why you shouldn't seize the opportunity."

Many students can take a jaded perspective on the roles that teens choose to play out for their peers, aware of the rules that can govern online performances of self. On the physical side, "If you are really attractive or often post scantily clad pictures (e.g., beach shots) you are likely to have a larger audience," wrote one, echoing the sentiments of many others. "People who post political rants or attention/pity-seeking rants usually have very small audience as NO-ONE IS INTERESTED IN THAT." Other students noted how people position themselves as particular types: "It's very common to see people taking the 'social activist' role by liking or passing on photos that state a message or alarming statistic … they can send the message of being a passionate activist by simply 'upvoting' or 'liking' a powerful image." Students can struggle to maintain their own voice within the competition for attention online. Ultimately, however, most feel that "the 'you' online is a general you—it is like an actor addressing the audience from behind a curtain. He/she is unaware of who exactly is watching, but the audience is scrutinizing the actor."

Given the many parallels between life online and live theater—the drama, the role-play, the manipulation of audience, even the narratives—could it be that students' need for theater is satisfied through social media? Are they living and breathing drama every time they log on to Facebook? Is theater, therefore, irrelevant to them?

The Relevance of Live Theater to Teenagers

For the third finding, I would like to make reference to one of the focus group discussions as well as to written comments submitted online. This focus group featured five students, all in grade 12 and looking forward to university in the fall. The students were articulate about their appreciation for live theater, partly because they liked how original it can be, and partly because it allows for a night out with friends and a more meaningful experience than spending the evening surfing the web or cruising around social media sites.

"Whenever I'm doing whatever on my laptop I feel often like I've wasted a few hours of my life," said Alisha, a socially minded and ambitious student with work experience in international women's issues. Theater is "a more rewarding experience," she noted, "and it's obviously more cultured. You feel like you've done something with your evening." Her friend Claire agreed, and offered a very personal reflection on the downside of being raised in the digital era. "There's some nights where I'm literally just cycling between 10 websites every few minutes," she said. "I'm just so bored I keep going. It's like I don't know why I don't just get up and leave. It's stupid. I think when you go to theater, especially a good theater … it's so much more rewarding." The group nodded their assent as she went on. "I almost wish I grew up in *not* a laptop era … Sometimes I wonder, 'What if I had actually grown up in the '60s or the '70s or the '80s and I didn't have that?' … I love the Internet. I'm not saying that I don't, but sometimes I just wonder what it would've been like." Ingrid, a student from Germany who planned to return home to study mechanical engineering, agreed. "I think people go to the theater to escape from technology," she said. "I think in today's world we're just so consumed by technology that people look forward to going to the theater."

The students were aware, however, that theater offered a more restrictive environment than the online world to which they were more accustomed. Gabe, the one boy in the group, described how, since subscribing to Netflix, "I tend to start like five movies before I find the one that I want to watch." This leaves him fearful in the theater, where he is locked in his seat. Ingrid agreed. "With smartphones now," she said, "if you're getting bored with one game you can just download another. I think that we're so used to having things at a fast pace, we've gotten sort of spoiled … there is that fear of being bored." The relative lack of special effects in theater can also impede the students' enjoyment. "We're used to those action-filled movies, so we get bored easily when there's just monologues or dialogues," said Alisha. Still, the students felt that theatre can be relevant to young people, seeing it partly as an antidote to the digital life and partly an entertaining option. "I think there could be a misconception that all theater is boring," said Claire. "It's all Shakespeare plays and that's it. If you're exposed to different types of good theater, especially if you're younger, then you'll be aware of the possibility of being entertained."

The focus group comments were echoed in a number of ways by the written, online survey responses. "A play engages you mentally and you never know what to expect, whereas when you are participating in various online activities, your brain is not being stimulated in a good way," wrote one student. "Going to see a live play is a lot better for both your mental and physical health than sitting at a computer like a vegetable." Live theater has "real sweat and tears and real life in it which is directly visible and not separated through cameras, screens etc." wrote another. "There is a certain exhilaration seeing live actors performing right in front of you."

The students who did not enjoy theater often focused on the slow pace and their lack of freedom and choice as audience members. "Plays are long and self-indulgent," shared one respondent. "They cannot be paused, fast-forwarded or rewound." "I do not enjoy the fact that theater forces one to sit through plays regardless of how entertaining they are," wrote another. Most, however, viewed theater as relevant to their generation. "Theater portrays emotions and the struggles that everyone goes through and everyone can relate to that," wrote one teen. "You need to find something that works for you," offered another. "The greatest challenge is being detached from technology but if the play you're watching interests you then it shouldn't be a problem." Some students struck a regretful, elegiac tone: "It was a better time than I expected," wrote one, "and it's a shame it's a dying art form."

Discussion

The arrival of smartphones in the pockets, backpacks, and purses of youth audience members disrupts and complicates the relationship between the performer and the audience member in a variety of ways. By checking a smartphone during a show, or by feeling it vibrate, or even by just knowing it is there, audience members take power away from the performers by directing their attention elsewhere. The possibility is there for the youth audience member to signal in the "blue glow from the back row" displeasure with the performance and to slip from the theater building into the enormously complicated, infuriating, sometimes dangerous, yet often compelling drama of cyberspace. Within cyberspace, many of the elements—role play, audience, story, conflict—are present for an alternate form of dramatic engagement within networked publics that teens can call their own.

And yet to dismiss live theater as irrelevant to young people would be an over-simplification. Many students were clear in their belief at the end of the series that live theater is relevant to young people, so long as the topics and themes are of interest to youth. Many were sorry that more young people do not have the opportunity to experience live theater, and pointed out the importance and value of school trips so that exposure can be gained and lifetime theater-going habits possibly nurtured.

It would also be inaccurate to say that student responses to live theater are somehow immature, or compromised by their online lifestyles. In terms of student responses to each of the four individual plays, I have yet to find in the many pages of transcripts I collected a single case where I do not agree with the student evaluation, pro and con, of a production. In looking over the comments, I was also struck by the many notes of poignant regret that surfaced during much of the feedback, regret for what has been lost in the flood of data that characterizes the Internet era, a sense that amidst the texts, likes, and uploads, something quieter and more contemplative may have been sacrificed, and an appreciation for the opportunity provided by theater to go out with people, to sit with people, to watch people performing for people. Speaking to students and reading their commentary led me to admire the ways in which young people seek to make meaning of the digital environments delivered to them by the major corporations, and to feel empathy for them as they articulated an awareness of what may have been lost in the midst of all that they have gained.

Perhaps the biggest consequence of Mindset Number 6, the shift in attention from the theatrical space to the virtual space, is that educators will need to take time prior to their trips to the theater to build bridges (Hosenfeld, 1999) between the students' digital culture and the theater (Richardson, 2013). Teachers like myself, raised in the analogue world, may vaguely assume that students have the same base understanding of live theater that we do. In reality, there is a need for educators to teach students about what theater really is, how it differs from film and online entertainment, and how the overall effect of a show can be largely dependent upon the relationship between the actors and the live audience. This provides a wonderful opportunity to discuss the nature of digital culture and to explore the significance of drama—whether it be on stage or online—and what it means to act, to perform, to be human at a time when many of us tend to interact with the world through a screen and a keyboard. It also provides the opportunity to discuss, experience, and explore the role of the arts in the students' lives.

Conclusion

Maxine Greene (1991) referred to John Dewey when she wrote about how important it is "to attend actively" and "to pay heed," to strive for "the energizing encounter that counteracts passivity" in order to "begin to experience art as a way of understanding" (p. 36). Her words have particular relevance in the Internet era and to the work of English and drama teachers today. The research suggests that theater producers, meanwhile, will have to work extra hard to select and create plays that appeal to the audiences of tomorrow: fresh takes on the world kids live in now, provocative viewpoints, and skillful acting. Without that quality and relevance, young people will choose pixels over people, while those who do make it through the theater doors will always have what Jane called "that comparison" in mind—between what is transpiring on stage and what they could be doing online.

My conclusion after analyzing the data from this study is that the students in the back row, faces bathed in the blue glow, are not merely distracted. They are hopeful.

"If theater disappeared, would that change anything?" Jane was asked. "Would we even notice?"

"I think that would suck," she replied. "You'd lose a lot of humanity. You'd lose a lot of that creative part of what it means to be human and want to convey ideas and emotions and make people feel something. We need it."

References

Abercrombie, N., & Longhurst, B. (1998). *Audiences: A sociological theory of performance and imagination.* London, England: Sage.

Alvermann, D. E., & Hagood, M. C. (2008). Critical media literacy: Research, theory and practice in "new times." In M. Mackey (Ed.), *Media literacies* (pp. 21–47). London, England: Routledge.

Bagnoli, A. (2009). Beyond the standard interview: The use of graphic elicitation and arts-based methods. *Qualitative Research, 9*(5), 547–570. doi: 10.1177/1468794109343625

Barker, M. (2003). "Crash," theatre audiences, and the idea of liveness. *Studies in Theatre and Performance, 23*(1), 21–39.

Bennett, S. (1990). *Theatre audiences: A theory of production and reception.* London, England: Routledge.

boyd, d., & Marwick, A. (2011). *Social privacy in networked publics: Teens' attitudes, practices, and strategies.* Paper presented at Oxford Internet Institute's "A Decade in Internet Time: Symposium on the Dynamics of the Internet and Society," Oxford, England. Retrieved from http://ssrn.com/abstract=1925128

Bucheli, R. J., Goldberg, M. R., & Phillips, A. (1991). Symposium: Arts as education. *Harvard Educational Review, 61*(1), 25–26.

Buckingham, D. (2003). Media education and the end of the critical consumer. *Harvard Educational Review, 73*(3), 309–328.

Burwell, C. (2010). Rewriting the script: Toward a politics of young people's digital media participation. *Review of Education, Pedagogy, and Cultural Studies, 32*(4–5), 382–402. http://dx.doi.org/10.1080/10714413.2010.510354

Clapp, E. P., & Edwards, L. A. (2013). Editor's introduction: Expanding our vision for the arts in education. *Harvard Educational Review, 83*(1), 5–14.

Creswell, J. W. (2007). *Qualitative inquiry and research design* (2nd ed.). Thousand Oaks, CA: Sage.

Creswell, J. W. (Ed.). (2008). Collecting qualitative data. In *Educational research: Planning, conducting and evaluating quantitative and qualitative research* (3rd ed.) (pp. 212–242). Upper Saddle River, NJ: Pearson.

Dixon, S. (2007). *Digital performance: A history of new media in theater, dance, performance art, and installation.* Cambridge, MA: MIT Press.

Feldman, E. B. (1973). *Varieties of visual experience.* New York, NY: Abrams.

Friedman, T. (2007). *The world is flat: A brief history of the twenty-first century.* Vancouver, Canada: Douglas & McIntyre.

Gallagher, K., & Riviere, D. (2007). When drama praxis rocks the boat. *Research in Drama Education, 12*(3), 319–330.

Gee, J. P. (2010). *How to do discourse analysis.* London, England: Routledge.

Goffman, E. (1959). *The presentation of self in everyday life.* New York, NY: Anchor Books.

Greene, M. (1991). Texts and margins. *Harvard Educational Review, 61*(1), 27–39.

Harper, D. (2005). What's new visually? In N. K. Denzin & Y. Lincoln (Eds.), *The Sage handbook of qualitative research* (pp. 747–762). Thousand Oaks, CA: Sage.

Hosenfeld, C. (Ed.). (1999). Louise Rosenblatt: A voice that would not be silenced. In *Expanding our vision* (pp. 110–129). Oxford, England: Oxford University Press.

Ipsos. (2009). What's your child doing on Facebook? [Press release]. Retrieved from http://www.ipsos-na.com/news-polls/pressrelease.aspx?id=4437&wt.mc_id=1110042&link=4437&top=

Jenkins, H. (2009). *Confronting the challenges of participatory culture.* Cambridge, MA: MIT Press.

Kamberelis, G., & Dimitriadis, G. (2005). Focus groups: Strategic articulations of pedagogy, politics, and inquiry. In N. K. Denzin & Y. S. Lincoln (Eds.), *The Sage handbook of qualitative research* (pp. 887–907). (3rd ed.). Thousand Oaks, CA: Sage.

Klich, R., & Scheer, E. (2012). *Multimedia performance.* Basingstoke, England: Palgrave Macmillan.

Kress, G. (2009). *Multimodality: A social semiotic approach to contemporary culture.* London, England: Routledge.

Kuksa, I., & Childs, M. (2010). But a walking shadow: Designing, performing and learning on the virtual stage. *Learning, Media and Technology, 35*(3), 275–291. doi: 10.1080/17439 884.2010.509352

Lankshear, C., & Knobel, M. (Eds.). (2007). "You won't be needing your laptops today": Wired bodies in the wireless classroom. In *A new literacies sampler* (pp. 25–48). New York, NY: Peter Lang.

Lee-Brown, E. (2002). Performativity, context and agency: The process of audience response and its implications for performance. *Text and Performance Quarterly, 22*(2), 138–148.

Lenhart, A. (2012). *Teens, smartphones & texting.* Retrieved from the Pew Research Center website: http://www.away.gr/wp-content/uploads/2012/03/PIP_Teens_Smartphones_and_Texting.pdf

Lewin, T. (2010, January 21). Media junkies: Kids wired 7.5 hours a day. *The Globe and Mail.*

Marwick, A. E., & boyd, d. (2010). I tweet honestly, I tweet passionately: Twitter users, context collapse, and the imagined audience. *New Media & Society, 13*(1), 114–133. doi: 10.1177/1461444810365313

Marwick, A., & boyd, d. (2011). To see and be seen: Celebrity practice on Twitter. *Convergence: The International Journal of Research Into New Media Technologies, 17*(2), 139–158. doi: 10.1177/1354856510394539

McCarthy, C., Giardina, M. D., Harewood, S. J., & Jin-Kyung Park. (2003). Contesting culture: Identity and curriculum dilemmas in the age of globalization, postcolonialism, and multiplicity. *Harvard Educational Review, 73*(3), 449–466. Retrieved from http://www.hepg.org/her/abstract/80

Miles, M. B., Michael Huberman, A., & Saldana, J. (2014). *Qualitative data analysis* (3rd ed.). London, England: Sage.

Morley, D. (2003). The nationwide audience. In W. Brooker & D. Jermyn (Eds.), *The audience studies reader* (pp. 95–111). London, England: Routledge.

Murray, J. (2004). From game-story to cyberdrama. In N. Wardrip-Fruin & P. Harrigan (Eds.), *First person: New media as story, performance, and game* (pp. 2–11). Cambridge, MA: MIT Press.

National Endowment for the Arts. (2008). *2008 Survey of public participation in the arts.* Washington, DC: Author. Retrieved from http://arts.gov/publications/2008-survey-public-participation-arts

The New London Group. (1996). A pedagogy of multiliteracies: Designing social futures. *Harvard Educational Review, 66*(1), 60–92.

Phelan, P. (2010). Performance in the age of social networks, or, Facebook as theater. Retrieved from iTunes University.

Radway, J. (1991). *Reading the romance: Women, patriarchy, and popular literature.* Chapel Hill, NC: University of North Carolina Press.

Reason, M. (2006). Young audiences and live theatre part 2: Methods, participation and memory in audience research. *Studies in Theatre and Performance, 26*(3), 221–241.

Reason, M. (2008). "Did you watch the man or the goose?": Children's responses to puppets in live theatre. *New Theatre Quarterly, 24*(4), 337–354.

Richardson, J. M. (2010). *The blue glow from the back row: The impact of new technologies on the adolescent experience of live theatre* (Master's thesis). Retrieved from https://www.ruor.uottawa.ca/handle/10393/19609

Richardson, J. M. (2011). "Such tweet sorrow": The explosive impact of new literacies on adolescent responses to live theatre. *Language and Literacy, 13*(1), 98–110. Retrieved from http://ejournals.library.ualberta.ca/index.php/langandlit/article/view/10273

Richardson, J. M. (2012). The blue glow from the back row: Live theater and the wireless teen. *English Journal, 102*(1), 88–91.

Richardson, J. M. (2013). Taking it to the tweet seats: How teachers can use new technology to create "theatre knowledge building communities" in the English language arts and drama classrooms. *In Education, 19*(1), 50–61.

Rideout, V. J., Foeher, U. G., & Roberts, D. F. (2010). *Generation M²: Media in the lives of 8- to 18-Year-Olds.* Retrieved from http://files.eric.ed.gov/fulltext/ED527859.pdf

Rosen, J. (2006). The people formerly known as the audience. *Pressthink.* Retrieved from http://archive.pressthink.org/2006/06/27/ppl_frmr.html

Saldana, J. (2013). *The coding manual for qualitative researchers* (2nd ed.). London, England: Sage.

Salter, C. (2010). *Entangled: Technology and the transformation of performance*. Cambridge, MA: MIT Press.

Selwyn, N. (2009). Faceworking: Exploring students' education-related use of Facebook. *Learning, Media and Technology, 34*(2), 157–174. doi: 10.1080/17439880902923622

Selwyn, N. (2012). Ten suggestions for improving academic research in education and technology. *Learning, Media and Technology, 37*(3), 213–219. doi: 10.1080/17439884.2012.680213

Tulloch, J. (2000). Approaching theatre audiences: Active school students and commoditised high culture. *Contemporary Theatre Review, 10*(2), 85–104.

Wardrip-Fruin, N., & Harrigan, P. (Eds.). (2004). Cyberdrama. In *First person: New media as story, performance, and game*. Cambridge, MA: MIT Press.

Willis, P. (2003). Foot soldiers of modernity: The dialectics of cultural consumption and the 21st-century school. *Harvard Educational Review, 73*(3), 390–415.

Zamaria, C., & Fletcher, F. (2007). *Canada online! The Internet, media and emerging technologies: Uses, attitudes, trends and international comparisons: Year two highlights, 2007*. Retrieved from The Canadian Internet Project website: http://www.omdc.on.ca/AssetFactory.aspx?did=6324

· 8 ·

MACKLEMORE

Strong Poetry, Hip Hop Courage, and the Ethics of the Appointment

Awad Ibrahim and Adriana Alfano

Introduction

Life is a struggle, it seems, a beautiful struggle. So, for Haggerty and Lewis (2012, track 6), it is both our ethical duty and moral challenge to "record it." In doing so, however, *true artists* emerge, and in the process, they occupy a category of/on their own. Part and parcel of navigating the challenges of courageous and visionary artistic production is that these true artists will most likely never be fully satisfied. Their dis-satisfaction, Haggerty and Lewis contend, is a small price to pay and a sacrifice to make. True artists, moreover, regardless of their medium of choice, provide testaments to the human experience. In the process of engaging with life's *beautiful struggles*, as Haggerty and Lewis put it, they manage to articulate, depict, or represent those struggles in a way that captivates others' attention, often reflecting common experiences, and at times challenging normative ways of thinking. In responding to such a tall order, the artist must be strongly reflexive, and acutely aware of the difficulties inherent in the task of representing the complexities of reality, sharing what they—and those around them—see when they look upon the world. It is this fluid process of seeing with open eyes and sharing what one has seen in a uniquely identifiable manner that is also needed from revolutionary leaders.

Becoming a revolutionary leader—one who cultivates awareness through true communion with others—necessitates clarity of thought. A leader cannot challenge others to engage with reality if they do not exercise this capacity within themselves. Awareness is key to what Maxine Greene (2000) termed *wide-awakeness*, denoting "a plane of consciousness of highest tension originating in an attitude of full attention to life and its requirements" (p. 121). A key aspect of this attention is that it is "an active one," which "lives within its acts and its attention is exclusively directed to carrying its project into effect, to executing its plan" (p. 121). It is this active and focused attention to the execution of a plan that attracts the attention of the "strong poet" (Rorty, 1989). With a revolutionary vision, and an awareness of what it is to *be* in the world, the strong poet confronts and walks through, so to speak, "the blind impresses"; that is to say, "the gaps and blind spots of thoughts, ideas and practices" of everyday life (p. 43).

The "strong poets," Richard Rorty (1989) explained, do not simply write verses. They are those individuals who understood that, as humans, "We are condemned to improvise. We are like actors dragged onto the stage without having learned our lines, with no script and no prompter to whisper stage directions to us. We must decide for ourselves how to live" (Gaarder, 1996, p. 457). In this improvised theatre that is called life—and thanks to their strong conviction and clear mind and language—the strong poets' articulation, ideas, and the totality of their script are so freshly new that one cannot resist reading and wrestling with them, and may even take them in as her or his own. This is (the power of) the "strong poet." This is, we are arguing, the case with Ben Haggerty, also known as Macklemore, and his lyrics. As a strong poet, we will show, Macklemore has the courage and audacity to engage, look for, and think through the "blind impresses": those difficult knowledges—problems, if you like—that society prefers not to face, be they aggression, consumerism, war, xenophobia, homophobia, or ethno-and-White-supremacy.

Here, it is worth noting, while Rorty's (1989) conception of the strong poet does not forcibly describe one who writes verses, it would be appropriate to conceive of Hip Hop artists, with their use of poetry and language to share their visions of the world, as strong poets. According to Maxine Greene (2000), "poets help us to penetrate the darkness and the silences and move on to visions of possibility" (p. 275). It is this balance between engaging with, and penetrating, darkness in the hopes of future possibilities, we contend, that characterizes the oeuvre of the independent Hip Hop artist Macklemore. Macklemore and Ryan Lewis' (2012) debut album, *The Heist*, is aptly titled

MACKLEMORE153

as it provides a hijacking of normative values, one which requires the listener to actively and strongly (in Rorty's sense) consider the context within which they find themselves and to engage with their reality. As we shall see, they require us listeners to see things that, although present, we may not be accustomed to *seeing*, or rather acknowledging. This Hip Hop artist's capacity to dig up and strongly articulate issues with which we are familiar, while presenting truths in ways we have not yet heard, speaks to Macklemore's identity as a strong poet and a wide-awake witness to life's beautiful struggles (Rorty, 1989).

As a decidedly political genre of music, Hip Hop can be a site for testifying, consciousness raising, and bearing witness in the world (Chang, 2014). A medium which traditionally gave voice to the voiceless, Hip Hop continues to represent a space within which to interrogate what may at times seem like fixed realities in contemporary societies. This interrogation and consciousness-raising is essentially what Freire (1970) referred to as *conscientization*—an essential exercise in becoming human and in becoming aware—which is contingent on wide-awakeness in seeking to truly bear witness to the world. This chapter aims to analyze Macklemore and Ryan Lewis' (2012) album *The Heist*, among other works, in relation to Maxine Greene's notion of wide-awakeness, and through Paulo Freire's *Pedagogy of the Oppressed*. While the genre itself is complex, and different artists use its different components in different ways, this chapter will focus on what Macklemore raps—as rap is the poetry that contributes to the meanings garnered from Hip Hop as an art form (Ibrahim, 2013; 2014). Using the conceptual framework of Freire's essential elements of witness, we propose to read *The Heist* strongly, conceiving of Macklemore himself as a strong poet who manages to work as an ally to the oppressed, a guide to the oppressors, and whose dynamic reflection and engagement with reality can impact others' naming of the world, and, in its own way, contribute to wide-awakeness en masse.

Bearing Witness and the Significance of Reflection

To properly analyze *The Heist* as an artifact of Hip Hop through which the act of rapping acts as a poetic medium to transmit a message (Ibrahim 2013), some notes are required on the elements of witness, as well as the significance of reflection. According to Freire (1970), the essential elements of witness include:

> *consistency* between words and actions; *boldness* which urges the witnesses to confront existence as a permanent risk; *radicalization* (not sectarianism) leading both the witnesses and the ones receiving that witness to increasing action; *courage* to love …; and *faith* in the people, since it is to them that witness is made. (p. 176)

We argue that Macklemore's strong poetry in *The Heist* reflects each of these essential elements, therefore making the album a valuable testament to the conscious-raising capacity of Hip Hop music and culture. Furthermore, the album and its reach will be analyzed using Freire's (1970) specification that reflection is not a stagnant exercise, but rather an indispensable aspect of action. He wrote, "true reflection … leads to action" (Freire, 1970, p. 66). Freire also wrote of praxis—a blending of meaningful reflection and action—which is deeply rooted in consciousness-raising. In Freire's view, "when [a] situation calls for action, that action will constitute an authentic praxis only if its consequences have become the object of critical reflection" (1970, p. 66). Freire specified that consciousness of the historical moment, as well as the "concomitant conscious involvement" of both oppressors and oppressed is essential for authentic praxis (p. 66). A detailed analysis of *The Heist* will demonstrate Macklemore's engagement in authentic praxis, as well as the value of continuous reflection in the struggle to live consciously.

Hip Hop and the Ethics of the Appointment

The witness or the appointee, Shoshana Felman (1992) argued, cannot relieve her/himself by any delegation, substitution, or representation. This is because testimony cannot be simply relayed, repeated, or reported by another without thereby losing its function as a testimony. "No one bears witness for the witness," Felman concluded, since "[t]o bear witness is to bear the solitude of a responsibility, and to bear the responsibility, precisely, of that solitude" (p. 3). This is the ethics of the appointment and, as we shall see, Macklemore is a primary example of the artists who are conscious of this ethics. Similar to Dori Laub (1992), to occupy the position of the witness for Macklemore is to recognize three distinct levels of witnessing: "the level of being a witness to oneself within the experience; the level of being a witness to the testimonies of others; and the level of being a witness to the process of witnessing itself" (p. 75). Though we have a particular connection and affinities with the first level as two people who listen to, consume avidly, research, and write about Hip Hop, our interest in this chapter lies within the second level. Here,

Laub explained, one is a participant "not in the events, but in the account given of them," that is to say, a "companion on the eerie journey of the testimony" (p. 76).

Thinking through Macklemore and his artistic production, we are arguing that: (a) Hip Hop in general is testimony, a form of speech act that usually speaks to social realities of the marginalized; (b) Macklemore is a strong poet who is exceptionally mindful of the ethics of the appointment; and (c) what makes Macklemore a strong poet is his ability to bear witness and speak truths we are not accustomed to hearing. The questions we want to ask in this chapter therefore are: How one does one become a strong poet? Within the Hip Hop scene, how is one appointed to speak? How is this done and/or accomplished? As we attempt to answer these questions, on the one hand, we approach testimony not as a completed statement or a totalizable account, but a *langage en procès*—a language-in-process, a discursive practice, an unapologetic testimonial speech act that borders on hope and absolute hopelessness. Significantly, on the other hand, even though we come from two different locations and subject positions, this chapter is an act of love for Hip Hop. We recognize that naturally, one's identification with and consumption of an artist is partially contingent on the consumer's own positionality. Adriana is a racialized White woman with a keen interest in Hip Hop, and she acknowledges that her consumption of Macklemore has been in some ways problematized by his own positionality—a straight White rapper. Awad is a racialized Black man who had done a number of research projects on the topic of ethics of the appointment, Hip Hop, witnessing and testifying from a Black perspective.

Before we proceed, we want to make it absolutely clear that we do not aim or claim to make a messiah out of the artist, but we do attest to his power—and that of Hip Hop artists in general—to transmit messages through strong poetry. Strong poets, Rorty (1989) explained further, become strong poets precisely because "they are products capable of telling the story of their own production in words never used before" (p. 28). And for this reason their vocabulary is not free-of-error. Yet, their lives are wrapped around the ethical responsibility of storytelling: that one *has to* tell one's story. If "poets help us to penetrate the darkness and the silences and move on to visions of possibility" (Greene, 2000, p. 275), it is this balancing act between engaging with, and penetrating, darkness in the hopes of future possibilities that characterizes the work of Macklemore. Oscillating between the dark side of consumerism, racism, and addiction, and the bright side of possibility, especially in *The Heist*,

Macklemore is able to dig deeper, expose, and talk with a language that can only speak to his identity as a strong poet and a wide-awake witness to life's beautiful struggles.

"All My People, Stay True": Biographical Notes[1]

Roland Barthes (1989) cautioned against biographical notes. He called for the death of the author or the artist when we are reading or viewing their work. That is to say, we need to take the author's work on its own terms. In the case of Macklemore, however, we think biographical notes are necessary and helpful, especially because Hip Hop is exceptionally biographical and Macklemore is no exception. Born in 1983, Macklemore began writing rhymes at the age of 14 in his home of Seattle, Washington. He cites his captivation with Hip Hop music as beginning around the age of 6, and notes that it is a style of music that has always drawn him in. A great deal of emphasis will be placed on Macklemore's awareness of his (pedagogy of) place as an artist and his identity as a rapper, as these are defining characteristics of both his personality, as revealed in interviews, and his oeuvre. While one cannot exclusively rely on an artist's creations to get a full understanding of them, Macklemore's songs provide a strong poetry and a valuable testimony for considering his identity, as he frequently employs a style similar to life-writing in his witnessing and testifying. In "Ten Thousand Hours" (Haggerty & Lewis, 2012, track 1), Macklemore raps that he is a product of a liminal space where Malcolm Gladwell meets David Bowie meets "Kanye shit." This self-professed description is extremely apt for the artist, who combines a conscious and thought-out, sometimes existentialist, perception of the world with originality and lyrical skill and tact. By comparing himself to a renowned modern thinker, a trail-blazing rock star who defied convention, and a prolific Hip Hop artist who himself is an innovative and strong poet, Macklemore expresses his own self-perception as a multi-faceted individual who wishes and dares to occupy more than a singular category. How does one arrive at such a distinct identity? Certainly, through experience, inner-work, and engagement with the world.

In what follows, we elaborate upon the experiences that pushed Macklemore to arrive at such a distinct identity. For example, Macklemore is a rapper who raps about the very act of rapping and what it means to be a rapper. His authenticity in projecting messages is manifested in the recurrence of the theme of wide-awakening in different songs and situations, and the way in which awareness is a tool of choice that is fundamentally necessary for the way in which Macklemore navigates life and produces his music. We identified four themes that seem to recur in Macklemore lyrics: Church, White Privilege, Addiction, and his need not to be boxed in a particular category.

Talkin' to God: Church Hip Hop

An analysis of Macklemore lyrics demonstrates that he often uses church discourse in his songs and poetry. Macklemore described his own engagement with music as something spiritual. In "Church" from "The Unplanned Mixtape," released in 2009, Macklemore rapped that the only time he felt he was talking to God "was with [his] Walkman, walkin' with Nas" (Haggerty, "Church," 2009, track 7). This line is revelatory for the power of rap music as a medium to connect to something outside oneself. While connecting to music on a spiritual level is not in and of itself a revolutionary idea, the notion that connecting to Hip Hop music could be so spiritual is not a widely embraced notion. In a radio interview with ZMTV in 2013, Macklemore describes his engagement with music as a spiritual force, and as a manifestation of his awareness and engagement with the world around him:

> If you're aware, if you're present, if you're open to the universe, it will provide in a certain way, and that's what music is to me. Music is about capturing a moment that's bigger than yourself, but being aware for it, and you need to let it transfer to you [,] through you and to the music; and that's where the best music is created ... That's what music is to me—it acts as a higher power and it's my conduit to something bigger. (ZM, 2013)

In this quote, Macklemore exposes his way of living and being in the world, and, by extension, his philosophy as an artist. His emphasis on the importance of the spiritual aspect of his connection to music demonstrates a key aspect of his personal and artistic identity, and the crucial importance of *awareness* in order to witness and understand the potential effects of Hip Hop music's influence.

White Privilege: Writing a New Verse

In "White Privilege" (Haggerty, 2005, track 2) Macklemore rhymes about a global cultural and musical space that is dominated by a (White) race that is appropriating and exploiting more than consciously engaging the Other (Black). As a racialized White man, Macklemore holds a contentious place in Hip Hop, and as an artist, he is acutely aware of this fact. There is a long history of White performers making it big on the back of Black music, musicians, and artists; from Elvis to The Beatles (Ibrahim, 2014). A key manifestation of Macklemore's awareness is his acknowledgement and engagement with a concept too often ignored and taken for granted: White Privilege. The rapper is intently aware of the benefits conferred to him as a result of the way in which he is racialized and makes no pretense in acknowledging this fact in both interviews and in his music. On his first album, *The Language of My World*, Macklemore demonstrates his critical engagement with his contentious choice to rap on a track called "White Privilege" in which he acknowledges his status as a White Hip Hop artist. In that track, he acknowledges that Hip Hop started on a block he has never been to; that Hip Hop is rooted in a struggle he has never been through; and that, if he wants to keep-it-real, he needs to speak authentically, about what he knows.

This is no small declaration for a racialized White rapper. It acknowledges Hip Hop genealogy as an inner-city Black cultural phenomenon and product; yet the declaration also shows his discomfort with making it big, which may hint to Whiteness more than his talent. Put this way, that is, he cannot be totally sure of what holds more weight in light of the gentrification of Hip Hop: his Whiteness or his talent. Reflecting upon his own positionality and subjectivity, Macklemore differentiates himself from those who contribute to the gentrification of the genre, and acknowledges the irreconcilable way in which his body may be read as a racialized White rapper. In the spirit of wide-awakeness, he rhymes that even though he gives it all when he writes a rhyme and that he may have paid his dues, as a White MC however, Hip Hop culture is not his ("White Privilege," Haggerty, 2005, track 2). In addressing the penetration of White artists into Hip Hop, Macklemore demonstrates his awareness of his place in the music industry, as well as his privilege in having the means to pursue music. While he calls attention to his problematic role in Hip Hop, he also describes his authenticity with which he aims to produce music and respect the genre that speaks to him the most. Here, he calls on White artists to be themselves, to rap about what they know and at the same time to acknowledge the undeniable and deep-rooted cultural theft throughout history—musical and otherwise—that has permeated the experiences of Black people ("White Privilege," Haggerty, 2005, track 2).

It is certainly a unique and seldom-heard statement to proclaim that White rappers contribute to and abuse the theft and cultural appropriation of Hip Hop, and a remarkable proclamation from a White Hip Hop artist.

Such a subversive proclamation and a strong verse demonstrate Macklemore's ability to implicate himself in his music, even when such an action puts him on the line. The rapper makes similar subversive proclamations on *The Heist*, in the tracks "Same Love" and "A Wake." These tracks present the strong poet's engagement with awareness and the challenges that come with working through his newfound incapacity to silently accept the injustices he witnesses, as well as the anticipation of resistance to expressions of such boldness. It is this self-implication that presents an aspect of difficulty, as Macklemore is compelled to address such contentious topics as White privilege, same-sex marriage, consumerism, and self-awareness. In doing so, the rapper demonstrates great courage in putting himself on the line to not only be scrutinized professionally but also targeted personally, since his work is rooted in his personal perspective in looking upon and naming the world. The cultivation of such courage takes time; and while his largest commercial success has come with *The Heist*, the artist has been working—personally, musically, and spiritually—for years to develop his characteristic "voice," and the courage with which it speaks volumes. This cultivation, and the perceptible truths that come with such development, are the result of personal difficulties, most poignantly, addiction.

The "Otherside": Addiction

While Macklemore is vocal about his privilege, such privilege (and financial stability, for example), are not the makings of a tumult-less life. Macklemore is very vocal about his struggles with addiction, both in interviews as well as in his songs. In fact, his track with Ryan Lewis, "Otherside" (Haggerty & Lewis, 2010, track 3), released in 2010, has resonated deeply with fans. Engaging his own experiences and sharing them in a style akin to life writing, Macklemore invites his listeners to see his perspective, but without alienating them by acting as an expert. Instead, the struggle is palpable in his words, whether they are about his difficulties with addiction or simply the struggle to see the world as it really is, in all its contradiction and complexity. He and Ryan Lewis garnered much attention for their song, "Otherside," released in 2010 on the *VS. Redux* EP (track 3). This track exposes a conscious engagement with his influence as a rapper, especially on young people. Rappers, Macklemore argues, need not only be conscious about their ethical responsibility of witnessing, but should also be sure not to rap about "some shit they haven't lived."

A concern for talking about lived experience is a crucial part of witnessing. The witness does not pick and choose favorable experiences to share—true witness accounts for both positive and negative experiences, and unearths truths that are often difficult to face. Some of the most poignant examples of such accountability and witness are "Neon Cathedral" and "Starting Over," two tracks from *The Heist* in which Macklemore testifies to his struggles with addiction. Having announced 2 years of sobriety in 2010 after spending time in a rehabilitation center in 2008, the track "Starting Over" (Haggerty, Lewis, & Bridwell, track 14) provides an artifact of accountability, as Macklemore describes the strife and personal struggle of relapsing. There is extreme bravery in the kind of honest life-writing which comes through in "Starting Over." He testifies to having relapsed and talks about his worries of how audiences may find him disingenuous for having done so after so publicly sharing about his addictions and perceived arrival at recovery.

He resolves, however, that it is his duty to document his struggle through his lyrics, as he would prefer to live truthfully and incur judgement for his mistakes rather than be falsely lauded as a squeaky-clean success story. Here, Macklemore uses poetry and music to convey an authentic, though imperfect, part of himself. Dealing with addiction is no easy feat, and it takes bravery to address such struggles honestly. Yet, Macklemore takes this experience as a responsibility, where there are no magic solutions, and where getting sober means putting oneself through the arduous task of starting over (Haggerty, Lewis, & Bridwell, 2012, track 14). His success in relating to fans and striking a chord with those who have faced addiction is a direct reflection of his own effective praxis—reflection upon his situationality—and expression of the experience through his art. Furthermore, he takes on the challenge to *be an example*—to inextricably live what he raps about, and to prepare himself to face the consequences of others' consumption and scrutiny in sharing his personal ideas and struggles.

Though he has been sober since 2010, in an interview with Jabari (Johnson, 2012), Macklemore described the difficulty of overcoming his addictions. He noted that substance abuse would affect his ability to be creative and would bring him to a place of fear and guilt, in which he would convince himself that he was incapable of succeeding as a rapper. Furthermore, he noted he felt stagnant, as if he was closing his connection to God and in its place, just smoking weed. Much of our reading of Macklemore has to do with *becoming*. One such aspect of Macklemore's becoming is his efforts to become sober. Becoming a strong poet is about overcoming both external and internal obstacles. Evidently,

Macklemore is aware of this, and continually lives this struggle, rooted in a desire for balance. When speaking about such struggles and his publicly addressing them in his music, Macklemore has said: "I think that I'm *becoming* and I'm not there yet; none of this stuff I'm like 'there' yet, like I don't have it figured out" (Johnson, 2012, italics added).

Macklemore does not claim to be an expert in anyone's experiences other than his own, and even in sharing his experiences he is honest and upfront about his ongoing struggles, holding himself accountable at every turn. He talks about feeling like he wasted time but talks a great deal about gratitude as well—noting that he is fortunate to have come out alive from his struggles with addiction. His road to becoming a strong poet was rooted in spirituality, hard work, good fortune, and timing, and fighting his way out of stagnancy. Escaping the numbing effects of addiction was essential to Macklemore's becoming a strong poet. He realized he had another shot and took that opportunity, and he stuck with his goals in spite of personal difficulties. Notably, and integral to our reading of the artist, Macklemore is resistant to contemporary music trends where the artist is to follow a formula, a formula whose ultimate guiding principle is not the ethics of witnessing but the climbing of record sales (Haggerty & Lewis, 2010, track 3). With a fierce commitment to rapping authentically, writing strongly, and resisting formulaic approaches to music rooted simply in profits, Macklemore rises above convention and truly demonstrates his independence as an artist.

Don't Box Me In/Becoming Mack and Hijacking Hip Hop

A truly remarkable aspect of *The Heist* and its success (the album has earned platinum distinction) is that the album was released independently, and that Macklemore and Ryan Lewis are not signed to a commercial record company. It is this very thread of independent artistry that weaves itself through the album and characterizes the very essence of these artists' authenticity and conscious approach to rapping about the world. For example, the album's breakout single, "Thrift Shop" (Haggerty & Lewis, 2012, track 3)—which touts the benefits of thrift shopping in comparison to blind allegiance to brand names—comes in conjunction with "Wing$" (Haggerty, Lewis, Wear, & Joslyn, 2012, track 11), a song about the pervasiveness of consumerism and the tendency to define one's identity through possessions. While the sounds and subject matter on the album are diverse, the album itself reflects a har-kening back to old-school "backpack rap" ("White Walls," Haggerty, Lewis, Hanley, & Wear, 2012, track 9). Furthermore, one thing is clear: awareness is a tool of choice that Macklemore uses to navigate the world and produce his music.

As artists with their own (rather than a corporate) agenda, Macklemore and Ryan Lewis exercise their agency and demonstrate that their work is not "a copy or replica" (Rorty, 1989, p. 43). In a declaration of their originality, Macklemore proudly raps that he has chosen to refuse limiting offers presented by conventional record labels, and that he and Ryan Lewis have opted instead to directly spread their messages to the masses ("Can't Hold Us," Haggerty, Lewis, & Dalton, 2012, track 2). As an independent artist, he actively chal-lenges available discourses that otherwise lead us to believe that it is necessary to play the game's rules as they have been set out. Unbound by corporate whims, Macklemore challenges hegemonic, hetero-normative, and neo-liberalist discourses in his work, calling upon his listeners to envision their world with clarity—to become wide-awake, and to join him in acting as an ally with those who are being oppressed and dispossessed. The seamless inter-weaving of the subject matter and professional conduct by Macklemore and Ryan Lewis demonstrates the very "consistency between words and actions" that Freire (1970) described as necessary for authentic witness (p. 176). *The Heist*, its independent release, and its widespread success thus symbolize the power of conscious reflection in affecting the strong poet's message, both in its authenticity as well as in its potential to shed light on reality for its listeners.

This Is Not a Conclusion: Becoming a Strong Poet

The Heist demonstrates contemplation of Hip Hop itself as a medium, and in many ways, Macklemore's words are subversive of contemporary understand-ings of the genre, as he calls attention to the commodification of Hip Hop artists themselves ("Jimmy Iovine," Haggerty, Lewis, Stevens, 2012, track 10). The artist's wide-awakeness to the reality of manipulation within Hip Hop representations is demonstrated as he contends that rappers who are rapping to simply possess the candy-painted Cadillac and to get "the girls in the back" are pimping their arts and themselves to Uncle Sam; that is, to making money ("Make the Money," Haggerty & Lewis, 2012, track 6).

At his end, there is a conscious reason why Macklemore raps, but it is not rooted in stereotypical means of success in commercial rap music (Alim, 2006;

Ibrahim, 2014; Love, 2012). While one could argue this is a result of privilege, *Make the Money* demonstrates the strong poet's awareness of his potential place in the Hip Hop industry—a role that comes with responsibility—and the recognition that he indeed has the capacity to rise above the confines of conventions of commercial interests. Such reflection is the very reason why we call Macklemore a strong poet.

The idea of not being boxed-in is key to our reading of Macklemore as an artist. Whether he is speaking about consumerism, about sexuality, or about his struggles with addiction, it is clear that the artist does not wish to be relegated to a singular category. In a mainstream musical epoch rooted primarily in marketability and being forced to choose a genre and target audience, this is not only unique, but in many ways an act of courage. The way in which Macklemore and Ryan Lewis produced and released *The Heist* exemplifies, for us, their desire to not be boxed-in by conventionality. Rather than searching for wealth or empty fame, Macklemore addresses them as he notes: "My intention was to make music that *spoke to people*, and not like 40 people. Like, hundreds and thousands if not millions of people can connect with what I'm writing about" (Johnson, 2012). It is this wide-awakeness, this courage, vision, and ability to use language that makes Macklemore a strong poet who is deeply conscious of the need for an ethics of testifying, an ethics of the appointment. Here, Hip Hop becomes a pedagogical space for testifying, consciousness-raising, and self-expression. Macklemore echoes these words himself in a song that expresses the vital role that Hip Hop played in his personal development as he raps: "And as a public school student, I learned from my teachers, but *became* through my music" ("The Town," Haggerty, 2009, track 1). It's high time to testify, to tell our own stories and to be courageous and daring. Indeed, we need more strong poets, those who tell us what we know differently or use language in original ways that encourage us to develop the very same audacity in and for ourselves.

Note

1. This is a line from the song, "Make the Money" (Haggerty & Lewis, 2012, track 6).

References

Alim, S. (2006). *Roc the mic right: The language of Hip Hop culture.* New York, NY; London, England: Routledge.

Chang, J. (2014). *Who we be: The colorization of America*. New York, NY: St. Martin's.

Felman, S. (1992). Education and crisis, or the vicissitudes of teaching. In S. Felman & D. Laub (Eds.), *Testimony: Crisis of witnessing in literature, psychoanalysis, and history* (pp. 1–56). New York, NY; London, England: Routledge.

Freire, P. (1970). *Pedagogy of the oppressed*. New York, NY: Herder & Herder.

Greene, M. (2000). *Releasing the imagination: Essays on education, the arts and social change*. San Francisco, CA: Jossey-Bass.

Haggerty, B. (2005). White privilege [Recorded by Macklemore]. On *The language of my world* [CD]. Seattle, WA: Macklemore, LLC.

Haggerty, B. (2009). Church [Recorded by Macklemore]. On *The unplanned mixtape* [CD]. Seattle, WA: Macklemore, LLC.

Haggerty, B. (2009). The town [Recorded by Macklemore]. On *The unplanned mixtape* [CD]. Seattle, WA: Macklemore, LLC.

Haggerty, B., & Lewis, R. (2012). Make the money [Recorded by Macklemore & Ryan Lewis]. On *The Heist* [CD]. Seattle, WA: Macklemore LLC.

Haggery, B., & Lewis, R. (2010). Otherside [Recorded by Macklemore & Ryan Lewis]. On *VS. Redux* [EP]. Seattle, WA: Macklemore LLC.

Haggerty, B., & Lewis, R. (2012). Thrift shop [Recorded by Macklemore & Ryan Lewis]. On *The Heist* [CD]. Seattle, WA: Macklemore LLC.

Haggerty, B., Lewis, R., & Bridwell, B. (2012). Starting over [Recorded by Macklemore & Ryan Lewis]. On *The Heist* [CD]. Seattle, WA: Macklemore LLC.

Haggerty, B., Lewis, R., & Dalton, R. (2012). Can't hold us [Recorded by Macklemore & Ryan Lewis]. On *The Heist* [CD]. Seattle, WA: Macklemore LLC.

Haggerty, B., Lewis, R., Hanley, Q., & Wear, H. (2012). White walls [Recorded by Macklemore & Ryan Lewis]. On *The Heist* [CD]. Seattle, WA: Macklemore LLC.

Haggerty, B., Lewis, R., & Mansfield, C. (2012). Ten thousand hours [Recorded by Macklemore & Ryan Lewis]. On *The Heist* [CD]. Seattle, WA: Macklemore LLC.

Haggerty, B., Lewis, R., & Stevens, H. (2012). Jimmy Iovine [Recorded by Macklemore & Ryan Lewis]. On *The Heist* [CD]. Seattle, WA: Macklemore LLC.

Haggerty, B., Lewis, R., Wear, H., & Joslyn, A. (2012). Wing$ [Recorded by Macklemore & Ryan Lewis]. On *The Heist* [CD]. Seattle, WA: Macklemore LLC.

Ibrahim, A. (2013). *Race, language and globalization: What can "Global Hip Hop Nation" teach us about citizenship?* Paper presented at Intercultural Counseling and Education in the Global World, University of Verona, Italy.

Ibrahim, A. (2014). *The rhizome of blackness: A critical ethnography of Hip Hop culture, language, identity, and the politics of becoming*. New York, NY: Peter Lang.

Johnson, J. (2012, October 23). *Jabari presents: Macklemore & Ryan Lewis (Documentary)* [Video file]. Retrieved from https://www.youtube.com/watch?v=JErUzr8GSvU

Laub, D. (1992). Testimony. In S. Felman & D. Laub (Eds.), *Testimony: Crisis of witnessing in literature, psychoanalysis, and history* (pp. 57–78). New York, NY; London, England: Routledge.

Love, B. (2012). *Hip Hop's li'l sistas speak: Negotiating Hip Hop identities and the politics of the new South*. New York, NY: Peter Lang.

Macklemore. (2005). *The language of my world* [CD]. Seattle, WA: Macklemore, LLC.

Macklemore. (2009). *The unplanned mixtape* [CD]. Seattle, WA: Macklemore, LLC.

Macklemore & Lewis, R. (2012). *The heist* [CD]. Seattle, WA: Macklemore, LLC.

Rorty, R. (1989). *Contingency, irony, and solidarity.* Cambridge, England: Cambridge University Press.

Ryan Lewis. (2011, August 31). *Macklemore X Ryan Lewis—Otherside remix feat. Fences [Music video]* [Video file]. Retrieved from https://www.youtube.com/watch?v=fvDQy53eldY

ZM. (2013, February 24). *ZMTV—Macklemore interview* [Video file]. Retrieved from https://www.youtube.com/watch?v=_VB3xmaNsBI

· 9 ·

IMMIGRANT CANADIAN NEW YOUTH

Expressing and Exploring Youth Identities in a Multicultural Context

Handel Kashope Wright and Maryam Nabavi

This chapter is based on findings from an ethnographic study with 12 first-generation immigrant youth in Vancouver, Canada, on how they articulate and perform notions of belonging/alienation in relation to Canada and Canadian multiculturalism, through both interviews and participant observation at a summer-long program that employed Theatre of the Oppressed (Boal, 2002) techniques. Findings include: (1) youths' expression of nuanced articulations of multiculturalism (e.g., as both marker of belonging and segregation and nominal indicator of cultural diversity); (2) ambivalence about both emigration (romanticization of home country and relief of escape from homeland strife) and immigration (longing for acceptance within Canada and rejection of Canada); (3) complexity of identity and belonging in a multicultural context (troubling sexual identity categories, insider/outside status, and identification of language fluency and accent as markers of belonging/ alienation). Drawing on work on diaspora, transnationalism, hybridity, the nation, and *New Youth* (Wright, 2009), the study reveals that Canada as a multicultural nation is, at best, an incomplete project and that immigrant youth as New Youth are ambivalent about Canadianness and the multicultural project.

Introduction

Canada self-identifies as a multicultural nation, an identity performed through official policy, academic discourse, national philosophy, and everyday practices (Kymlicka, 2007; Taylor, 1994). However this official and commonsense cohesive multicultural nation image text is contested, often by "minorities" and immigrants (Bannerji, 2000; Thobani, 2007). Furthermore, the national contexts of citizenship and belonging within multicultural Canada are troubled as a consequence of the post-colonial (Gunew, 2004). Categories of identification and belonging, often unacknowledged by hegemonic, national discourses of multiculturalism, are increasingly contesting for individual and group identity. Thus, national belonging and identification is no longer bound by substantive citizenship (Nabavi, 2010). Rather, transnational (Ong, 1999), diasporic (Werbner, 2002), religious (Zine, 2001), and cyber (boyd, 2007) identities and identifications compete with the nation-state for location of identity and primary allegiance. It is useful, therefore, to explore new Canadians' experiences and impressions of the nation, Canadian multiculturalism, and multicultural identity in relation to other identities and identifications.

For new immigrant youth, in particular, their Canadian experience is made not just by multiple identifications and belongings—such as ethnicity, religion, language—but also by their *liquid* (Wright, 2008) identities, which includes maintaining their space in both the national and global, familial and peer, and contributing to their social and political learning within the national discourses of multiculturalism and institutionalized spaces, such as schools, in which they are embedded. Our interest in exploring the notion of being a new Canadian and about Canada within an immigrant youth culture, we recognized, could not be limited to how youth talked about their experiences, but rather it was necessary to explore how immigrant youth performed as new immigrant youth to Canada. We were interested in hearing their creative expressions of identity and belonging, thus, there was a need for an embedded understanding of participants, lived experiences and how that was articulated.

Thus, we worked with a youth program in a large immigrant-serving agency in Vancouver, which had a program that employed Augusto Boal's (2002) Theatre of the Oppressed as a vehicle for helping youth address issues of interest to them. In the version of the exercise we developed in collaboration with the program's facilitators, we focused on the topic of our research, thus developing an exercise involving utilizing Theatre of the Oppressed as a medium for having youth explore and articulate issues of belonging and alienation, multiple identities and identifications, and the experiences of emigration and immigration for youth in multicultural Canada. Who these youth were, are, and are becoming (not in singular conception but in multiple, overlapping, and sometimes contradictory identity formation), what they thought of Canada, the local community, diversity, and Canadian multiculturalism were all issues we were interested in exploring collaboratively.

This study troubles the traditional conceptions of youth identity, the nation, and multiculturalism. For example, while much of the literature relies on psychological conceptions of youth based on developmental stages (youth being an age between childhood and adulthood), we were more interested in what a cultural studies approach viewed youth as. Our commitment to exploring issues pertaining to youth is informed by a cultural studies approach. The current realities for youth are articulated in Hall's (1996) classic call for a "new politics of representation," wherein the social markers of identity are no longer fixed and secure, challenging the ways in which identities have traditionally been constructed. We explored this idea through the exploration of newly immigrated youth as New Youth (Wright, 2009). New Youth includes youth who self-identify as new immigrants, multiracial or multiethnic, and/ or queer.

For the remainder of this chapter, we discuss how, theoretically and methodologically, we troubled the traditional, liberal, hegemonic notions of the nation and traditional theoretical approaches to youth identity. Further, we articulate our methodological approach and how it served to disrupt traditional youth-focused ethnographic research. Finally, we will discuss the intersections between these areas in the context of interview findings with participants.

Theoretical Scope

We were interested in troubling the notion of "youth"—as not just a linear stage of development, but rather a stage of political learning. We approached this study taking into consideration the ways in which youth are politicized (Giroux, 2006); the complexities of hybrid identities (Hall, 2006); relationship with geography/spatiality (Massey, 1998); and consumer cultures (Nayak, 2003). For immigrant youth in particular, the notion of youth—in the traditional sense—needs to be further troubled, as they must also deal with experiences of emigration; socio-cultural adaptation; and managing two or more cultures, ethnicities, languages, and nationalities. Thus, we define three central characteristics to exploring immigrant youths contexts and conditions as New Youth; these include youth who self-identify as new immigrants, multiracial, or multiethnic, and/or queer. In other words, it is those identities that are in these "new times" more visible or articulated.

We were also interested in troubling the notion of nation and, in particular, the multicultural nation. The experiences of immigrant youth are useful for articulating new understandings of the nation. The social identities of New Youth in particular challenge traditional notions of belongings, identities, and the citizen within a nation. For New Youth, their location as a diaspora population in addition to their age positions them as not quite a citizen within dominant social, political, and institutional sites. We draw on Benedict Anderson's (1983) notion of *imagined communities* to explore how the experiences of New Youth contribute to an imagined understanding of the nation. Traditional conceptions take the nation for granted as given, solid, with immigrants expected in the past to assimilate into their new nation. Of course Canadian immigration policy now aspires to the more nuanced notion of integration of immigrants. However, theoretical reconceptions of immigrants variously as diasporic, cosmopolitan, and nomadic subjects are contributing to a necessary reconception of the nation as a leaky category at best, one which may in fact not be the immigrant's primary or immediate alliance or even residence.

Methodological Scope

Methodologically, we were interested in troubling how research is conducted. There were various traditional approaches and conceptions we could have taken to this research exercise. Firstly, we could have simply studied the students in their "natural environment" as in a traditional ethnography, outside of the TO exercise. Secondly, we could have taken the Theatre of the Oppressed exercise as a given, albeit constructed, environment in which activities took place and we as researchers conducted observations and interviews (as full observers). Thirdly, we could have gone farther along the participant observer continuum and participated in some way as participant observers. However, what we ended up developing was an exercise in which research and activity were blended such that the Theatre of the Oppressed exercise was simultaneously a theatre exercise and research exercise and the research elements were integrated as aspects of the TO exercise.

Paradigmatically, e.g., in Denzin and Lincoln's (2005) useful identification of positivist, postpositivist, constructivist, critical, and postmodern research paradigms, we are both situated in the critical paradigm, and the research exercise was conceptualized as a critical ethnography (Carspecken, 1996). However, there was always an assumption that the performative would be incorporated into the research in some ways (reflecting Judith Butler's notion of identity as performative) (Butler, 1988), and going beyond it to including explicit performance in some way. While the tenets of critical ethnography drove the methodological approach, the process of creation, development and enactment of the performance contributed to the methodology in the actual research exercise. The combined process served as a method of inquiry, a way of knowing; a method of reporting knowledge and ideological critique; a method of critical response; and as an interpretive tool (Alexander, 2005). In other words, the process of what was learned and what was known for immigrant youth were intricately linked.

Furthermore, as researchers, we were present not just observing and interviewing the participants, but engaging as participant observers. We participated in all the exercises with the youth and therefore were both seen as members of the program, and neither our position as researchers nor our age positioned us as having an expertise they could not identify with. Rather, since both of us are also racial minority and immigrant subjects our location as racialized immigrants who also shared our experiences of migration, belonging, and identity aided in flattening the power differences, developing trust and a sense of respect and reciprocity throughout the process. Most significant in our methodological reflections is whether our engagement with the program was a research study wherein theatre was the tool for exploring youth identity or whether this was an experience in theatre and, in light of the population, issues of youth identity were brought to the forefront. The combined approach of a traditional research agenda, collaborative research goals, and fused methods, for us, was an attempt to trouble the traditional approach to research as expert-driven and outcome-focused.

Findings

Through the unique methodological approach of this study and by drawing theoretical developments of New Youth as well as troubling the concept of the nation to explore alternatives such as diaspora, transnationalism, and hybridity, this study reveals three central findings: (1) youths' expression of nuanced articulations of multiculturalism (e.g., as both marker of belonging and segregation and nominal indicator of cultural diversity); (2) ambivalence about both emigration (romanticization of home country and relief of escape from homeland strife) and immigration (longing for acceptance within Canada and rejection of Canada); (3) complexity of identity and belonging in a multicultural context (troubling sexual identity categories, insider/outside status, and identification of language fluency and accent as markers of belonging/alienation).

Youths' Expression of Nuanced Articulations of Multiculturalism

First, youths' expression of nuanced articulations of multiculturalism (e.g., as both marker of belonging and segregation and nominal indicator of cultural diversity). Peter McLaren (1995) and other American critical multiculturalists have helpfully indicated that there is a continuum of multiculturalisms from conservative through liberal and left-liberal to critical multiculturalism. In Canada, where multiculturalism is official policy, it is clearly what could be identified as liberal, celebratory multiculturalism that is the hegemonic conception, firmly instituted as official policy and marking everyday multiculturalism as well. Not surprisingly, therefore, when asked directly about their understanding of, and attitudes toward, multiculturalism, participants' responses generally focused on their appreciation of the Four-Ds of multiculturalism (dress, dance, dialect, dining) and of the sense of harmony suggested in many cultures being brought together. Generally, hegemonic liberal, celebratory multiculturalism, as a concept, was a nominal indicator of belonging for the participants.

> It's people from different culture being together as in creating a sense of community and yeah, like in our school, we have people coming from different countries and we all study together and we can study together and we can be really good friends, close friends. Yup.—Mary, 17.

However, when asked more specifically what aspects of multiculturalism did or did not work, participants revealed the ways in which cultural differences did not always enable a picture-perfect, romanticized multiculturalism as constructed by dominant discourses in their lives. Said one participant:

It's not necessarily that I don't like about specific about multiculturalism. It's how people approach it. Because it can be overpowering. A lot of times pride gets in the way. So it can be that, that maybe I'm the one doing it, that I think so highly of my own culture that I become neglected of others. That what may be accepted in my culture may not be accepted in someone elses.—Lida, 19.

Similarly, exposure to a myriad of cultures promotes stereotypes and using the cultural context of individuals to turn against them. One participant spoke about a bullying experience in which she was called a "deeper," a derogatory reference to Sikhs, which draws on the suffix "deep" in first names (e.g., Sandeep). The term has been expanded to all people who look South Asian. She talks about her attempts to challenge the stereotype:

One girl, every time she walked passed by me, she's be like "deeper." [They] turn around and was like, you call deeper people who have Indian accent, how do you know I'm Indian. And they're like, "you're a brown kid" I was like, "just in case you don't know, I'm from Bangladesh." And they are like "where is exactly Bangladesh?" [laugh]—Carrie, 21.

Furthermore, although participants expressed an understanding of accepting other cultures and differences, their own multicultural experiences were constituted by stereotypes, labels, and segregation:

We speak 33 languages at my school. Yeah, so there is a lot of multiculturalism. You can't be racist in there because there is a lot people from other countries. If you're racist, I don't think you're going to fit in there because somehow you have to get along with all of them. And if you don't get along with them, you're gonna suffer a lot. They're not your culture but you have to respect them.—Perla, 15.

Ambivalence About Both Emigration and Immigration

As New Youth, negotiating two or more cultures, languages, ethnic and religious backgrounds while negotiating aspects of identity yields ambivalence about both their experiences of immigration and emigration. Faced with peer pressure to ascribe to social and cultural norms within their adopted country, participants' responses are clearly reflective of the ways in which they had thought about and consider the differences between their two cultures. In articulating their impressions of "who" a Canadian person is, they clearly identify Canadianness with a cultural capital that they feel, as immigrants, they simply do not possess, a performance they are incapable of reproducing.

Like I start to follow the trends. Like the clothing and ya, all that. 'cause it's quite different than the style in Hong Kong ... um, they [Canadians] watch hockey and they know what's on the TV, the show. 'Cause I don't watch TV actually and they speak English.—Amy, 19.

There's a picture in the media, in the mainstream that white, and then, your parents have been here for a while and then, especially it has a lot to do with your accent. The way you talk, the way you behave, and the way you look—the way your dress plays a huge role. Huge huge role.—Lida, 19.

Rather than focus only on immigration, we tried to have participants explore their perspectives on both emigration and immigration. Our primary finding was that the dominant reaction was one of ambivalence: ambivalence about emigration (marked by a tension between a romanticization of home country on the one hand and relief of escape from homeland strife on the other) and ambivalence about immigration (longing for acceptance within Canada and rejection of Canada because of the perception of being always already rejected by Canada). Further, ambivalence about being Canadian is indirectly linked with a fear that they will lose the cultural identity with which they have come to Canada:

Well, I feel Canadian and Persian. But I feel more Iranian ... Because, that's where I was born and that's where my dad and my grandparents and mom was from.—Shahram, 19.

A nostalgia and romanticization of their home country set the context for rejecting (or perhaps coping with) the troubling aspects of their Canadian experience. Shortly after expressing his experiences with racism in Canada, one respondent discusses his native country with great admiration and pride:

Yeah, the problem is that racist people, we don't have. No one is racist in Egypt 'cause for example, here black and white, they always keep fight together and being racist and everything or from different religion or from different country. We don't have that ... Yea, we're all like, one person.—Nathan, 15.

One participant's Canadian experience is made up of distrust for "Canadian people." She qualifies that Canadian people are "fake" and people from her home country are not:

It's this country is more perfect. It's like how you see in a movie. The streets are the same, the buses are the same, people who are biking on the street have Suzuki everything and everything that you see in a movie back home. In a Hollywood movie, it's practically the same. I was completely thinking that every character you see in a movie, it does exist in real life in here. So I kind of felt like people are faking all the time. Back home, whatever you see on TV does not exist in real life. It's completely the opposite. And I have the issues of trust in here. I barely trust people in here.—Carrie, 21.

In spite of a feeling of pride and romanticization for their home country, participants discuss their gratitude for no longer having to deal with issues such as a poor education system, censorship, corruption, and poor living conditions. These new "luxuries" in their lives make them appreciate the different systems and institutions that they have come into contact with in Canada. These opportunities have enabled them to attain a cultural capital impossible without emigration.

Yah, we were planning on coming for like 7 years, or, 6 years. Something like that. Because my father told me that, here is the best way to learn. A lot of people say that. We come here to learn, because you know ... for example a doctor here, the study here is way better than our country. Yah, 'cause in our country schools are really bad. They don't teach you. They just come for money—the teachers. That's why I really hate it there.—Nathan, 15.

Complexity of Identity and Belonging in a Multicultural Context

As immigrants, their feelings of belonging and identity are complicated in their individual processes of identity formation, linked with their stage in development. For example, one participant shares her process of questioning her sexual identity. However, she is quick to dismiss the possibility that she may not be heterosexual as it is not accepted in her church community, which is also the main space where this participant feels like she belongs. The sense of national and cultural identity is complicated for participants who are embedded in transnational migrations and are, thus, both insiders and outsiders to Canada and their home country. In one case, a participant discusses the complexity of her sense of belonging and identity:

um actually I was born in Vancouver. But my parents took me back 'cause the, um, the government issue, when I was born, was not stable in China. They decided to came to Canada, yah, gave birth ... when I was in Hong Kong, I didn't think I belonged to Hong Kong too, 'cause you know, you're already in there and don't think much about and when I leave Hong Kong, I came to Canada and I don't feel like I'm a Canadian too. Although I've got a Canadian passport.—Amy, 19.

Participants' feelings of being both an insider and outsider in Canada are informed by both their ability to adapt and integrate into Canadian society while recognizing that their parents do not have the same luxury. Their parents' professional, cultural, and social context complicates their relationship with their parents as well as how they negotiate being an insider in Canadian society (compared to their parents) and being an outsider (compared to their peers).

> it's been worse for my parents then it's been for me. Because it was a lot easier for me to adapt here than for them because it actually strained my parents' relationship with me. It has something to do with the kind of job my Dad used to have. He doesn't have the same level of jobs and he's not happy with what he has. And it frustrates him and when it frustrates him, my Mom, it immediately affects the whole family.—Lida, 19.

Conclusion

Findings from this study reveal that for new immigrant youth, as New Youth, how they articulate identity with the context nation, in general, and a multicultural nation, in particular, is complicated by competing and conflicting loyalties between Canada as an *imagined nation* and their home country. Articulations of multiculturalism as it plays out on the ground, juxtaposed with their understanding of the national discourses of multiculturalism, feed into existing ambiguities of emigration and immigration and complex dimensions of youth identity, demonstrating that for participants, Canada as a multicultural nation is, at best, an incomplete project, and that immigrant youth as New Youth are ambivalent about Canadianness and the multicultural project.

References

Alexander, B. K. (2005). Performance ethnography: The reenacting and inciting of culture. In N. K. Denzin & Y. S. Lincoln (Eds.), *The Sage handbook of qualitative research* (3rd ed.). Thousand Oaks, CA: Sage.

Anderson, B. (1983). *Imagined communities*. London, England: Verso.

Bannerji, H. (2000). *The dark side of the nation: Essays on multiculturalism, nationalism and gender*. Toronto, Canada: Canadian Scholars' Press.

Boal, A. (2000). *Theatre of the oppressed*. London, England: Pluto.

Boal, A. (2002). *Games for actors and non-actors* (2nd ed.). New York, NY: Routledge.

boyd, d. (2007). Why youth (heart) social network sites: The role of networked publics in teenage social life. In D. Buckingham (Ed.), *The John D. and Catherine T. MacArthur*

Foundation series on digital media and learning—Youth, identity, and digital media (pp. 119–142). Cambridge, MA: MIT Press.

Butler, J. (1988). Performative acts and gender constitution: An essay in phenomenology and feminist theory. *Theatre Journal, 40*(4), 519–531.

Carspecken, P. (1996). *Critical ethnography in educational research: A theoretical and practical guide.* London, England: Routledge.

Denzin, N. K., & Lincoln, Y. S. (Eds.), *The Sage handbook of qualitative research* (3rd ed.). Thousand Oaks, CA: Sage.

Gunew, S. M. (2004). *Haunted nations: The colonial dimensions of multiculturalisms.* London, England: Routledge.

Kymlicka, W. (2007). *Multicultural odysseys.* Oxford, England: Oxford University Press.

McLaren, P. (1995). White terror and oppositional agency: Towards a critical multiculturalism. In C. E. Sleeter & P. McLaren (Eds.), *Multicultural education, critical pedagogy, and the politics of difference.* New York, NY: State University of New York Press.

Nabavi, M. (2010). Constructing the "citizen" in citizenship education. *Canadian Journal for New Scholars in Education, 3*(1).

Ong, A. (1999). *Flexible citizenship: The cultural logic of transnationality.* London, England: Duke University Press.

Taylor, C. (1994). The politics of recognition. In D. T. Goldberg (Ed.), *Multiculturalism: A critical reader.* Oxford, England: Blackwell.

Thobani, S. (2007). *Exalted subjects: Studies in the making of race and nation in Canada.* Toronto, Canada; Buffalo, NY: University of Toronto Press.

Werbner, P. (2002). The place which is diaspora: Citizenship, religion and gender in the making of chaordic transnationalism. *Journal of Ethnic and Migration Studies, 28*(1), 119–133.

Wright, H. (2008). *New youth, new time, liquid identities.* Paper presented at the Canadian Society for the Study of Education, Ottawa, Canada.

Wright, H. (2009, November). *Ambivalence about the "M" word: Multiculturalism with new youth and in liquid communities.* Paper presented at the Visiting Professor lecture delivered at the Centre for Educational Research, University of Western Sydney, Australia.

Zine, J. (2001). Muslim youth in Canadian schools: Education and the politics of religious identity. *Anthropology & Education Quarterly, 32*(4), 399–423.

PART IV

RESEARCHING YOUTH AND PLACE

· 1 0 ·

HISPANIC YOUTH
LEADERSHIP IN TEXAS

Creating a Mexican American College-Going
Culture in West Texas

Mary Frances Agnello

Creating a college-going cultural movement of Mexican Americans has taken many years. Given that Mexican Americans gained the right to attend school with white Texans during the Civil Rights Movement of the 1960s, remarkable changes have occurred in 50 years. Despite the gains in Civil Rights, however, rates of Hispanic high school and undergraduate degree completion are low in Texas and throughout the U.S. Despite progress made in these areas through the Generation Texas, P-20 Councils all over the state, and local efforts to increase Hispanic, especially male, graduation rates, the statistics show little gain. Yet, progress has been made in local areas, with initiatives from the Texas Higher Education Coordinating Board, diversity-focused hires in upper university and public school administration, and through leadership assumed by Hispanic and Mexican American students as they find their voices in and through education.

At Texas Tech University, Hispanic student groups on campus have formed six Hispanic fraternities and sororities, as well as 12 Hispanic Registered Student Organizations (RSOs). These groups plan and implement cultural programming, including talks, panel discussions, film viewing, and others to promote Hispanic culture on campus. University administration and RSOs have created scholarships, outreach, Red Raider Guarantee, and merit awards targeted at high-achieving Latinos in Honors classes both at the sec-ondary and college level. Fundraisers, T-shirts that announce Yo Soy Texas Tech, Cinco de Mayo celebrations, aguas frescas and palettas sales of at least five Latino RSO groups are quite routine on the Texas Tech campus reaching out to the West Texas and greater Texas regions.

The strides made in Texas and at Texas Tech have not come easily or quickly, and they have not come without promoting other cultures in addi-tion to Hispanic culture on campus in ethnic and cultural elements, foods, music, religion, issues-related work careers, professions, and programs directed at understanding policies related to immigration and language. The promotion of Mexican American culture is not siloed or exclusive, but rather is inclusive of other cultures visible in events focused on Chinese New Year with Dragon Dancing, Anglo, Indian, Celtic, Vietnamese New Year, the West Texas Turkish Student Association Kite Festival, among many others.

This chapter focuses on three Mexican American affiliates of higher edu-cation, a Hispanic male who is vice provost for Undergraduate Education and vice president for Institutional Diversity Equity, and Community Engagement at Texas Tech (José), a male graduate student who is a Mexican immigrant from a border town in Southwest Texas (Diorio), and a female Mexican American, longtime advocate for Mexican American education (Juanita). Interviews were done with these individuals during spring 2013. The infor-mation that they shared in response to 13 questions was regarding their views on the progress made by Mexican Americans, their contributions to Mexi-can American educational success, and what they believe will help promote the college-going success of future generations. The pseudonyms José, Diorio, and Juanita will be used in reference to these three individuals. The terms Hispanic and Mexican American are used interchangeably throughout the chapter.

Hispanic matriculation and graduation from Texas Tech did not begin until 9 years ago, when José Martinez accepted a dual appointment in upper administration and as assistant professor in the College of Education, but it has accelerated because of many of his efforts as the vice provost for Under-graduate Education and vice president for Institutional Diversity Equity, and Community Engagement. University president John Whitmore saw the need to include diversity initiatives in his administration, and he recognized the talent and insight that José possessed. His work most of the last decade has built on preceding successes and extended deep into local communities, as well as across the state.

Perspective of the Vice Provost for Undergraduate Education and Vice President for Institutional Diversity Equity, and Community Engagement

Throughout the state, adversities to Mexican American matriculation persist. Few Hispanic families have the financial wherewithal to continue paying their children's way through university. They do not like to send their children far from home to attend school, and this is especially relevant at Texas Tech, where most students live more than 3 hours away from the university. Also, schools in general have not advocated for Hispanics to matriculate at the university, often pushing students toward the trades and service industries. Yet, marked and extraordinary results have been achieved over the last 9 years in the estimation of the vice provost for Undergraduate Education and vice president for Institutional Diversity Equity, and Community Engagement. Persistence, improved retention, with enrollment rates going from 5% in 2004 to 18% in 2013, and impetus achieved through university efforts combined with initiatives around the state and nation to close the gap for Hispanic and African American students have achieved a rate three times higher than the national average. In business, for example, the Master of Business Administration graduating class at Texas Tech now exceeds 25% Hispanic graduates. Ranked by Education Trust as one of the Top 25 campuses for closing the achievement gap for African American and Latino students, Texas Tech was the only research university in Texas to make the list (Menard, 2013).

The efforts of the vice president and vice provost for Diversity Affairs have built increased university enrollments on such events as the Back to School Fiesta that occurs every August prior to the start of public school. A recent Families Access to College Education Symposium with 400–500 attendees gathered educators from public schools, the university and junior colleges, and families to educate families about the requirements and possibilities for college education through the Regions XVI and XVII Education Service Centers. Promoting Hispanic academic success on the Texas Tech campus has come through the Cross Cultural Center, Pegasus, Mentor Tech, Hispanic Student Society, Unidos Por Una Lingua Misma, football game presentation of awards including Raiders Rojos scholarships, among other organization and planned events to promote the success of Mexican American students.

José's role as vice provost for Undergraduate Education and vice president for Institutional Diversity Equity, and Community Engagement has enabled Hispanic influence on various administrative committee roles, allowed funding of organizations, promoted taking Mexican American students to leadership training, and served to provide individual mentorship. He has worked with the Higher Education Coordinating Board led by a Hispanic. Concomitant to academic improvements for Mexican Americans, there is evidence of political progress made, with Hispanics elected to the Lubbock Independent School District Board, and to the Lubbock City Council and U.S. Senate. And the Texas Tech influence and interest in Hispanics reaches far into the South Plains region, as well as across Texas, to attract and address the needs of the Mexican American community.

Texas Tech's drive to address the needs of diverse students, including Mexican American students, promotes the hiring and tenuring of more diverse faculty, including women of color, and promoting women and other diverse associate faculty to full professor. The University has millions of dollars invested in diversity in every area, including athletics, as well as academic advisory positions, and at every administrative level including offices of the president and chancellor.

Yet, Mexican American families still face adversity in sending their students to university. Some of the challenges include low-income and under-preparedness, as well as the family ties that keep students close to home, high-stakes testing, and isolated acts of prejudice. Overall, however, the University will not tolerate staff members who are belligerent to Hispanics because no office is foolish enough to dismiss serious students—regardless of their backgrounds. Such an attitude toward students leads to a campus marked by pervasive acceptance and little prejudice.

Areas of improvement on the horizon include the need for the administrative hierarchy from upper administration to college departments and programs to promote the academic success of all Hispanic students that come to Texas Tech. In the words of José, we will have achieved the administrative feat of graduating all those Hispanics who come to Tech when we understand that "a student's failure is our failure." Such an approach toward the promotion of Mexican American academic achievement at Texas Tech is the mantra of the vice provost for Undergraduate Education and vice president for Institutional Diversity Equity, and Community Engagement. His personal recommendation to Hispanic students is, "Don't ever let anyone else define your potential. Tenacity will always overcome talent."

A Mexican American Graduate Student Perspective

Diorio Amada (a pseudonym) came from a border town in southwest Texas with some family on both sides of the border. Because of the strong Mexican culture, all signs and advice for him during his formative years indicated that he should stay home, get married, raise a family, and not pursue education. However, his parents told him, "Strive for more. Get educated."

Since there were no immediate role models for him, Diorio got involved with high school organizations, with "elite groups." He did everything he could to develop academic traits. He went to the counselor's office at school and asked random questions; he talked to his band director who really wanted him to pursue music education. Diorio knew his destiny lay elsewhere: he wanted to be an academic and not an extracurricular professional. He learned how to study, take notes, and collaborate with students successfully. What he did, he achieved for his parents who told him to stand up against his peers when pressure became very influential. His uncle told him that he would "be back home in a semester because he could not make it"; Diorio had to prove him wrong. Through the constant battle with individuals to prove that he was worthy enough to go to a university, as well as smart enough to excel and graduate, he endured.

Diorio and his friend who wanted to study biology talked about going to university. His friend went to, and graduated from, Odessa College because he did not have money to go to university. He now works in Odessa. In contrast, Dioro wanted to go to Texas Tech, so his family gave him $200 and told him, "Good luck!" He had some scholarships also, but the most difficult thing for him has been paying for school, rather than achieving in classes, which he handles well. He has decided to get loans, and eventually secure a job in university administration or in a governmental agency that works with educational policy.

Upon enrollment at Texas Tech, Diorio felt he was different racially and ethnically because of language and his background. He also hated the word, "Latino." He still thinks of himself as Mexican American, part of the Latino population. He felt like people like him were all generalized into one group. Although open to the idea of meeting new groups of people, he needed to have a sense of belonging and thus started to seek out Latino cultural groups, the Hispanic Student Society, for example. The Society promoted itself by going to predominantly Hispanic schools, doing the Cesar Chavez walk, and showing students that they had identity and were working for a good cause.

One of the main things that Diorio (and a lot of his peers) has done personally to promote Hispanic culture is to go back home to their schools to spread the word, work continuously, and show fellow Mexican Americans that securing a degree is difficult but doable and important to gain some economic success. He asserted that these students need motivation because many are first-generation college students and do not have role models. As a model for the next generation Hispanics, he and others in the Hispanic RSOs mentor the 10% of honor students in his former high school, and they maintain communication with some of the students, answering questions about university life wherever they enroll. One of his mentees is in graduate school and another in law school. He said he does not sugarcoat what it is like at the university, telling the mentees that in some classes they can sail by and in others they will be fighting for 1/10 of a point to pass. He tells them that he pushed himself to excel academically and they can also do it.

In Diorio's view, the Hispanic population is still underserved because the population of Hispanics in the university does not mirror that of the society. Until it becomes part of the campus culture to promote Hispanic success, there remains a majority of white students on campus. He believes that more work with high schools promoting the success of minority populations is necessary, as well as bringing them to the university. He sees progress in the shift in demographics of some businesses and careers to respond to the population that will be the driving force in those professions. Politicians, in Diorio's view, have thrown the needs of Hispanics "under the rug," but now they will need to focus on Hispanics, coming to political understanding that their election and re-election will be determined by their efforts and abilities to work with the Hispanic community.

Diorio cited the initiatives of President Obama to increase graduation rates of minorities as the beginning of what can lead to a "successful" minority population. The Dream Act would give undocumented Hispanic people the desire to stay to contribute to the welfare and initiatives of the U.S. This would help the prosperity of the U.S. and lead to more economic success in general. He thinks it would be a mistake to disallow those educated individuals to become a part of society. He believes that the white culture is visibly dominant at Texas Tech, showing in every activity, and leaving much room for improvement. Although there is a Back to School Fiesta and Hispanic Heritage Month, there is a long way to go, with campus Hispanics now being a "group of flies in the milk" rather than just "an individual fly in the milk." Grossly outnumbered, Hispanics have a long way to go.

Remaining work to be done includes closing the educational gaps of the population, evening out the numbers, success in K–12 retention and graduation, college and university matriculation, more work in recruitment, and improved ways of recruiting. Diorio emphasized that there need to be Hispanic recruiters that look, sound, and speak like Latinos, rather than those who speak no Spanish or use English pronunciations for their names. Otherwise, Hispanics will not be open to the idea of going to Texas Tech. Also, although visible in the immediate region and in the cities across Texas where recruitment efforts are focused, Texas Tech can do a lot to seek students who are in the outlying areas and smaller towns. He said, "No one reached out to me; it was through my own research that I found out about Texas Tech."

The way in which Diorio remains connected to his Hispanic roots is through mentorships, finding others who have been through the university process, remaining active with Hispanic/Latino associations. We become our own advocates through the Spanish Honor Society (Sigma Delta Pi), and others like Beso and Unidos Por Una Lingua Misma, as well as the American Association for Hispanics in Higher Education (AAHHE) that brings "lonely only Hispanics together from around the country in higher education to form a network of support."

Diorio was awarded the AAHHE and Ford Foundation Fellowship in 2013 and was able to connect with 27 Hispanic individuals from across the country. These are people who will be Hispanic leaders in education, government, business, and banking. He was instilled with the mission that they have the responsibility to push forward, "be outspoken, and take leadership in any realm." Citing Ghandi, Diorio said, "If we want to see change, we have to be the change." He clarified that if people are unhappy about aspects of politics and education, they have to stand up to positively influence change. His advice was, "Be the change in every aspect of life, make a difference, persevere, and push forth."

Juanita—Longtime Advocate for Hispanic Education

Juanita's parents bought her and her siblings Texas Tech shirts and memorabilia for Christmas every year, not because they were loyal alumni, but because they were janitors at Texas Tech who loved the university and the idea that one day their children would be alumni. That day has arrived because not only are their children alumni, but now their grandchildren are as well. Juanita works in community outreach for Texas Tech and has been instrumental in creating events such as the Back to School Fiesta and in establishing local organizations such as the Hispanic Student Society, as well as the local Generation Texas Chapter affiliated with the Generation Texas movement around the state and the regional chapter of the P-20 Council. She worked on Project Future that promoted bringing Hispanics into the teaching profession, as well as the East Lubbock Neighborhood Promise Grant, an Obama administration initiative.

As Juanita contemplates the success of her efforts and other Hispanic efforts over the last quarter century, local politics surfaced as one of the biggest impediments to Hispanic success in Lubbock. Infighting, non-support of Hispanics in power through overthrow, power struggles to be county commissioner or city council representatives, perception that one candidate supports the success of Hispanic business over petty politics, and more such intrigue can be found on the front page of the local newspaper. All of these recent community interactions do not go unnoticed by the mainstream Anglo power structure, nor do they go uncovered by the local press. Such a political atmosphere that engages Hispanic in-fighting precludes the need for other power wielders to do much except sit back, watch, and observe the Hispanic constituency undo its political accomplishments. This kind of behavior is not helpful to the movement to achieve more and better political and educational power in and for the Hispanic community.

On the other hand, Juanita worked with students to raise an endowment established by the Hispanic Student Society from $18,000 to $25,000 this year. Such an effort enables the awarding of several $500 Texas Tech University scholarships to deserving Hispanics every year. Juanita's goal is an endowment of $100,000 to secure this educational support into perpetuity.

Juanita attributed the success of this kind of educational scholarship program to those who do the hard work of making it happen, but also to those in positions of power, such as the Texas Tech chancellor who donated $2,000 to the effort this year. She is on a first-name basis with the chancellor and many people in power like him because she has been a community organizer for so many years. Because she has done work to promote Hispanic success in education in the state, region, and local communities, Juanita went to Washington, D.C., to receive an award last year. Many plaques and certificates on her office walls attest to her undying support for the cause of Mexican American education. This year, the Hispanic Student Association that she sponsors honored the Lauro Cavazos Family for their contributions to Texas Tech. Lauro Cavazos served as the first Hispanic president of Texas Tech and secretary of education under Ronald Reagan. His children and their children have Texas Tech degrees. Pride in such accomplishment runs deep.

Juanita proclaimed that Hispanics who used to be only the janitors at Texas Tech have made great strides in education and in the professional and business world as well. Her own children work in international business and the arts, living on the east coast and abroad. They have traveled around the world, along with their children. Juanita beamed as she described this progress achieved by her family in just two generations because of educational opportunities provided and taken. In contrast, she sighed as she expressed the difficulty she and others experience as they attempt to educate families who have no hope for education because of lack of money about the opportunities they have, because they have so little.

Preparing the next generation of advocates is the most important work that lies ahead for Juanita. Because of the political climate in which the Hispanic community has not been its own best advocate, there remains much work to do. Yet, much of the work that is being done in communities, neighborhoods, and schools is being realized because of the networks built by Juanita and others like her. The same can be said for much of the success of José and Adorio. They have each built on aspects of work done by Juanita and her predecessors. All three of these individuals are extending the network of possibilities for the Mexican American community from the older generation to the younger, working in and through established channels and forging new paths. Such efforts are necessary to turn around centuries of educational neglect of Mexican Americans and to create Hispanic college-going culture. Juanita's efforts have made present leadership positions such as that of José possible, and such future leadership of those such as Diorio probable.

Reference

Menard, V. (2013, February/March). Eye on the prize: Latino leaders in Texas keep tabs on Latinos in higher education. *Poder: Intelligence for the Business Elite, 91*(79–81).

· 1 1 ·

CONOCIMIENTO

Mixtec Youth *sin Fronteras*

Elizabeth Quintero

Conocimiento, for Anzaldúa, is

an overarching theory of consciousness ... all the dimensions of life, both inner—mental, emotional, instinctive, imaginal, spiritual, bodily realms—and outer—social, political, lived experiences ... the awareness of *facultad* that sees through all human acts whether of the individual mind and spirit or of the collective, social body.

—Hérnandez-Ávila & Anzaldúa (2010, p. 177)

In this chapter we explore examples of Conocimiento Theory through the interactions of a senior level university student working with migrant youth from Mixtec backgrounds (from Oaxaca, Mexico) in an urban high school in southern California. A segment of a conversation between Fabiola Martinez and a high school student she tutors hints at the need for a theoretical approach such as Conocimiento, according to Anzaldúa. This is a way to view and support the strengths and challenges of youth in migrant situations. Fabiola noted in her journal:

A young tenth grader approached me asking about my own living situations. "Maestra, usted vive sola?" she said. I went on to say I had a roommate, then I had to explain what a roommate was, and that I take care of my personal things.

She asked if I missed my family, but specifically she asked if my missed my mother. At the moment this wasn't awkward, later I made the connection. A while later that day ... she went on to share with me that she had lived in Mexico while her mother lived in California. This student had to go to school, work, and maintain a home for her eight younger siblings. Three years ago her mother brought her here to California and here she is. She is a straight "A" student speaking English very well, soaking in information and was well on her way to college and to being a success story.

But ... now, she is being taken out of my program. Worse than that, she is being taken out of school as a whole. Her mother is moving her to Las Vegas with no plans to enroll her in school. (Martinez, 2013)

We discuss the strengths of the youth from this group of students, the challenges they face, and the multidirectional learning between the university student and the high school youth she interacts with in a student support program. Critical literacy will be a framework within the theory of Conocimiento to view this work.

This research story addresses issues of access and quality in education for children of migrant farmworkers. Migration, language, culture, power, ethnicity, race, and class enter into the complex consideration of how the education serves the needs of this population. Fabiola Martinez is graduating from an Early Childhood Studies program in a state university in California. The students in the program approach curricula from a participatory critical theory framework study and work to create responsive, high-quality education for children and youth of migrant farmworkers. The university students rethink curriculum for children and youth through their university coursework by learning from the families and children of the migrant workers working in Southern California. Research has shown that quality early care and education positively influences children's success in school and later in life (Loeb, Fuller, Kagan, & Carrol, 2004; Schweinhart, Barnes, Weikart, 1993; Shonkoff & Phillips, 2000). This is true for all children and particularly important for children of recent immigrants, who are often beginning to learn English and who have a rich cultural history as well as diverse needs.

From Conocimiento as Theory to Critical Theory

As stated earlier, Conocimiento Theory, for Anzaldúa, is

an overarching theory of consciousness, ... all the dimensions of life, both inner—mental, emotional, instinctive, imaginal, spiritual, bodily realms—and outer—social, political, lived experiences ... the awareness of facultad that sees through all human acts whether of the individual mind and spirit or of the collective, social body. (Hérnandez-Ávila & Anzaldúa, 2010, p. 177)

Anzaldúa urged the generation of theories based on those whose knowledges are traditionally excluded from and silenced by academic research. She further asserted that beyond creating theories, "we need to find practical application for those theories." Anzaldúa advised that we de-academize theory and "connect the community to the academy" (Anzaldúa, 1990, p. xxvi). Anzaldúa (2002) also noted that "Change requires more than words on a page—it takes perseverance, creative ingenuity and acts of love" (p. 574).

Family History and De-academization of Theory

Through the persona of Fabiola Martinez, her own historical and cultural influences, and her dedication to working with youth from migrant families, we see illustrations of the de-academization of theory. Multiple examples of Conocimiento Theory appear as all the dimensions of the lives of migrant students and their tutor interconnect. Fabiola Martinez has documented memories from her childhood that influenced her strong feelings about her home language, her family, and her passions and interests. These experiences reflect the importance of viewing family, learning, and opportunities through Conocimiento Theory and point to her passion for supporting Latino youth from all backgrounds, and especially those from migrant families.

Martinez wrote a summary of memories about maintaining home language. When asked what influenced her to nurture and use her home language, complete her education, and persevere in general, she said:

> My dad! He always made it a point to (insist that we) keep our Spanish. He would always complain about cousins that spoke Spanish with an accent or didn't know how to conjugate properly while speaking. I definitely have him, and my mom, to thank for my not forgetting Spanish ...

> Also, ever since I can remember it was imprinted in my head that college was not an option. It was elementary, middle school, high school and college. NO OPTIONS! ... And all that is due to my parents. Now that I have moved out and I see the graduation light so close, I definitely have to thank my parents. I appreciate them more now that I am away from them compared to when I saw them every day.

In a class focusing on methods for teaching multilingual students, Fabiola wrote an "I Am ..." poem (Christensen, 2003) that reflects Conocimiento Theory in her own life:

Where I am From …
I say I am from a breeze
From a golden globe that warms my every step
From a place where mountains decorate my surroundings
With their white tops on hot summer days
From a place where dreams are supposed to come true
With white picket fences
From a place where people run on their own clock
Places to be and people to see
From a place where gold started it all
And diamonds are a girl's best friend
From a place where stars decorate the floor we walk on
And the stars in the sky hide behind our bright lights

But this is all a lie …
Where I am really from is a place full of spirit
And culture is everything
From "Donde esta Fabiola?"
And "Todo el mundo es un coral …"
From a place where family is priority
And priority means leaving them behind to better their life
Like my father …
So now I can say I am from a breeze …

—Martinez, 2012

Fabiola explained that California Mini-Corps is a migrant tutoring service provided through Butte County Schools. It began in 1967 and was designed after the Peace Corps program. While working for the program she has been able to go to different districts each school year and work with the migrant students and their families. She noted, "We do assessments, SMART goals and make home visits in order to help us better understand our students" (Martinez, 2013).

During the summers Fabiola Martinez had the honor of attending Mini-Corps Professional Development sessions in Sacramento. Travel expenses were covered, as well as their lodgings at Sacramento State University for the weekend. All summer tutors were offered educational and informational workshops. Martinez said, "This has helped me grow as an individual and as a future educator. Through Mini-Corps I received a well-rounded experience in all levels K–12 in different districts in California."

Fabiola Martinez, her family, her tenacity, and her dedication to what we've come to see as Conocimiento Theory illustrates what many critical and postmodern scholars call transformation. Critical theory encourages the production and application of theory as a part of the overall search for transformative knowledge. Paulo Freire (1985) promoted critical theory that emphasizes participation through personal histories, the sharing of multiple ways of knowing, and transformative action.

Critical Race theorist Gloria Ladson-Billings (2009) stated that the critical turning point of transformation might be the stage educators would be most interested in seeing their students achieve. This is a stage where the student becomes qualitatively renewed, with a commitment to compassionate understanding; in some ways, it shares affinities with the goals of culturally relevant pedagogy, in that educational work be transformative (Ladson-Billings, 2009). When this happens in students, what are the factors that contribute to it? We believe that this transformation is multidirectional and can occur for both the learner and the tutor/teacher. We believe that by approaching Conocimiento through critical theory and critical literacy, participants in learning situations have the opportunity to fully participate knowing their history and languages will be respected and become an integral part of all learning, share multiple sources of knowledge—traditional and non-traditional—and have the opportunity to make decisions about transformative knowledge. We also believe that until approaches such as these are instituted with youth from backgrounds rich in diversity and experience, their struggles will remain very difficult.

In our work, we use critical theory and critical literacy as a process of both reading history (the world) and creating history. Whose stories are important and in what ways? What ways can we learn from the stories? Whose background knowledge will we respect and include and in what ways? Whose and which knowledge is power and in what ways? What ways can we use literacy for specific transformative action? (Quintero, 2009).

Context of Current Study

The contemporary poet, Francisco X. Alarcón (1997), asked us if we can "hear the voices between these lines?" (p. 28). Scholars, dedicated teachers, and community activists have documented the fact that many immigrant students come from a variety of backgrounds with different "funds of knowledge" (Moll, Gonzalez, & Amanti, 2005; Quintero, 2010; Steinberg & Kincheloe, 2009) for contributing to our communities and educational programs. Acculturation and language acquisition are impacted by the process of aligning new societal expectations and requirements of immigrants with previous cultural norms, individual perceptions, and experiences preeminent in their lives; yet, these urgent issues are often ignored. By virtue of the fact that many immigrant students come from a variety of backgrounds with different "funds of knowledge," as Moll, Gonzalez, and Amanti (2005) reported, it is urgent that university education students learn the complicated practice of recognizing, acknowledging, and incorporating learners' background knowledge while providing them access to new and necessary knowledge for successful participation in the 21st century. The research described provides a focus on this work in ways that currently aren't often discussed in literature in the field.

Agricultural workers in our county include families from Mexico and Central America and a large, close-knit indigenous group of families from Oaxaca and Mexico, known as the Mixtecs. The Mixtecs are indigenous inhabitants of southern Mexico whose language and culture predate the Spanish conquest by hundreds of years. There are an estimated 500,000 Mixtec speakers today, almost one-fifth live in the United States for at least part of their lives. Mixtec language and culture are as different from Spanish as Navajo is from English. The Mixtecs' beliefs about health, religion, and family include many traditional concepts and are often at odds with Western concepts. Along with other indigenous cultures, the Mixtec's unique language, art, and culture are in danger of being lost forever. Many of the immigrant families who arrived in the United States in the 1970s and 1980s raised their families here—and now have children in college or who are successfully employed. Many have become U.S. citizens (Fox & Rivera-Salgado, 2004).

However, there are barriers for many of the Mixtec people living in California. Many are illiterate, and some speak neither Spanish or English but only their native language, Mixteco, or another indigenous language. As a result, they face exploitation and discrimination in labor, housing, and everyday life. Most live in extreme poverty and lack basic provisions such as adequate housing, food, clothing, and other necessities of life. Central to their struggle is the fact that they cannot communicate with people beyond their own indigenous community, thus impeding their ability to obtain appropriate health care, educate themselves and their children, negotiate with their employers to improve their work situation, and exercise their basic civil rights (Wright, 2005).

Fabiola explained her work with this group of learners from infant/toddler programs through middle school and high school:

> Working with migrant students ages three to eighteen has been an experience unlike any other. When I was focusing solely on the younger ages, I had been witness to

children struggling to identify a language to speak. What is going to happen to the children when they enter the elementary years and are expected to read a language that no one in their home speaks?

I am the oldest sibling and from my experiences with younger children, I wonder who do these kids go to for help? How are parents supposed to be involved parents if this language barrier also stops them? With this, I believe that a well thought out literacy plan will greatly impact these kids and their families. (Martinez, 2013)

A migrant child is defined as a child who has parents or guardians that are migratory agricultural workers. Due to this lifestyle the child is at risk of possible health problems, poverty, constant relocation, discrimination, and language barriers. The problems can have an intense influence on the educational accomplishments of children of migrant laborers. These are not new elements of struggle to any one of us in this society. Some of these conditions happen to many of the poor populations here in the United States. However, the consequence of having to constantly move and readjust creates a new set of obstacles for the child and for their education. Migrant students may attend as many as six or seven schools per year (Jachman, 2002).

Fabiola, as a part of her university study, read "Classroom Teaching and Instruction Best Practices: for Young English Language Learners" by Linda M. Espinosa (2010). She reflected:

Something new that stood out to me right away is that the number of programs for students who are learning to speak another language other than English is increasing. Due to my tutoring with migrant students I have gotten the chance to meet these students. When I think of students learning a second language my mind automatically jumped to students learning English. However, I had students that were learning Spanish as a second language and English as a third. As simple as the idea is, I had never seen it from that point of view. And the number of these students is increasing? It is something amazing to me. (Martinez, 2013)

She went on to reflect,

When I was learning English, around the age of 4 or 5 (still young), I would go back to my Spanish to make connections. I would say a Spanish word and put an awkward accent to it and call it "English." Then as I grew up I used my knowledge of Spanish to learn how to spell. Since in the English language we don't pronounce every single letter in a word (i.e., Wednesday/because) and in Spanish we do, I would say "w-e-D-n-e-s-d-a-y" or "b-e-C-A-U-s-E" just to make sure I got all the letters down. This article by Espinosa states that ELL students make relationships between the language they are learning and their primary language. And it is true. I think that this is something important to keep in mind when working with children.

I had a student last week ask me "how do you spell tender?" They were writing sentences about the colonial times so I was confused as to how the word "tender" fit in her sentences. So I asked her how she was trying to use it. She said "In the morning I tender my bed." I honestly couldn't help but laugh a little bit. She was using the Spanish word "tender" which means "to make." So she translated the Spanish verb over to English. She went to her Spanish knowledge to figure out her sentence. She was a fourth grader learning English and the fact that she's trying to use what she knows is a good step. (Martinez, 2013)

Tying this information from Espinosa's article to her personal history and her work with children and youth from the migrant community, Martinez (2013) said:

Knowing how kids think and accepting it as a positive step forward I think is a key lesson for teachers. Being patient and accepting that each child will slowly accept and grasp the new language at her/his own pace is important. I've had students that refused to communicate with me in English (given these were kids that first spoke Mixteco, while learning Spanish in a bilingual classroom). I had to ask questions and converse in Spanish. Only later I learned that the parents of one boy pushed learning Spanish so much that he didn't want to learn English. (Martinez, 2013)

Anzaldúa might have smiled at Martinez's final thoughts about the article she had been thinking about. Martinez (2013) said, "Reading articles makes us knowledgeable and it is important to learn what others have found and concluded. But nothing beats personally working with these kids and first hand verifying that what one is reading in academia is true."

So What? Conocimento Literacy

Martinez (2013) found that some children are introduced to the school system when they haven't had any school knowledge at all. She commented,

Being introduced to math, how to read, a schedule is something new and unnatural to these kids. Then after they are getting settled in a school, it is time to move and time to readjust to a new curriculum and procedures.

If we think about Conocimiento Theory,

all the dimensions of life, both inner—mental, emotional, instinctive, imaginal, spiritual, bodily realms—and outer—social, political, lived experiences ... the awareness of facultad that sees through all human acts whether of the individual mind and spirit or of the collective, social body.

then we have to really interrupt assumptions about "school readiness" and other stereotypical expectations for performance and narrow approaches to knowledge. Children who are migrating with their families are not only disrupted in the typical school processes and expectations, but they must also make new friends and learn to trust again. Again, some of the children are learning English as a third language. This inconsistency and the many challenges set the tone for the child's reading readiness and their ability to retain knowledge, or not (Martinez, 2013).

The complexity of all of it, in particular the overarching theory as an important lens to view complex strengths and struggles, is illustrated through the brief segment of Fabiola's notes about working with two brothers, one in 10th grade (Student A) and one in 11th grade (Student B). Martinez (2013) wrote,

> Having a set of brothers gives me the opportunity to see how two different students raised in the same household, with similar experiences does not necessarily mean the same outcome will occur.
>
> Student B tries hard to do his work even though I can see in his eyes that he knows that he can't do it without me. It takes a lot of guidance and one-on-one attention to help him do the work instead of just letting him work with a group and simply copy answers. Having him in a group causes the group to slow down because then I have to work with students that are in two different paces.

She noted that teachers often do not have the time to slow down for that one student who needs more attention because then the other 25 students are not given attention. She says, "Student B slides by and copies work if I do not sit with him and allow him to slowly but surely work out the homework" (Martinez, 2013).

She noted a disturbing experience with this student:

> While working on a packet for his English 101 class I was made aware of something huge that even made me feel guilty for assuming. The page consisted of fixing what was wrong with the sentence: "There are 33 seconds in a minute." All students had to do was correct the bold word. I ASSUMED he could at do this much on his own and simply translated the sentence expecting him to know the answer in Spanish. To my surprise the first answer he gave me was "One?" and the guessing just continued from there. After I told him that this was "easy" I was made aware that at 11th grade, he had never been taught his numbers in Mexico. (Martinez, 2013)

Then Martinez (2013) described his brother, Student A, who, on the other hand, has totally given up. "Para que maestra? Si voy a reprovar." "Why bother? I'm going to fail anyways." She said,

I know the correct response to that is supposed to be something positive, but what do I do when even I know that this student will most likely not graduate? Do I lie? All I can do is do my best to set up this student to be motivated. I know the student is involved in gang related activity. He does turn in homework, but only when I sit with him and help him. While reading short stories in English it takes him a good while to get through it and with a lot of errors along the way.

Martinez (2013) went on to say,

Student A did confide in me one day that their mother and four sisters are in Mexico while they live here with their father. The dad wasn't working so it made me wonder how things were getting paid. A few months later the student stayed after school for tutoring for the first time in 8 months. I couldn't help but ask why. Looking down and hesitant, he told me that due to their dad not working they had to leave their small house and rent a room in a stranger's home. Now the 3 men live in one room. He said that the owner told them that they can't do their homework in the living room, so now he stays after school with me for 3 hours to make sure his work is done before he goes home. This is helping his grades! I hope this is the beginning of a positive ending.

Heartfelt Questions for Teachers

Through critical approaches to how things are and things could be/should be for this population of students, Martinez said,

I have noticed from teachers teaching Specially Designed Academic Instruction in English (SDAIE) that often they seem to forget what it is that they signed up for. While tutoring a U.S. History class, a boring subject for students right from the beginning, I noticed the teacher did not even teach. The class was full English Language Learners (ELL's) and with them the migrant students I tutor. The teacher never left the desk, never lectured the chapters and never controlled the class. This alone made the class a problem for me, making me be the disciplinarian when that is not my job, it's hers.

   Eventually I decided to just focus on my migrant students and made sure they got ahead. The teacher would randomly show a power point on a television screen up on one corner of the room that was hardly visible. Power points don't work for my students and they can't keep taking notes. They are at a huge disadvantage with "teaching" techniques like this. She would pass out packets about chapters and simply put a due date, give a test on that day and move on to next chapter. Needless to say, all students were failing. As a tutor I can only do so much to attempt to help them understand a chapter and translate for them along with translating the packet. Why take a SDAIE class if one isn't prepared for what it takes to make those students succeed? It is documented that "The SDAIE teacher is a facilitator of learning; the teacher is the essential expert in a classroom typified by social interaction and the construction of meaning" (Sobul, 1995).

Martinez asked, "How will the Common Core affect ELL's and migrant students that are learning Spanish as a second language and English as a third?"

What Can We Do?

Martinez suggested that we can support migrant youth in spite of the struggles beyond their control by creating a positive environment and displaying respect for diversity and values. Her suggestions reveal work she has considered and internalized based on Critical Theory and Critical Literacy, with the overlap of exploring the knowledges of Conocimiento Theory. Critical theory stresses participation by all in the learning process, multiple sources of knowledge, and transformative action. Conocimiento Theory stresses the merging of the individual and the collective, the academic and the social, the whole person. Martinez suggested having older students mentor the younger ones. This would give them a chance to be mentors and share experiences and demonstrate trust. She noted that the teacher can personalize lessons based on the student's experiences. This can help the learners feel confident in the classroom. The teacher can implement assessments based on language proficiency that are appropriate to the student's academic needs (this would be transformative for the teacher as well as the students). It is also important that the teacher does some research about the learners' culture and language. This can help open the communication between parents and teacher.

Linking community resources (such as adult education programs or existing parenting programs) and schools has the potential of creating positive learning environments for both children and families (St. Clair, Jackson, & Zweiback, 2012). It is no secret that parent involvement is a huge factor in any child's education. Parents of migrant children suffer from the same challenges as their children: language barriers, confidence and education barriers. Programs that help the parent are useful and necessary.

Despite all of the challenges that migrant students go through due to their lifestyle, they also gain many advantages from the experiences of their lifestyle. The necessity of having to adapt to new environments is a skill that many people cannot grasp. These students also have the ability to solve problems on their own. They meet new challenges and are able to problem-solve and adapt with ease. Migrant students also have a wide-ranging knowledge of cultural and geographical diversity. Using this knowledge and these skills these students can develop confidence and a sense of self that can lead them towards a successful academic future.

According to Anzaldúa (1999), our muse for this work,

> To survive the Borderlands
> you must live sin fronteras
> be a crossroads. (p. 195)

References

Alarcón, F. X. (1997). *Laughing tomatoes and other spring poems* [Jitomates risueños y otros poemas de primavera]. San Francisco, CA: Children's Book Press.

Anzaldúa, G. (1990). *Haciendo caras* [Making face, making soul: Creative and critical perspectives by women of color]. San Francisco, CA, Aunt Lute Press.

Anzaldúa, G. (1999). *Borderlands: The new mestiza* [La frontera]. San Francisco, CA: Spinsters/ Aunt Lute Press.

Anzaldúa, G. (2002). Now let us shift … the path of conocimiento … inner work, public acts. In G. Anzaldúa & A. Keating (Eds.), *This bridge we call home: Radical visions for transformation* (pp. 540–578). New York, NY: Routledge.

Christensen, L. (2000). *Reading writing and rising up: Teaching about social justice and the power of the written word*. Milwaukee, WI: Rethinking Schools.

Espinosa, L. M. (2010). Assessment of young English language learners. In E. Garcia & E. A. Frede. *Young English language learners: Current research and emerging directions for practice and policy*. New York, NY: Teachers College Press.

Fox, J., & Rivera-Salgado, G. (Eds.). (2004). *Indigenous Mexican migrants in the United States*. Stanford, CA: Center for Comparative Immigration Studies.

Freire, P. (1985). *Politics of education*. Granby, MA: Bergin Garvey.

Hérnandez-Ávila, A., & Anzaldúa, G. (2010). Interview. In A. C. Elenes (Ed.), *Transforming borders: Chicana/o popular culture and pedagogy*. Lanham, MD: Lexington Books.

Jachman, A. (2002). Reading and the migrant student. *SEDL Letter*. Retrieved from http:// www.sedl.org/pubs/sedl-letter/v14n03/4.html

Ladson-Billings. G. (2009). *The dreamkeepers: Successful teachers of African American children*. New York, NY: Jossey-Bass.

Loeb, S., Fuller, B., Kagan, S. L., & Carrol, B. (2004). Child care in poor communities: Early learning effects of type, quality, and stability. *Child Development, 75*, 47–65.

Martinez, F. (2012). Unpublished manuscript.

Martinez, F. (2013). Unpublished manuscript.

Moll, L. C., Gonzalez, N., & Amanti, C. (2005). *Funds of knowledge: Theorizing practices in households, communities, and classrooms*. New York, NY: Lawrence Erlbaum.

Quintero, E. P. (2009). Young children and story: The path to transformative action. In S. Steinberg (Ed.), *Diversity: A reader*. New York, NY: Peter Lang.

Quintero, E. P., & Rummel, M. K. (2010). Problem posing, reflection, action: Literature and our lives. In C. Rhodes (Ed.), *Literature and social justice*. Newark, DE: International Reading Association.

Schweinhart, L. J., Barnes, H. V., & Weikart, D. P. (1993). *Significant benefits: The High/Scope Perry Preschool study through age 27. Monographs of the High/Scope Educational Research Foundation* (Number 10). Ypsilanti, MI: High/Scope Press.

Shonkoff, J. P., & Phillips, D. A. (2000). *From neurons to neighborhoods: The science of early childhood development*. Washington, DC: National Academies Press.

Sobul, D. (1995). Specially designed academic instruction in English. ED391357. Retrieved from http://files.eric.ed.gov/fulltext/ED391357.pdf

St. Clair, L., Jackson, B., & Zweiback, R. (2012). Six years later: Effect of family involvement training on the language skills of children from migrant families. *School Community Journal, 22*(1), 9–19.

Steinberg, S., & Kincheloe, J. (2009). *Christotainment: Selling Jesus through popular culture*. Boulder, CO: Westview.

Troia, G. A. (2004). Migrant students with limited English proficiency: Can Fast ForWord Language make a difference in their language skills and academic achievement? *Remedial and Special Education, 25*(6), 353–366.

Wright. A. (2005). *The death of Ramón González*. Austin, TX: University of Texas Press.

· 1 2 ·

THE SCHOOLING OF AFRICAN YOUTH IN ONTARIO SCHOOLS

What Have Indigenous African Proverbs
Got to Do With It?

George J. Sefa Dei
[Nana Sefa Atweneboah I]

Acknowledgments

I would like to thank the many Ghanaian, Nigerian, Kenyan, and Canadian local research assistants and consultants, students, parents, and elders who have in various degrees assisted in the cause of this longitudinal SSHRC-funded research. In Nigeria, there is Lateef Layiwola, Joy Odewumi, Chinyere Eze, Provost Hakeem Olato Kunbo Ajose-Adeogun, Tola Olajuwon, Dr. A. O. K. Noah, not to mention the many students and educators at the Adeniran Ogunsanya College of Education in Otto/Ijanikin, Lagos State, and the Lagos State University, Lagos. In Kenya, mention can be made of Samuel Njagi, Grace Makumi, Moodley Phylis, students and educators at Eggerton University, Ngoro, Nakuru and the University of Nairobi, Gichugu Primary School, Kandori Youth Polytechnic in the Embu area, Kenya. In Ghana, special thanks to Anane Boamah, Osei Poku, Kate Araba Stevens, Daniel Ampaw, Ebenezer Aggrey, Paa Nii, Alfred Agyarko, Professor Kola Raheem, and the many students, educators at local universities and parents and elders who generously gave their time and expertise to ensure the success of the field study. At the University of Toronto in Canada, contributions from Dr. Paul Adjei, Dr. Lindsay Kerr, Harriet Akanmori, Jennifer Jaguire, Isaac

Darko, Yumiko Kawano, Jadie McDonnell, Dr. Bathseba Opini, Shaista Patel, Mini Tharakkal, and Michael Nwalutu have all been enriching to the study. Finally, I want to thank Sarah Papoff of the Ontario Institute for Studies in Education of the University of Toronto for reading through, editing, and commenting on an earlier draft of this chapter.

Introduction

I begin this chapter with a story I recently heard when I gave a community address. Three adults appear before a Roman Catholic priest to confess their sins. One man is an ordained pastor who confesses that despite his calling, he cannot help looking at attractive young women. The second man claims he is an alcoholic who can hardly control his drinking spree. In fact, for no apparent reason, he feels he must take a drink every now and then. The third man confesses he is a habitual gossiper, and right at the moment of these confessions he can't control himself and is eager to get out of the room to gossip about what he has heard. My question is: why would someone even ask which of these three men has a serious problem? To me, all three have serious problems and it serves no purpose trying to create this hierarchy of sins. However, I also see this example as a problem of larger society in terms of our collective desires for hierarchies. We must find a way to address our culture of hierarchies. I find it necessary to start with this story, given that in raising issues of schooling, one is always trapped in a discourse of hierarchies in terms of the severity of issues for our youth in schools. Whatever the problems are, we owe it to ourselves as a collective responsibility to search for common ground and respond to the challenges.

The subject of youth culture is an interesting study in part because of the difficulty of understanding just what exactly constitutes a study of youth culture or sub-culture. For the purpose of my chapter, I conceptualize youth culture as both a knowledge system and social practice. Youth cultures would refer to the social experiences, everyday political practices and struggles, cultural productions and identity formations and expressions that characterize the ways youth engage society. Culture is about education and a transmission of knowledge about individual and community practices and social ethics. In broaching African/Black youth cultures and education, four interrelated areas can be identified: (a) how schools themselves are implicated in the production of such cultures (e.g., the role of schools in the production of Black youth cultures and sub-cultures of resistance); (b) how off-school (out of school?) knowledge helps sustain these cultures (e.g., how the youth tap into the wealth of community knowledge to build and strengthen their own cultural resistant practices); (c) how schools can tap into the wealth and richness of youth cultures to assist the delivery of education (e.g., pedagogically, how can educators use off-school knowledge gained from popular/media culture in the education of young learners); and (d) how local/Indigenous knowledge can be used to strengthen youth cultures (e.g., specifically, how can we use the teachings of African Indigenous proverbs to assist youth in the acquisition of positive/solution-oriented cultures and sub-cultures). This chapter will focus more on the latter.

There is much that can be learned from a critical study of youth cultures. Our youth of today—notwithstanding challenges they encounter in daily life—can and do demonstrate skills, talents, capabilities, and innovation when given the chance to excel. Often, youth come into conflict with adult and adult culture. We cannot cast this attitude as simply a question of intergenerational differences. I believe misunderstandings about youth and adult cultures often stem from a lack of deep appreciation of what youth in particular offer to society and what adults can learn from a critical engagement with youth. Of course, this is not to say youth practices and actions are not in need of adult critiques, guidance, and direction. In order to build youth cultures to sustain lives and communities educators have a responsibility to mould learners to be socially conscious. The schooling experiences of youth offer opportunities for educators, parents, and community workers to come together to assist the youth of today as they negotiate the tensions and challenges of contemporary society. There are questions about what educators can teach youth in schools, how and why that needs some focus and re-direction to ensure the strengths, capabilities, and contributions of youth are realized. Understanding the role of schooling and education in the cultivation of youth cultures is an important area of study.

This chapter begins a conversation about coming to understand Black and racialized youth experiences in the Canadian school system and what can be done to improve learning. For example, youth can develop a sense of self and collective identity, pride, social and collective responsibility, and community belonging. The task is far from being informed by a perspective that would deride the youth as being socially irresponsible. As noted, a number of youth have developed a commendable sense of community, social responsibility, personal probity, and collective pride in who they are and what they see as their

responsibilities to a larger citizenry. The problem is, we seldom hear about
these dimensions to Black youth life and cultures. Many youth daily exhibit
their creative tendencies/skills/attributes in popular culture, arts, literature,
and the sciences. Yet, we more often hear daily about Black youth violence,
crime, deviancy, and truancy. There is more that can be said about the making
and exhibition of Black excellence. In fact, the complex nature of Black youth
cultures and identities requires a critical examination of questions about what
it means to educate, how and why and what the youth learner of today can do
with their education. How do Black subjects come to learn to appreciate self,
collective, social responsibility? What role does education play in nurturing a
positive (solution-oriented) Black culture? How do we understand the complexity of Black youth cultures and experiences in the schooling contexts?
While this chapter may not have all the answers to these questions, it offers
an entry point into teaching about community, responsibility, and self-respect
and appreciation for/of oneself, peers, and authority.

My learning objective is to emphasize ways of teaching and learning to
improve educational outcomes for youth in a way that shows the purpose
of education as self and collective development and a transformation of our
communities in terms of what it means to be human. My goal is to focus on
particular teachings embedded in Indigenous African knowledge systems, particularly proverbs, and how these teachings can assist the work of educators
as they deliver education to contemporary learners. In fact, I take the notion
of character education as more than simply educating about self-discipline,
respect for oneself, peers, and authority. "Character education" has been so
individualized that it loses the collective implications for a community of
learners. Character, like discipline, can be talked about as if it is something to
be imposed rather than taught. I approach character education as fundamentally a sort of anti-colonial education that enables young learners to develop
a strong sense of self and collective identities, personal respect, agency, and
empowerment to community building and to work to create schools that
are healthy, working communities (see discussions in Dufault, 2003; Nucci
& Narváez, 2008; Salls, 2007; Smagorinsky & Taxe, 2005; Toulouse, 2011).
This education embraces local Indigenous knowings to challenge oppressive
structures and relations of schooling by promoting social values of community membership and responsibility, ethics, community belonging, and moral
fortitude. Such teachings are also about re-visioning schooling and education to espouse at its centre such values as the fight for social justice, equity,
fairness, resistance, and collective responsibilities. In other words, as argued

elsewhere (Dei, 2013), such education is about looking at "character and civic education" differently—placing power and equity at the centre with a critical understanding of community and the role of communities.

Consequently, the chapter moves beyond a critical interrogation of the systems and structures of educational delivery. It focuses specifically on the pedagogical possibilities of African Indigenous proverbs to educate youth about notions of community; responsibility; character development; self and collective discipline; respect for oneself, peers, and authority; a consciousness of identity; and a politics of mutual interdependence for collective survival. My argument is that when these values are well ingrained in learners, they are able to bring a sense of personal responsibility to their education not only to challenge schooling and its relations, but also to carve a path for their own education—notwithstanding some of the conventional processes and aspects of schooling that fail to produce effective learning outcomes for Black youth. I use "Indigenous" to refer to these African teachings because they are part of the local philosophies of education, and coming to know that is taught to the young from infancy until they mature into adulthood. These teachings are based on "long-term occupancy" of particular communities and the knowledge consciousness that emerges with an awareness of the interdependence of society, culture, and nature. They are teachings associated with understandings of Mother Earth, teachings of the land, environment, and the social ecology of a place. While it may be argued that these teachings are context-specific, we point out that their lessons cut across cultural boundaries and social spaces. It is the responsibility of the teacher to work with different knowledge systems in educating the youth so as to appreciate global diversity of knowledge.

Decolonizing Education

To create a decolonized education, attention must be paid to subverting structures of schooling rather than maintaining dominance and hegemony. Colonizing relations of schooling must be understood in terms of the maintenance of a culture of hierarchies, merit badges, privileging certain bodies of knowledge, experiences, histories, cultures, and identities. There is a role of local/Indigenous knowledge in subverting the internalized colonial hierarchies of conventional schooling by promoting Indigenous teachings that focus specifically on social values, community building, and different understandings of character education such as fighting for social justice and equity.

Among the many challenges facing educators and youth on school and education is how learners can be assisted to develop a sense of connectedness to the processes of educational delivery. These would include issues relating to teaching, learning, and administration of education in ways that make meaningful sense in terms of how youth live their cultures in society. The question of how schools have become sites of disenfranchisement and marginalization for many bodies, rather than sites of opportunity and possibilities, is still pertinent. The questions of equity and inclusion are still begging for redressing in our schools (Dei, Mazzuca, McIssac, & Zine, 1997). In calling for the "boundaries to be redrawn" we are asking for new ways of educating young learners using multiple knowledge systems, including some of the teachings of Indigenous communities that highlight personal and collective development, mutual interdependence, social ethics, accountability, and responsibility to each other and our social and physical environments.

Of late, I have enthused about the intervention of "education as a right," in terms of the right to education beyond all borders, as a component of "global education" and as a spiritual understanding of what education is and ought to be for all learners. For many, the high cost of education and question of access globally is making it increasingly clear that education has become a privilege. But we need to challenge this trend. I have also become more cynical of how the neoliberal discourse in education has co-opted progressive educational language particularly around issues of responsibility and accountability. The neoliberal agenda in education has ushered in individualism, competitiveness, deregulation, standardization, quality with equity, and restrictive competencies. A neoliberal agenda has seen schools run as profit-making ventures, and finances and financial imperatives define what constitute academic programming and quality. In such ventures we seem to lose all that it means to to be human or create persons with a deeper conscience and understanding. While we crave efficiency and perfection, we must simultaneously take questions of humanhood, emotions, and feelings along the ride. What is rational does not simply have to make economic sense. We do not necessarily have to maximise profits. There is a place for the logics of intuition that is not defined by what is rational and intelligible to a particular way of reading our worlds.

In a neoliberal context, responsibility and accountability are spoken of in individual terms. The individual learner and the parent are being asked to be responsible for their own education. States are not only shedding collective responsibilities but also a troubling discourse of personal responsibility and ethics has dwarfed any calls for a systemic implication and a critique of the institutionalized structures for educational delivery. I am also amazed about how the neoliberal discourse has co-opted and mobilised individual "success" for public consumption. Of course, no parent would want their child not to succeed in school. But when youths fail at school it is only intellectually hon-est that we ask why and what perhaps are the responsibilities of schools them-selves and the wider community at large in not only producing such failures, but also ensuring collective success for all learners. We acknowledge that we must speak about the responsibility of the young learner herself or himself. But this must not quickly slide into pathologizing and blaming communities, parents, and learners who may in fact be victims of an oppressive school system.

I use the term oppressive in the sense of power relations of schooling: schools forcing a culture of individualism upon young learners, a language of what is normal, neutral, reasonable, and objective fails to account for dif-ferences in knowledge systems or a recognition of the multi-centric ways of knowing about ourselves. We are speaking of the terror of the culture of same-ness (see hooks, 1992) and the "one size fits all" syndrome. And yes, it is equally problematic when we speak of the experiences of all Black youth as homogenous just as when schools adopt an approach that hardly deals with difference and diversity in the student population. Educators may have good intentions and care about their learners succeeding at school. That goodwill may not be in dispute. But expressing and harbouring such good intentions and goodwill does not mean the system does not have inherent problem spots that contribute to youth failures. Correspondingly, we note that schooling is too important for parents, communities, and learners to leave it to school teachers and administrators alone. This is where all efforts at grounding the learner in the purpose of education, responsibilities of learning, and the teachings of values of shared/collective responsibility become important. The neoliberal educational agenda's preoccupation with well-trained, professional teachers, school administrators able to deliver "measureable success" work-ing with well-defined learning aims and goals to ensure that all learners have equal opportunities in education may be well-intentioned. But it is problem-atic when the discourse ignores the fact that the learning process occurs both within the institutionalized structures and processes of schooling as well as forces and development outside the formal classroom.

The foregoing raises the nebulous question of inclusion. I say nebulous because the "inclusion" talk has become very seductive talk of late. We all crave inclusion, but what are the particular responsibilities of those who are already included? How do we take up critical inclusion in a meaningful way that involves critical questions of power, knowledge production, creating new and counter spaces, and holding people accountable for maintaining and sustaining exclusion? I want to move away from a discussion of inclusion as always entailing some other forms of exclusion. We can have genuine inclusive space that is not about excluding anyone, in other words, ensuring that inclusion and exclusion do not exist simultaneously. To achieve such ends, critical inclusion should be about creating new spaces, having a power-centeredness, and the pursuit of shared responsibilities to ensure the mutual existence of all. The power-centering means giving up unearned privilege. But it must not be viewed as a net loss nor as a form of exclusion. This reading is only possible if we freely contest the notion of "inclusion." Inclusion has become bland, very liberalized, with no recourse to power, accountability, and transparency. Furthermore, as we aspire for inclusion, we must ask inclusion into what? Inclusion should be transformative of existing power structures that either oppress, devalue, or marginalize certain bodies. Inclusion should be about centering experiences and not being made to be tangential to a dominant experience.

In effect, inclusion is about power and knowledge. Many of us, especially those who have been forcefully displaced/bodies of colour have found ourselves sitting on the margins for quite some time now notwithstanding the fact that we may continually assert our agencies. So what does it mean then for us to think critically about belonging to schooling communities in an era of inclusion and diversity? It is more than becoming a part of something meaningfully. It is about being valued, accorded power, and an acknowledgement of our own knowledge and cultural knowing in concrete terms. There are inherent dangers associated with the pluralism/democracy discourse as far as schooling is concerned. While we may call for spaces for multiple histories/ perspectives to persist in our institutions, many times this notion of "plurality" is co-opted—especially in "all sides of an issue" and "freedom of speech" scenarios. This avoids particular bodies (the dominant and those with power) being held responsible and accountable for their actions. It fails to recognize the severity of issues for certain bodies. Therefore, there is a need to target schooling responses to particular populations even as we claim "social justice for all," as in the particular reference to school policy or platitude. "Social justice for all" may be the ideal thing to do, but it is not the only model of social justice. Another model of social justice calls for a recognition of the particularity of justice as well as the severity of experiences and a need to direct educational measures that address specific problems facing our respective diverse schooling population. When we approach inclusion this way we end up serving the interests of a collective.

We cannot approach inclusion as if it is objective, neutral, normal, and reasonable in a context when what is normal, objective, natural, and reasonable has become about the particularity of a dominant experience that tends to be imposed on all. Reading inclusion and justice this way does not mean there are no shared values nor that in pursuing such ideology one stands the risks of Balkanizing the school curriculum (a curriculum already fragmented). It certainly does not imply we are giving preferential treatment to certain segments of the schooling population. It is only a recognition of the power of history and the possibilities of privilege that position bodies differently in our school system to make claims regarding earned and unearned advantages. It is noteworthy that many times the privileges that the dominant seek to assert are unearned privileges (e.g., right to be the main, authoritative voice—their norms become the standard-bearers and the tacit norms of collective reference). Today, the democratization of education can generally be perceived as mutually beneficial, and we may be right in explicitly aiming for this, as consistent with Paulo Freire's (1970) articulation of the inclusive community education in his *Pedagogy of the Oppressed*. We need education to be beneficial to all in that all learners can decolonise and liberate ourselves. Yet, I also want to suggest that for Black, marginalised/colonized, and Indigenous bodies and communities we are not looking for this desire of democratization of education explicitly. We put the politics of decolonization at the centre of schooling more so than democratic politics of schooling. We must simply see the benefits of (democratic) education for all as a by-product of critical pedagogies of liberation as they require decolonisation.

The Schooling Experiences of Black/Racialized Youth in Euro-Canadian Contexts: What Educational Research in Ontario Tells Us

The fact that the Ontario schooling population is diverse is not in dispute. In fact, a brief context of Ontario's diversity through the lens of the specific case of Toronto District School Board (TDSB) statistics is in order. In a fact sheet put out by the School Board it is noted that "visible minorities make up 43 percent of the Toronto city population" (Statistics Canada, 2009) and that the "TDSB student body alone speak 75 different languages (not including regional dialects). English is spoken at home by 53% of the TDSB students, followed by Chinese and Chinese dialects (11.8%), and then Tamil (5.6%). About 24% of TDSB students were born outside of Canada, in more than 175 countries. More than 11,500 (12%) of secondary students have been in Canada for 3 years or less" (http://www.tdsb.on.ca, fact sheet). This clear evidence of growing diversity can be described in a relative sense for other provincial school boards. The pressing challenge for educators has been how to take advantage of this growing diversity in the student population to educate young learners of today. It is simply not enough to acknowledge this diversity and not engage in concrete educational change to transform the way we teach, learn, and administer schools today.

There are many successes in the current school system one can point to. We definitely have committed educators, administrators, policy makers, parents, and community workers hard at work to provide education to diverse youth. Many students continue to excel in the system despite the odds against them. These students are a credit to themselves, their schools, parents, and educators. But we cannot be complacent because there are mounting challenges. Not all students are doing well or feel engaged in the system. In fact, it is only the privileged body who will deny that we still have a long way to go to ensure that our schools meet the needs and concerns of a diverse student body. Educational research in Ontario, for example, points to the fact that race and poverty constitute the two most powerful drawbacks to our current school system (Toronto District School Board, 2009). For many Black students, race and class work together to produce social alienation and disengagement. Race and poverty continually demarcate the experiences of Black and minority bodies in the school system. Feelings of students' disengagement, alienation, exclusion, and a lack of a sense of belonging to their schools can be placed on the doorstep of experiences relating to race, class, gender, sexual, linguistic, and religious differences and oppressions.

The cultural politics of schooling affect racialized bodies negatively as they are not able to tap into their rich traditions of history, culture, and identity in ways that make them feel empowered in schools. There is the denial of race and social difference. Approaches to classroom pedagogies and instruction often operate on the assumption of one size fits all. Diversity is acknowledgement, but what it takes to respond to such diversity and difference in schools requires concrete action rather than lip-service acknowledgment. "Standardization recipes" (Lewin, 2008) of schooling create a sense of normal as defined by the particular interests of dominant bodies. The "marketization of education," to use Kenway and Epstein's (1996) words, has actually intensified the differences in schools and the undercurrent tensions and divisions that can, and continue to, tear the fabric of society. The differential impact of the neoliberal educational agenda and the economics of schooling such as the high cost of going to high school, college, and university is apparent in the ever-increasing tuition and the abuse that many bodies have to contend with daily. The racialization of poverty for Black and other minority families (e.g., high unemployment; underutilization and non-recognition of [foreign] credentials and skills; unequal access to education; high drop-out rates for racialized youth; immigrant students disproportionately placed in basic non-academic level and special needs programs; and the differential impact of safe schools policy, expulsions, and suspension) are just a few concerns that have historically been enunciated (see Brathwaite & James, 1996; Dei et al., 1997; Zine, 2000). Many of our schools, particularly those serving diversified communities, are under-resourced. Consequently, schools need differential resources given the context and make-up of their populations. Funding is a key factor in doing any equity work, since schools are passing the buck, so to speak. As the same time as the effects of racialized poverty become clear we have cutbacks to frontline workers (e.g., school community advisors and equity officers) who are confronting the effects of racialized poverty.

There are other contemporary challenges. When it comes to representation, there is the challenge of visual representation (i.e., representing diversity in the visual culture of schools); knowledge representation (i.e., the active learning of multiple cultures, histories, experiences, and knowledges); and physical representation (i.e., proactive recruitment, retention, and promotion of diverse physical bodies/staff and students) (see Codjoe, 1997, 2001; Dei, James, James-Wilson, Karumanchery, & Zine, 2000; Dei, James-Wilson, & Zine, 2002). Identity and the link with schooling is another concern. Race is salient for engaging schooling. As already noted, as far as schooling of minority youth is concerned, race and social difference provide the context for power and domination in schools. Yet rather than place race and difference on the table, a particular intellectual gymnastics avoids a serious discussion of the issues. This is ironic in a culture that is continually trafficking race and social difference.

On the question of culture, a liberal understanding of culture sees culture as a problem rather than a pursuit of a critical education of youth and home cultures. Culture can be a site of empowerment and a source of disempowerment, and what critical education can do is to engage culture and pedagogy as sites and sources of knowing. The links of culture and pedagogy (e.g., different learning and teaching styles in cultures) offer important lessons of how we rethink schooling for diverse youth. Also, there is the question of language. There is a failure to promote and enhance local/Indigenous, minority and first languages in schools to assist in youth learning. This is critical, given that language is a mode of transmission of culture, history, identity, and ancestral knowledge. Language as identity and liberation—challenging learners to question and subvert the (dominant) language that minimizes, denigrates, and penalizes. Language can also be about resistance. We can challenge English (specifically correct grammar) as a barrier to success (see Gill, 2012). Rather than promote youth cultures in schools we see the ways cutbacks to equity work impinge upon the teaching of culture, Indigenous language, and identity. Since the mid-1990s, the repeated cutbacks to frontline education services such as school community advisors; equity departments; and programs such as ESL, African Heritage, and adult education have all affected Black youth schooling success. Underresourced and underfunded community organizations have been forced to step in and fill the gap to make sure that the needs of children from racialized communities are being met.

Many Black youth find themselves disconnected from the school system. Elsewhere, we spoke of how these students are "pushed out" (Dei, Campbell, Holmes, Mazzuca, & McIsaac, 1995). We made a distinction between "dropping out/push out" and "disengagement." A number of youth may appear physically present in school but are disengaged mentally, emotionally, and psychologically. It is such disengagement that often leads to dropping out. Because more often than not forces beyond their immediate control lead students to drop out (although they make the direct decision to leave prematurely), we argued that technically the students have been forced/pushed out. School polices that have worked in some jurisdictions to lower dropout rates have included having a strong equity focus in education (e.g., curriculum, pedagogy, teacher representation, multiple knowledge); programs that address issues of accountability and transparency in educational delivery and hold schools and teachers accountable for students success/failures; as well as having/employing inclusive schooling practices that address the needs of all students, taking into account racial, class, gender, disability, religious, and sexuality barriers to education. We know that when students feel a sense of ownership in their schooling and learning process they become engaged learners. Creating schools as communities with parents and families having central roles also helps in enhancing learning for youth, as do school-to-work transitions programs that give youth a sense of a future. Educational policies that also target specific vulnerable groups (while seeking the welfare of all students) help to enhance youth learning because such policies also recognize the severity of issues for different bodies. Addressing questions of learners' identities (race, class, gender, sexual, disability, etc.) is significant for schooling outcomes. Schools that have such orientations and employ educational policies guarded by these ideas have succeeded. There is data for this. Contextual learning is critical. For example, for Aboriginal students, we need to think seriously about Indigenous/Aboriginal schooling where local teachings are emphasized and there is a place for elders, families, and communities in schooling. The curriculum is targeted to students' lived experiences, cultures, and histories. Addressing the issue of teacher representation is also significant. After all, conventional schooling may not work for all. Aboriginal control of education is critical, as are community programs that seek working relations with local communities, educators, teachers, youth, and other caregivers.

Pedagogical Re-visioning of Schooling and Education

Faced with the above mounting challenges, critical research must explore multiple strategies of educational delivery for young learners. I highlight specific responses around pedagogy and classroom instruction as one of the approaches to strengthen young learners' ability to deal with the challenges of schooling and ensure equitable learning outcomes. There is a need for a pedagogical re-visioning of schooling and education in order to build a sense of identity, purpose, and meaning in life for the young learner. This is important in order to empower the young learner to engage schools and education effectively. Understanding what "self-empowerment" means in youth learning is a starting point. Self-empowerment is a question of power, knowing who one is, and having a sense of self-identity. It also means learners developing in themselves an ability to do things for oneself and becoming a socially responsible individual. It also speaks about respect for oneself, one's peers, and authority. With such teachings, educational success is that which is meaningful and purposeful to oneself, our families, peers, and communities. This helps young learners bridge their social and academic success, i.e., striving for a combination of the two. It also means understanding one's culture, history, and heritage, coming to know about oneself as a person with an identity (e.g., what it means to be African, African Canadian). It is also about appreciating the relevance of knowledge. Knowledge is meaningful if it compels action, brings about social change. This is knowledge that makes a difference and helps improve upon the place where one belongs. It is also about coming to voice, speaking out on racism and other oppressions. The empowerment of the learner comes with an appreciation of community and social responsibility. It is about creating and becoming a community. Any community is as good as we collectively work to make it! In schools the learner works with a community of learners and community work is pursued as helping others and oneself.

The question is, how can educators teach these ideas to the young learner? There are several ways to educate, and at this juncture we want to take up the issue of the teachings, pedagogic and instructional relevance of Indigenous African proverbs. While proverbs are specific to a given context their inherent teaching are words of wisdom that an educator can work with in different contexts to educate youth to be socially responsible and mature. I am interested in the ways in which Canadian educators working with African and other youth can bring some of the ideas and moral teachings of African proverbs to help in the education and empowerment of the Canadian learner. Indigenous teachings have relevance across borders and spaces. Such teachings borrow from other knowledge, and local communities do not work with the sense of a strict ownership and monopoly over such knowledge. There is an understanding that knowledge is co-created with others, it is shared and builds on its base through multiple applications in varied contexts.

The Place of African Indigenous Proverbs

African Indigenous philosophies include the use proverbs as a way of knowing and coming to know. Proverbs are discussed as a form of epistemology that show the interconnections of society, culture, and nature. Proverbs are about cultural interpretations and understandings of the social, physical, and metaphysical worlds of African peoples. The social meanings conveyed in local African proverbs have important lessons, including expectations for how individuals and groups are to live in communities. While these proverbs are culture-specific, their lessons transcend borders and boundaries. What do and can Indigenous proverbs, cultural songs, and cultural stories, fables, riddles, and folktales teach the contemporary youth? How do proverbs edu-cate the learner of today to be socially responsible? Do Indigenous proverbs of African communities have a place in our school system when it comes to the education of the contemporary learner? These questions are engaged in this chapter. Proverbs feature prominently in virtually all traditional African cultures. Ogiorumua (2007) wrote that proverbs lace everyday conversations, debates, and storytelling of elders and other cultural custodians. Proverbs are imbued with deep thoughts in customary law, ethics, social relations, cul-ture, spirituality, education, politics, and economics. Proverbs embody the values, aesthetics, cultural generalizations, and philosophical precepts by which African peoples live their lives (see also Jablow, 1961). The Yorubas of Nigeria attest to the value of proverbs with a saying, "a proverb is the horse that can carry one swiftly to the discovery of ideas." Through an understand-ing of proverbs, one can be considered a wise man/woman. Opoku (1999) long ago noted that African proverbs express the wisdom of the African peo-ple and are keys to the understanding of African ways of life in the past and the present. This chapter uses the teachings of African Indigenous proverbs, songs, and cultural stories in the education of youth in Canadian schooling. The focus is on the relevance of teachings of Indigenous proverbs around social responsibility, community-building, mutual interdependence, ethics, and moral/character development, and how these teachings can enhance youth learning in pluralistic contexts. The chapter is informed by findings of longitudinal field research on Indigenous philosophies of selected African countries.

Since 2010 I have been a principal investigator in on-going Social Sci-ences and Humanities Research Council (SSHRC) longitudinal research in Ghana, Nigeria, and Kenya, examining Indigenous African philosophies (specifically knowledge systems embedded in local proverbs, songs, folktales, and story forms) for their pedagogic and instructional relevance in youth education (see also Dei, 2010). As part of this research I have also been working with Canadian educators to highlight the pedagogic, instructional, and communicative values in youth education through the development of lesson plans and curriculum units for using African proverbs in the education of young learners. The primary focus of this work has been to understand the use and meanings of local proverbs and their instructional, pedagogic, and communicative values, especially teachings about identity, self-worth, respect for self, peers, and authority, and the obligations and responsibilities of community belonging. To offer some specifics of data gathering, working with Canadian graduate and African undergraduate students and other local assistants we have interviewed a total of over 50 African educational theorists and practitioners in Ghana, Nigeria, and Kenya. We have interviewed over 60 key informants (elders, cultural custodians, including parents and guardians) known locally for their knowledge and theorizing of local proverbs, folktales, and stories, as well as over 100 college/university, basic/elementary, and vocational/polytechnic training institute students in the three countries. In all we have collected 402 proverbs from Ghana; 251 proverbs, 12 cultural stories, 87 riddles, 10 songs and five folktales from Kenya; and 332 proverbs from Nigeria, all from different ethnicities. Currently, I continue to work with teachers from selected Toronto and Ontario elementary and secondary schools in the school boards to develop and field-test the draft of lesson plans and curriculum units for teaching African proverbs in Canadian schools.

I will now explain more fully some of the deeply embedded meanings of these proverbs for the education of contemporary learners.

Kiembu of Kenya Proverbs

1) Ndukaie gutari kuratuka [We must not lose hope before it is dark].

Hope is all we have. Unless the day has ended, our time on Earth has come to an end, we must still cling to hope. To hope is to dream and work toward a future. This proverb has pedagogic and instructional relevance in the school system, particularly in a time when a number of youth have developed despair, nihilism, hopelessness, and a sense of feeling lost and living a dead-end existence. Therefore, this proverb could be used to counter the challenge of "stolen futures" and the fear of "wasted lives" that confront a number of our youth daily. The proverb can also be used to teach the youth to resist their futures being taken away from them and to believe that we make our own histories and create our own futures. It is about hope, responsibility, determination, agency, and resistance. It teaches about the power of human agency and that young learners can aspire to greater heights and believe in the power of human imagination. In so far as there is life there is hope. Young learners can be encouraged to be positive in life and make the best of all situations. A critical engagement of the proverb is also to discuss with youth the challenges that they are likely to confront and how to overcome such obstacles. It is to empower the young to control their own destinies and to believe that whatever they set their minds on, by believing in themselves and the power of destiny, they will be successful.

2) Ngunia irugamagua ni kiria kiri thiini [One is understood by others through his behavior].

It is the actions of a person that tell about their character, moral fiber, and the values they cherish and protect. People get to know a person by looking at what he or she does, what they stand for and the views they hold. The proverb teaches about the importance of good behavior, leading a life of humility, respect, and care for others. It can also teach about how youth can make their lives meaningful for the communities that they are part of. It is to remind the young that adults keep a watchful eye on the youth and are able to tell the sort of person one can grow up to be. If a youth gets into trouble, an adult can foretell how they may act as an adult from their immediate actions. One cannot hide their character as their actions will betray them. This proverb exhorts the young to always aspire to do good and be of impeccable behavior through their daily actions.

Igbo of Nigeria Proverbs

3) Miri masia ogazu, agwa ya adighi agbachapu [A bird does not change its feathers because the weather is bad].

Again, the Igbo would say no intensity of rain causes a guinea fowl to lose its spotted feathers. Hardship or adverse conditions often do not mar a person's destiny. This proverb literally suggests that a bird does not change itself, or its nature, just because of adverse conditions, so why should we? This proverb has deep moral and pedagogical relevance in today's increased crime and violence. Violence is common globally. Sometimes houses are vandalized, stores are looted, and people are violently attacked. However, we also know these actions do not happen at this intensity on a regular basis. So why should an adverse condition drive people to behave in ways in which they would not normally behave? It is in such instances that this proverb reminds us to be who we are, to trust our innate goodness and humanity, even when adverse situations provide us with the opportunity to behave otherwise. This proverb is valuable as a tool to remind youth to remain respectable citizens of the classroom, even when they are provided with the opportunity to behave in unruly ways. It reminds young learners to be responsible, disciplined, and remain true to themselves at all times, even when the gaze of the classroom teacher is absent. It is a teaching that exhorts youth to not indulge in vandalism or stealing, even if nobody is looking. It is such lessons of firmness, decisiveness, remaining true to oneself, etc., right from childhood, that will carry on as children grow up to become the future adult citizens.

4) Ihe nesi mkpi isi di ya nime aru [What makes the goat stink is inside its body].

The pedagogic lesson of this saying is that an individual's character lies deep within his or her personality. Character is an essential and priceless thing to have. It is what one is and what makes one's whole being and conveys much about a person. It is for this reason that character can never be hidden, and no matter how much one may try to hide it, one's true character will eventually be revealed. If one has a bad character, the negativity stems from inside the heart and soul; thus if one wishes to change their character, they must begin by examining what is in their heart and soul. Therefore, building one's personality also means building one's character and morals. In regard to schooling and pedagogy, this proverb teaches us that change begins from the inside, that we must always look deeply within a person to truly understand their true character. A critical pedagogic and instructional engagement of this proverb thus requires the educator to ask questions about the extent to which one's social environment, including peers and friends, shapes what is inside, the self. In other words, the analysis of this proverb requires a linking of the inner self to the outer environment in terms of prevailing structures as well as social and political conditions. Taken by its literal meaning, this proverb focuses on personal responsibility. If it is to be applied to the making of individual success and achievement in school, this proverb would seem to suggest that the world is more willing to help those people who help themselves or who are willing to self-assess. While the proverb is certainly note-worthy and greatly applicable to our educational system, it cannot be engaged in a way that places a great deal of the responsibility of success on the student's shoulders. A critical pedagogic engagement requires the classroom teacher to consider questions of equity, such as: are all students equally equipped to put their best efforts into scholarly matters? How do we account for differences in access, abilities, and learning styles? Should teachers only be motivated to teach students who are motivated to learn, etc.?

Akan of Ghana Proverbs

5) Se Aketetua benya animuonyam wo badwa mu a, na efri kahyire a, eda asee
[If a pot will get its glory, then it's from the potter's duster].

This is about the recognition of reciprocity and reciprocal relationships. This proverb implies that a pot is supported by a seat before it can stand still because of the way it's carved. This means for every success there are contributing forces and factors and we should acknowledge those who have created the path and whose hard work has made the success we carry today possible. We stand on the shoulders of those who have gone before us. Success is not through our own individual efforts. It is part of collective exercise and community sacrifice. Anyone who is successful in life must never forget all who have had a hand in their success. The proverb offers many useful lessons for the young learner. A parent, teacher, community worker, a classroom mate, or school peer have in various ways contributed to our success. While hard work is important, the successful learner is so because he or she has been part of a community of learners and has had parents and teachers all giving a helping hand. Very often the learner may falsely believe all their achievements, glory, and fame were due strictly to their own efforts. Understanding the notion of community sacrifice, especially for Black youth, is important because it helps restore a sense of giving back to their communities. It offers a justification for rendering community service, to be grateful to one's parents, teachers, peers, and community for their support. This helps restore in the learner a sense of community ethic and social responsibility to others. Just as in the Akan tradition a husband or wife is a sign of glorification on each other, so must the teacher and student or the child and parent be a sign of glorification on each other. As the saying goes, behind a successful man there is a good woman; likewise, behind a very successful learner there is a good, caring teacher. Far too often the youth of today forget the history of the personal, community, and collective sacrifices that paved the way for their success in life. They develop a sense of no obligation or responsibility unto others and become so individualistic that they feel no sense of accountability to anyone. The teachings of this proverb offer a different knowledge-base on which to ground contemporary youth to grow with a deep sense of community obligation, social responsibility, respect for others, self, peers, and authority, and an appreciation of history and sacrifices of others in life.

6) Prayetia etwi adwareye a, eho efiri no, na prayetia nso ho efiri [As a short broom is being used to clean the bathroom, it also gets cleaned].

This proverb is about humility in our claims to know and recognition of the limits of our own knowing. A humble youth has the chance to know more by their humility of knowing. No one has the entire repository of knowledge. Through the act of teaching others, the teacher herself or himself learns, and vice versa, through learning, the learner influences the teacher. The essence of this proverb is to teach about the learning process as a collective journey of the teacher and the student. While the student is taught by the teacher, the teacher also learns from the student. No one has a monopoly over knowledge. The teacher is not all-knowing, and a student can teach the teacher as part of a collective learning undertaking. This proverb accords knowledge-creation to students and they become co-producers of knowledge in the classroom. It teaches about humility in claims to know, and an appreciation that learning has no limits and that we all continually learn from each other daily. No matter how big, small, tall, or short the learner or teacher is, we learn from each other. Teaching and learning are processes of self-discovery of knowledge for both teacher and the learner. The classroom teacher can engage this proverb as part of classroom instruction to empower their students and build in them a sense of power to know and to produce their own knowledge that others can learn from. It can be used to educate about the mutual responsibilities of all learners in the classroom; that the learner who learns more by teaching the classroom friend will also be building upon their own knowledge-base. Sometimes we may not recognize how much others have impacted upon our own knowledge-base until we realize that learning is a collective undertaking and every social practice continues the seeds of knowledge that is shared and can be impacted upon multiple bodies in the learning and educational process. This proverb can also highlight the teaching that there is a causation for every human action, and the youth must understand that nothing exists in isolation or is mutually exclusive from everything else around them. In effect, the proverb teaches about mutual benefits in the spirit of reciprocity and reciprocal relationships.

7) Aboa Opra tubon enso owankyie a, onni dabre nti [An animal digs a hole for another to lie in].

Opra is the name of an animal in the Akan language that digs, and *owankyie* is an animal that likes to lie in a hole. Usually it is the opra that does the digging and the owankyie will take advantage of the hole and satisfy himself. The opra has never asked the owankyie to either reciprocate or pay him back for the hole but it knows this is common knowledge that the owankyie cannot easily take credit for. This proverb is about making sacrifices in life not just for oneself but for others as well. It is intended to teach about responsibility to others and not simply always looking to immediate gratification and reciprocal benefits in what we do for others. While the proverb recognizes reciprocity and reciprocal relationships, it also acknowledges that sometimes in life simply doing something for the benefit of others can be rewarding. It is an accomplishment that history and posterity will come to judge. This proverb also instructs that we all have been bestowed with different gifts and talents. The question is, what do we do with our talents and gifts and if we see our skills as something not only for our sole benefit but also something to share in life with others? The young learner who is smart has a responsibility to assist the student mate facing learning difficulties. There is a responsibility to put our knowledge to our own and others' benefit. This does not mean doing things to please others. One must please oneself first, but life is more than the individual. The expectation of community membership and social responsibility places the individual within a community and he/she only makes sense in relation to the community they are part of. A society that sees each individual as an island unto oneself does not hold together and is consumed by pettiness, rugged individualism, and destructive competitiveness. It is both the advent and privilege of history that someone has to create a path for others to pass through at a later point. The classroom teacher can engage this proverb to teach about history, power, responsibility, accountability, and ethics.

8) Se akokonini ye kese a, na ne were afri se ofri kosua mu [A cock becomes big forgetting that it comes from an egg].

In life we often forget our humble beginnings and start to act in ways that show pomposity, arrogance, and ingratitude. Yet we are fragile and life is like a shell. It can easily break. No matter how big someone is today, they must not forget that they started small. This proverb teaches about knowing one's history and beginnings in life as such knowledge offers checks and balances upon one's actions. The proverb asks the youth to know their roots, to know where they are coming from so as not to forget where they are going. It calls for a grounded-ness in history and culture in order to know oneself. It also abhors arrogance and ingratitude, especially when one forgets one's humble beginnings and the hard work on the part of others that it took to reach where one is today. The idea of knowing the history is to let the lessons of history teach us lest we soon forget. A poor person becomes pompous and arrogant when they get rich forgetting that she/he made it from grass to grace. Forgetting this history can be costly in life. To know one's history and roots is to know oneself and to begin to appreciate one's purpose in life. History is more than events and discoveries. It is about a totality of lived experiences, and a knowledge of one's beginnings can help mold the learner to understand the meaning of life and one's purpose and social existence.

The pursuit of knowledge as being about our social existence should broach history in order to understand the complete history of ideas and events that have shaped, and continue to shape, our continued social existence. When we forget our beginnings or lose touch with our history (just like culture) we are bound to be lost at some point. Similarly, we grow even stronger and bigger from our humility, not from our pomposity. These virtues need to be ingrained in the thought processes of contemporary youth for them to appreciate the true meaning of life, social existence, history, and humility. The proverbs can also be used to teach about respect for the elderly and those in authority positions. The proverb shows that the road to where they are now started from humble beginnings and was achieved through hard work, sacrifice, and appreciation of others.

Discussion

Increasingly, schools, educators, and community workers are exploring multiple ways to reach the youth. There is emerging understanding on the part of many critical educators, for example, that we have to diversify our teaching and instructional methods if we are to reach youth from diverse backgrounds. One style of teaching and instruction may not fit all. This means we must explore different approaches to convey knowledge and understanding. One such area that holds some possibilities for youth education is working with multiple knowledge and ways of knowing. This chapter has sought to establish an appreciation of African Indigenous proverbs as a way of knowing with instructional, pedagogic, and communicative relevance for youth education. My concern has not been with the how of integrating such knowledge into schools; that will call for the development of lesson plans and curriculum units around these proverbs (see Dei et al., 2007). Although our focus has been with African proverbs, it is maintained that the teachings of these proverbs, notwithstanding their specific contexts, speak to youth from diverse backgrounds. North American youth experience a culture that is highly competitive, individualistic, and emphasizes rights over responsibilities. While not passing any moral judgements and evaluations that can be dismissive of other people's values, I would assert that in order to educate youth on issues of peace, love, equity, and social justice, and to create a community of learners thriving in healthy, sustainable environments, the social values of community, responsibility, and cooperation have more to offer the youth of today. Our schools can thus educate using these principles and teachings of respect, discipline for oneself, peers, authority, and elders, community, social responsibility, mutual interdependence, expressed in local African and other Indigenous proverbs.

Clearly, the study of proverbs, like fables, folktales, story forms, Indigenous cultural stories, parables, and riddles, presents significant pedagogic, instructional, and curriculum challenges for schools and educators working with youth in our school systems. The foregoing has highlighted some of the instructional and pedagogic relevance of African proverbs that can assist in youth education. Proverbs have literal and metaphoric meanings, and both meanings can be engaged in the education of the youth. Sometimes the literal meanings of proverbs do not get the learner to the deeply embedded philosophical thoughts and ideas that need to be conveyed. This is why it is important for one to understand the cultural system and the languages in which these proverbs are spoken. Without the appreciation of local culture and languages the philosophical and metaphoric thoughts of proverbs whose true meanings are often hidden cannot be quickly deciphered. There are also other forms of proverbs whose teachings are direct and can easily be engaged in by an educator in his/her teaching with the youth. Proverbs are about culture, history, identity, and politics. In general, proverbs must be seen as a conveyor of Indigenous knowledge. It is also a source of social criticism and carries the conscience of a community. Most traditional songs are replete with proverbs. These proverbs highlight the knowledge, skills, and values of the community. Proverbs help organize and describe a people's thoughts, actions, and feelings. Educators can use proverbs to teach and to strengthen a learner's ability to work with others on creative projects and to develop an awareness, social sensitivity, and appreciation for other knowledge systems, cultural values, and interpretation of ideas. Proverbs can cultivate in the learner a positive sense of self and others. Proverbs are contextualized, and there are different sources of proverbs speaking to the culture and traditions of a people, their relationship to the land and environment, Mother Earth, understanding of gender and social relations, social etiquette and respect, politics, economic relations, and matters of spirituality. The study of proverbs entails an appreciation of the literary, metaphorical, poetic, and aesthetic beauty in the expression of Indigenous cultural knowing.

The teacher's ability to pedagogically work with proverbs from different social contexts is a gift of professionalism. A classroom teacher's ability to communicate to students the embedded meanings and significance behind these cultural knowings shows the effectiveness of the teacher to educate. Bascom (1965) long ago argued that proverbs afford people a means of psychological, cultural, and emotional release through "venting socially impermissible expressions that are permissible only through folkloric or proverbial cloak" (p. 279). In his important work, Bascom further enthused the role of proverbs in educating and socializing individuals in maintaining conformity to accepted patterns of behavior and validating institutions, attitudes, and beliefs. Bascom added that proverbs also serve to give consolation, approval, encouragement, emphasis, excuse, self-defense, rebuke or criticism, ridicule, or insult (pp. 279–298). John Messenger (1959) also described proverbs as "means of amusement in educating the young, sanctioning institutional behaviour, gaining favours in court, performing religious rituals, initiating ceremonies, and adding colour to ordinary conversation" (p 64). Okpewho (1992) observed that Indigenous proverbs are pieces of folk wisdom and knowledge expressed with terseness, beauty, and charm. While the "terseness" implies a certain economy in the choice of words and a sharpness of focus, the "charm" conveys the thought of literary or poetic beauty in the expression.

Knowing Indigenous proverbs is an acquisition of power. Proverbs are often told to the young to enable them to grow mentally, spiritually, morally into adulthood. They are a form of customary teachings and wise sayings that guide social conduct for all, including adults and elders, as cultural custodians. Elders and cultural custodians are generally seen as having a particular responsibility to teach and lead by example, and their ability to communicate in proverbs suggests wisdom and intellect. For youth who sometimes refuse to learn about their culture, traditions, and social mores, proverbs are a way to bring them back in line. The individual grows up responsibly through advice contained in proverbs. As a form of communication, proverbs provide forums of socialization around genders. They help keep communities and peoples together. Individuals learn from examples. All social gatherings provide avenues for teaching the young. Embedded in African proverbs are the bonds of African hospitality, generosity, and communionship.

In conclusion, let me reiterate that in contemporary society, where many of our youth are having to contend with many challenges, hopefully educators can help sustain youth cultures with some of the teachings of African proverbs. Youth cultures can assist the learner to develop a sense of identity, belonging, and connections with their communities, responsibilities to themselves, their peers, and their family, and appreciation of the individual's role in society, culture, and relationship with nature and the social and physical environments. The youth can also learn why it is important for them to fight for equity, social justice, and fairness, and learn to appreciate the collective sacrifices that communities make to ensure the survival of all. Despite the many successes we can point to when it comes to understanding youth experiences and cultures, it is also a fact that many youth struggle in life, feel a sense of alienation and nihilism. There are youth who can easily give up under the tremendous weight of social problems they encounter in their daily lives. We need such teachings that highlight the virtues of perseverance, collective hard work, a definition of success broadly to include social and academic and appreciation of a culture without hierarchies. Recently, a senior administrator at a Southern university made a comment I found very interesting. In asking his university to strive to be the best he said: "there is nothing wrong with competition provided one is on top." How do we all get to the top such that the top is not assigned to just one group or person? I would offer comment and a reading that says there is nothing wrong with a struggle to get everyone across the competition space into a shared space.

Every community has a set of proverbs or proverbial sayings that educate about how one moves through life. But not all communities place an emphasis on examining the pedagogical, instructional, and communicative relevance of these local cultural sayings. Educators are trained to work with ideas. Such ideas would constitute knowledge that informs social practices. The spotlight on Indigenous African proverbs is a recognition of the important teachings such community cultural knowledge offers for understanding contemporary educational practice.

As a Canadian of African descent now settled on Turtle Island I do not come to claim an African Indigeneity very lightly. Such claiming is a politics of identity, knowledge-creation, and resistance. It is also about awareness of complicities and responsibilities to how we produce and use knowledge. In fact, I root my claim to an African Indigenousness in the sense of a connection to culture, land, and place and a knowledge-base that resides in cultural memory and my body as an African. I have a particular intellectual interest in exploring the ways (African) Indigenous philosophies (e.g., proverbs, fables, folktales, riddles, cultural songs, and stories) offer key educational teachings to disrupt dominant knowledges and approaches to schooling. My politics is to speak about the possibilities of "something else" when it comes to knowledge production, interrogation, validation, and dissemination in schools and communities. African communities live with proverbs. Proverbs constitute a form of epistemology, a way of knowing attached to particular cultural systems. We understand proverbs in the broader context of a cultural system. While proverbs are relevant to a given culture, this chapter takes the position that we can engage proverbs outside their given cultural contexts to affirm the power of multi-centric knowledge and the importance of learning with multiple philosophies of thought and education. Hence, learning proverbs is about a search for multi-centric ways of knowing and knowledge production. Proverbs are community cultural knowledges that can be tapped into the development of theories, frameworks, and perspectives that explain human roles, expectations, and responsibilities. Our frameworks matter because like theories, frameworks come with particular discursive and intellectual politics.

Proverbs are cultural frames of reference that help individuals and communities capture the complexities of their social existence. We use proverbs to teach history, culture, identity, and community politics. Education must engage African proverbs as a discovery of ideas and learning about life and existence. There is power in writing about what a people live every day. This is the power of coming to know relationally and with others. In other words, we learn and know in communities. Consequently, in re-visioning schooling and education today particular efforts must be made in building healthy and sustainable communities that support all learners. Inclusion is a lofty ideal, but how do we pursue an inclusion of multiple knowledges in the education of young learners of today such that their education does not exclude their experiences, identities, and lived realities?

Creating communities of learners is to uphold the idea of "collective whole." This concept of collective whole needs to be theorized to understand the interdependence of persons and communities. There is a particular knowledge system embodied in local proverbs and cultural frames of reference that speaks to relations to communities and responsibilities of selves, others, and communities. More than simply the fact that identities are constructed, created, imposed, and resisted we must work with the understanding that identities are consequential. So how can we begin to decolonize the identi-ty-making process and to own it? We must begin by learning to understand ourselves in relation to others.

References

Bascom, W. (1965). Four functions of folklore. *The Journal of American Folklore*, 67(266), 333–349.

Brathwaite, K., & James, C. (Eds.). (1996). *Educating African Canadians*. Toronto, Canada: James Lorimer.

Codjoe, H. M. (1997). *Black students and the school system: A study of the experiences of academically successful African-Canadian student graduates in Alberta's secondary school* (Unpublished doctoral dissertation). Department of Educational Policy Studies, University of Alberta, Alberta, Canada.

Codjoe, H. (2001). Fighting a "public enemy" of Black academic achievement—The persistence of racism and the schooling experiences of Black students in Canada. *Race, Ethnicity and Education*, 44, 343–376.

Dei, G. J. S. (2010, February 1). *Reclaiming indigenous knowledge through character education: Implications for addressing and preventing youth violence*. A Final Report submitted to the Literacy and Numeracy Secretariat (LNS), Ministry of Education, Ontario (with the assistance of Jagjeet Gill, Camille Logan, Dr. Meredith Lordan, Marlon Simmons, and Lindsay Kerr).

Dei, G. J. S. (2013). African indigenous proverbs and the question of youth violence: Making the case for the use of the teachings of Igbo of Nigeria and Kiembu of Kenya proverbs for Canadian youth character and moral education. *Canadian Journal of Education* [Under review].

Dei, G. J. S., Campbell, R., Holmes, L., Mazzuca, J., & McIsaac, E. (1995). *Drop out or push out?* Report submitted to the Ontario Ministry of Education, Toronto, Canada.

Dei, G. J. S., James, I. M., James-Wilson, S., Karumanchery, L., & Zine, J. (2000). *Removing the margins: The challenges and possibilities of inclusive schooling*. Toronto, Canada: Canadian Scholar's Press.

Dei, G. J. S., James-Wilson, S., & Zine, J. (2002). *Inclusive schooling: A teacher's companion to removing the margins*. Toronto, Canada: Canadian Scholar's Press.

Dei, G. J. S., Mazzuca, J., McIsaac, E., & Zine, J. (1997). *Reconstructing "dropout": A critical ethnography of the dynamics of Black students' disengagement from schools*. Toronto, Canada: University of Toronto Press.

Dufault, Y. G. (2003). A quest for character: Explaining the relationship between first nations teachings and "character education" (Unpublished master's thesis). Ontario Institute Studies for Education, University of Toronto.

Duffy, A. (2005). *Black students still poorly served*. Toronto, Canada: Atkinson Foundation's Public Policy Series.

Freire, P. (1970). *Pedagogy of the oppressed*. New York, NY: Continuum.

Gill, J. K. (2012). *Minding the gap: Understanding the experiences of racialized students and parents in Toronto's special education programs* (doctoral dissertation). Ontario Institute for Studies in Education of the University of Toronto (OISE/UT), Canada.

hooks, b. (1992). *Black looks: Race and representation*. Boston, MA: South End Press.

Isidor, O. (1992). *African oral literature: Backgrounds, character, and continuity*. Bloomington, IN: Indiana University Press.

Jablow, A. (1961). *Yes and no: The intimate folklore of Africa*. New York, NY. Horizon Press.

Kenway, J., & Epstein, D. (1996). Introduction: The marketisation of school education: Feminist studies and perspectives. *Discourse: Studies in the cultural politics of education, 17*(3), 301–314.

Lewin, K. M. (2008). *Strategies for sustainable financing of secondary education in Sub-Saharan Africa*. Human Development Series World Bank (Working Paper No. 136). Washington, DC: World Bank.

Messenger, J. C. (1960). Anang proverb-riddles. *Journal of American Folklore, 73*, 225–235.

Nucci, L. P., & Narváez, D. (Eds.). (2008). *Handbook of moral and character education*. New York, NY: Routledge.

Ogiorumua, V. (1997). *African proverbs* (Unpublished paper). Department of Sociology and Equity Studies, Ontario Institute for Studies in Education, University of Toronto, Canada.

Ogiorumua, V. (2012). *The pedagogical use of indigenous proverbs and storytelling in African-Centered schooling* (Unpublished paper).

Opoku, K. A. (1975). *Speak to the winds: Proverbs from Africa*. New York, NY: Northrop, Lee & Shepard.

Opoku, K. A. (1997). *Hearing and keeping. Akan proverbs*. Accra, Ghana: Asempa.

Salls, H. S. (2007). *Character education: Transforming values into virtue*. Lanham, MD: University Press of America.

Smagorinsky, P., & Taxe, J. (2005). *The discourse of character education: Culture wars in the classroom*. Mahwah, NJ: Lawrence Erlbaum.

Toronto District School Board. (2009). *2008 Parent Census, Kindergarten–Grade 6: System Overview and Detailed Findings—Executive Summary* (Janet O'Reilly and Maria Yau, Research Coordinators). Toronto, Canada: Organizational Development Department, Research and Information Services, Toronto District School Board.

Toulouse, P. R. (2011). *Achieving Aboriginal student success: A guide for K to 8 classrooms*. Winnipeg, Canada: Portage & Main Press.

Zine, J. (2000). Redefining resistance: Toward an Islamic sub-culture in schools. *Race Ethnicity and Education, 3*(3), 293–316.

PART V

YOUTH LIVING LIFE AND RESEARCH

· 1 3 ·

MAKING SENSE OF NON/SENSE

Queer Youth and Educational Leadership

Mark Vicars and Tarquam McKenna

Introduction

Whilst the epistemic landscape around sexuality has radically altered over the last few decades, the literature focused on sexuality-related diversity has routinely centered interrogation on how the wider educational communities of practice reify dispositional, structural, and institutional heteronormative practices. Research in the inclusive educational field has indicated the problematics of making present marginal sexualities for educational practitioners (McKenna & Vicars, 2013). Conjoining the double problematic and/or deficits of youth and sexuality, it is not too surprising to find out who or what becomes reiteratively constituted as "the problem."

Ricoeur (1995) spoke of the summoned subject, "the self constituted and defined by its position as respondent" (p. 262), and the assumption that the heteronormative world view is the only "correct" or real view, tacitly or not, makes a problematic presence of Queer youth, rather than becoming a legitimate challenge to epistemic and democratic occasion. Gender Queer and/or Queer youth sexualities are not openly neglected, but are, we suggest, deliberately "blocked" from view. An assumption that the heteronormative worldview is the only "correct" or real view to be considered can be read in exemplars of anti-homophobic discourse that interpellate Queer youth to sustain a partial sexuality. The maintenance of an impossible psychic distance and detachment from pejorative name-calling and physical harassment is rewarded with the fallacious promise that "It gets better." As Queer male educators and researchers, we ask, where is the "Queer" agency in this message? Where is an emancipation of knowing that engages with the interpretation and disruption of unexamined, heteronorming privilege? What about a critical contestation of the unspoken and normatively constructed Queer youth as a pedagogical problematic? And, in truth, does it get better?

A Code of Our Own

In 1996, *Harvard Educational Review* ("Lesbian, Gay, Bisexual, and Transgender People and Education," 1996) released a special collection of writings on lesbian, gay, bisexual, and transgender thought, theory, and experiences, which expressed "a commitment to creating space to generate, share knowledge and theory about lesbian, gay, bisexual, and transgender issues in education" (p. ix). In 2013 the rhetoric that politicizes the American, Australian, and British educational systems is in intention democratic and inclusive and positioned by "the inclusive agenda." McKenna (2009) has noted how

> Educational policies, which emphasise inclusivity, now require that greater attention be given to the voices which have traditionally been excluded or made invisible. There has recently been a stronger perception of a need for inclusivity in education to accommodate those who have been previously categorised into marginality—the learning disabled, the gifted, women (or men), those of different ethnic backgrounds, and those from socio-economic subcultures. (p. 5)

In this chapter, we have been prompted by the shift(in) policy and social discourse to explore educational leadership on Queer issues in practice. The research presented is fundamental to the work we have been doing as educators and as a psychotherapist. Our belief in a theory of queer *enactments* and the expression of, rather than the *repression* of, Queer differences is our way of situating resistances to normalizing discourses and protocols. In this chapter, we suggest that the doxic habitus of youth on sexuality has a heterogendered visibility that is enacted daily, and we focus on how a Queer belonging can become accommodated in the context of post-16 sector educational leadership.

Having identified an atypical institution that provided a range of vocational and academic programs to 16–18-year-old students on full-time academic and vocational courses, we approached the Senior Management Team with an initial proposal. We provided an overview of the aims of the research, and explained how, in the implementation of "scenario-led" sessions, we sought to elicit personal responses to the efficacy of educational leadership in supporting Queer youth, and in the implementation of Queer-positive strategies, policies, and practices in the institution.

Self-selected participants from the 1,200 staff participated in a series of semi-structured, scenario-based interviews. Provided with a range of performative scenarios prior to the interviews, the participants were asked to reflect on how they had sought to address formations of—and resistance to—heterosexism, homophobia in curricula, learning, and teaching in their day-to-day relationships with students and colleagues. The scenarios were used to generate discussion, and the issues raised were subsequently considered in follow-up discussions. The scenarios were drawn from actual incidents that had occurred in educational domains and beyond, and the participants were invited to talk through them and consider how and to what extent leadership could have positively or negatively impacted on sexuality-related diversity and inclusion. The prompts focused the participants to think about their knowledge of current policy and legislation as it related to educational inclusion and the welfare of LGBTQ students. They were asked to talk about their experiences of supporting LGBTQ students, if any, within the institution, and to consider how, in their curriculum areas, they felt they had, or had not, met addressing LGBTQ equity. In summary, they were asked to generate recommendations, on the basis of their experiences, for developing a model of inclusive and equitable practices. The participants all acknowledged that historically, LGBTQ issues had not been adequately addressed, and that institutional policy required reviewing; that sexuality-related diversity and inclusion was seen as a social-justice issue; and that the members of the senior leadership team were endeavoring to promote a whole institutional approach to sexual diversity. Effective leadership was spoken of as making explicit that homophobic incidents are not to be tolerated. Also, by way of policy and training, it was felt that staff should be equipped with the knowledge and skills to effectively and confidently deal with such incidents when they occurred.

Over a period of 6 months, the semi-structured interviews and focus group scenarios and/or discussions were conducted with the self-selecting sample of senior management; curriculum leaders; and lesbian, gay, and bisexual students. Four in-depth, one-to-one, semi-structured interviews were conducted with members of the Senior Management Team, comprising the principal, the vice principal (with responsibility for teaching and learning), the Human Resources director, and the Diversity and Equality officers. The aim of these interviews was to examine the development of strategies in the development of policy and effective leadership in addressing LGBTQ issues in the post-16 sector. Encouraging the participants to critically reflect on rituals of conformity, sexuality, and gender practices in the institution, a range of embodied narratives emerged in which personal responses generated personal and professional reflections. Listening to the narrative recounts, themes emerged of resistance, submission, and resignation to how pervasive was the heteronormative capital within the institution. Seale (2001) has noted how individual, emotively charged narratives always belong to specific communities, and are aligned within scripts of moral, social, and cultural practices. The retold narratives highlighted how the personal values of the educator and/or leader had been instrumental in shaping professional practices of inclusion and exclusion.

The narratives, as illustrative exemplars of performative enactments, revealed how discourses of Queer youth and other Queer sexualities get positioned as deficit by hetero-hegemony. For Queer academics writing in the field of youth and sexuality, we are cognizant and mindful about revisiting the interpretive locations of the silencing pedagogies of normalcy. Sedgwick (1990), in *Epistemology of the Closet*, spoke of the power of the silence; how it is not just one silence, but several "that accrue particularity by fits and starts, in relation to the discourse that surrounds and differentially constitutes it" (p. 3). Our approach to articulating the (re)presentation of "data" and analysis in action is aligned with the concept of Transformative Artful Praxis, as outlined by McKenna (2012), where there is

- learning about Queer youth and others as experiential practice;
- collaborative inquiry and connectivity through artful engagement to build respectful and collective knowing/meaning-making of the world of the Queer youth;
- critical interrogation of assumptions and beliefs to recreate personal narratives that explore notions of their identity;
- relational knowledge creation related to psycho-social wellness as a core of the identity of Queer youth;
- exploration of tensions and anomalies generating opportunities for integration around the identities of Queer young people and others;
- making present the presence for discussions of social justice, equity, respect, and mutuality;

- occasion for reflexive knowing of self-hood and life-worlds for all involved in the research; and
- the generating of opportunities to co-create ways of respectful engagements and community building.

This was an approach that we drew upon to provoke deconstructive, critical, and potentially transformative involvements and responses between researchers and/or performers and "data"; researchers and/or performers and audience; and researchers and/or performers, audience, and data. Potentially raising questions about the reclaiming of power and identity in research relationships, we situated performative scenarios to "stir up feelings and provoke a critical social realization and possible response" (Alexander, 2005, pp. 411–412) to further explore the in-out dialectics between the margins and centers of power. Performatively messing around on the fringes of methodology (Wolfe, 1992), we sought to utilize perspectival dispositions constructed outside dominant discourses to further explore "what if" and "what could" become constituted. As Queer male educators and researchers, we are invested in, and have increasingly different, research relationships. Our investments of self in the research we choose to do is a conscious attempt to speak about how we, too, have been and are being shaped by our "dispositions, positions and position-takings" (Luke & Carrington, 2002, pp. 233, 243), and we are only too aware of how messy talking the Queer talk can be!

Talking the Talk: Scenarios

1. I remember that warm summer night in 1996 as I was standing on William Street. I had lived there 9 years. It was the early evening of The Gay Pride Parade. This is the annual event to celebrate the men and women who are "out" as people who identify as gay or lesbian. Looking back I don't think that in this period the term "Gay and Lesbian" pride was even used so inclusively. For me, Gay Pride as a performative statement became a place of looking beyond "a haven" of acceptance to a place and event of celebration. On recollection, I think this was the last year that I actually went to the dance after the parade. At the dance I remember meeting many colleagues, not necessarily known to me as lesbian or gay, but teachers working in the field of education. One colleague was the vice-principal of a prestigious Roman Catholic school; he wanted to be in some of my research, but thought it "unwise" at the time to engage in the work in case he outed himself. He admitted being aware of the challenge of belonging in a Catholic school and related how Leonie (a colleague and Catholic nun) had discouraged him from being open because of the Church regulation.

2. Another colleague at that dance was the head of an English Literature department in the same Roman Catholic school. Eight years on, she is dead. The alcoholism that brought about her death was directly related to the challenges she faced confronting her identity as a lesbian in school. She was well known to me and had several emotional and distressing discussions about the nature of her sexuality and her capacity to belong in the Catholic schools in which she taught. She gradually deteriorated and drank on the job over the 6 years until her early death.

Perry was also at the dance. He had been on the front page of the Westside Observer—a local gay and lesbian newspaper at the time. The article alluded to his ability to teach, and oppressive commentary he had experienced at a Metropolitan primary school. There was discussion as to his suitability to be a teacher because he was gay. Whilst clearly "gay," he performed his teaching with diligence and professionalism. About three years later, Perry suicided and his body was found in the car park of the school that he last taught in.

3. In my schooling there was no opportunity to be open, gay, and a primary or high school student. The one or two teachers that I had who were identifiable as "outsiders" because they were artists and musicians, and who might have been gay, gave up the profession. It was only in my university training years from 1972 that any considered sense of the self being so much a "teacher" and a gay man, occurred ... I seem to recall that I was known as gay but there was not any place to talk about this, and sexual expression was fairly much "on the run." One holiday I was cruising and the poofter-bashers were chasing gay men and the police were chasing the bashers and the gay men.

4. The shampoo container dripped in the shower. Five men drying and grooming themselves after workout and swimming. Some naked, and me the openly gay man in the changing room. The banter is jaw-dropping. The shower man starts with, "I could be in prison and the shower would be ready for me, eh?" Laughter. The men banter back, "Watch it—You bend over and you will get a XXXX full of XXXX." I am sickened. Shower man retorts as he exits the cubicle: "Once I was invited to a swim carnival. It was in Perth and after I applied I realized it was a gay Olympics event. Oh I went but you should have seen the poofs wiggle in the shower room." (He performs a feminized, stereotypic masculinity that is effete-mannered and poor in representation of a gay man). They all giggle. I am furious as I stand there naked and my anger sterilized by their privileged masculinities. I don't know how to interrupt the oppression—what could I do? Should I out myself again and say stop this nonsense?

5. *School wasn't problematic, I used to sit at the back of the class and get on with whatever was thrown at me. There was awareness at my school that I might play for the other team but I was a quiet lad and I never made a conscious effort to stick out. I was inconspicuous by perceived ability. I had to get through. Sometimes the people who don't fit in don't get through; they are the teenagers you read about that are found dangling in their bedrooms. Now, 20 years on, being homosexual is not a big thing for any of us but if you spend a night thinking Oh God, this is what I have got for the rest of my life … and you can't equate being yourself with having some kind of inner peace, then that is when you are found hanging the next day. A lot of young people are discovered that way because they can't get through that one bad night. We all have them, that one night when we think I have got to make a break. Do I do it or don't do it? I can't remember exactly when mine was but it happened.*

6. *At 14 I was increasingly cognizant that the heresy of growing up a sissy boy meant keeping a close watch on what I did and said.*

At 15, I tried to suppress and disavow my homosexual feelings through exercise and attempted to construct a body that would encase my desire in a hard protective shell.

At 16, having spent years listening to instructional voices, I was never quite sure if or how or when I should speak.

At 17, the spectre of AIDS stalked and prowled and I sought refuge in boy-on-boy sex.

At 18, just when I thought it couldn't get any worse, it did …

At 19, I waited and waited and waited for sanctuary from the coerced smile, the sideward momentary look, and the furtive gaze.

On being presented with "Queerly" embodied counter-narratives, the complex meanings of Queer actions of "belonging" were brought into focus. The embedded articulation of personal and professional conflicting experiences interrupted the constitutive silencing of Queer youth, and furthered discussion of the cultural and social settings in which Queer students become subjected to pervasive cultural definitions.

Walking the Walk

Throughout interviews and/or discussions, a sustained degree of caution about entering uncharted territory was articulated by the leadership team. A perceived major obstacle was overcoming *personal* discomfort in talking about Queer issues, especially with students, and uncertainty was expressed about how to challenge homophobic remarks made by colleagues and students. Also expressed was an uncertainty about how the introduction of policies, training, and resources could be managed. Sentiment was expressed about getting it wrong and causing more harm than good. The leadership team called for better guidelines and frameworks to be introduced that could be referred to in the event of an incident, and felt that there was a lack of procedural knowledge. Whilst some staff utilized the existing grievances policy, it was felt by other staff that a discrete policy needed to be introduced, that this needed to be made visible and communicated to all staff members and the student body.

It was acknowledged by all participants that post-16 institutions have a key role in delivering the most comprehensive social-inclusion agenda, and Wright and Cullen's (2001) research examining the changes in college students' attitudes after they had been exposed to information about homosexuality and had actual interactions with LGBTQ individuals was discussed. Suggested reasons for the change in attitudes, from negative to positive, were the dispelling of myths surrounding homosexuality, and that there was a correlation between having low levels of knowledge of sexual information and high levels of homophobia.

Charged with a responsibility to find ways to productively intervene in the social exclusion of LGBTQ youth, there was a general consensus that specialist brought-in training would ensure that all staff have the skills, confidence, and techniques to deal with homophobic incidents. It was also noted that whilst the college delivered an induction that sets out values, expectations, and requirements in relation to equality and diversity, sexual orientation was not being sufficiently addressed. Visibility was identified as a key issue in awareness of attitudes toward Queer youth.

The consensus amongst all of the participants was that the most effective way to overcome barriers for addressing sexuality equality was for senior management to act as an advocate for, and champion of, Queer issues within the institution:

I think the principle of leadership on LGBT issues is no different from leadership in other senses, in that you need to have some clarity of purpose, be aware of context, and have some vision of what you want to do. LGBT issues have a currency of discomfort. There is not a formulated plan at the moment for dealing with individuals in middle management that are homophobic. You have a choice whether you allow something like that to happen, as an individual, as a member of staff, and also as a manager. The question then arises, who is the one who is challenging? Who is the challenger? Would I be able to challenge another colleague? The problem is knowing how to effectively address a homophobic colleague. We have an inconsistency around our practice that is not acceptable. You can put all the frameworks in place, but what matters is what people believe and that they are challenged in their beliefs. How do you do that? We have got frameworks about discrimination, we have got frameworks for complaints, and we have got frameworks about grievances. What I am not sure about is where we, as managers, would be on the scale in terms of providing education and supporting individuals that have experienced harassment. What would that involve? Where do we need to be? The ethos and culture of an organization come from the principal and senior management team. Beliefs and values should cascade down, with the right support, for people to understand what it is we expect of them. As an organization we are strong on saying we will not tolerate any form of discrimination of any kind but I do not think we are overt enough with LGB. Any change in culture can be quite a slow process as there needs to be some reflection on where we are now and where we want to go and then develop an action plan that has clear strategies and clear targets and a time-frame attached. At the moment, we don't have that in place. There is still a notion that being racist is more serious than being homophobic and that needs addressing. We have people with prejudice who are behaving in a totally unacceptable way in our institution and our way of dealing with it is to embed LGBT in a global strategy instead of doing anything very overtly about LGB. It has sort of been buried in a way. The big barrier is convincing people it is a priority. The difficulty with education is that it is very target-orientated. There are retention and achievement and financial and performance targets. The difficulty is making people see this as a priority amongst targets that might make you lose your job or senior management lose their jobs. It is showing and justifying it as a priority. When you are under pressure, as a senior manager, there is limited time and people tend to do the priorities that they are measured on. Maybe one of the barriers is not having criteria or measurement on this issue. Whilst it sounds a bit mechanical, there might be a case for some sort of target-setting on these issues to see how we are dealing with it and to measure whether we are addressing it because changing hearts always sounds good but it is difficult to measure. (Manager)

We have tackled complaints of racism and disabilism because we have had alarm bells ringing that made us take action quickly. What we haven't had is the same sort of information back about gays and lesbians. One of the potential hurdles is that of the laddish, heterosexual culture that often exists in organizations. For these people there is the potential that LGB issues might be alien and those attitudes go potentially all the way up to the top and that includes the governors. Unless there is some concrete evidence it is very hard to deal with an individual who is being homophobic. Without a frame of reference, or a way of adequately reporting and recording incidents, how can it be challenged? LGBT is a high priority for us because I have decided anything to do with people who are disempowered; anything that affects an individual from reaching their potential has to be knocked down. Prejudice against gays or lesbians is a priority because it is a barrier block and anything that is a barrier needs to be attacked. Effective leadership is someone at a senior level prepared to show support and be proactive in driving the agenda. It is not just about the legal requirements, everybody has to meet those. I am interested in developing the concepts of equality and embedding non-discriminatory behavior in everything that we do. I think there has to be a champion at a very senior level and we have a lot of work to do here in driving LGB equality at a macro level. It is about linking up with the LGB community, having awareness days, and challenging prejudice. It is about embedding these issues in the curriculum, which has started in some areas. It is about integrating equality into the curriculum and it is about becoming part of the learning. We are not fully there at the moment. I am very interested in looking at diversity in the curriculum and that is where we need to turn our attention. We are committed to taking a stand on LGB in terms of celebrating diversity and being part of making a difference. (Manager)

We have policies about everything but to be honest my view on policies is that they are only as good as the people who implement them, embed them and believe in them. It is the practice that matters. I chair the Equal Opportunities Committee and I am at liberty to influence what is on their plan for the year. We are going to take the work that we are doing on LGB to that group. Membership of that group consists of all the directors of the organization, so there is quite a big impact. I also have a significant input in terms of what goes on in staff development week and I am making contributions there on LGB diversity issues. LGB is going to be one of the pre-eminent diversity strands that we target this year. I am interested that we develop the concepts of equality and non-discriminatory behavior, and in order to do that I think you need to have a champion at a very senior level. My work is driving these things at a macro level and we are making links with communities. We should be integrating LGB in the curriculum, including it as part of the learning ethos. I have insisted that at the start of every term we have a package on diversity issues and every lecturer is supposed to go through that with their students. As a diversity package it should be covering all the themes. It is updated regularly so when students come in they are briefed by the lecturers on the issues. We have already started to develop LGB training materials and that is part of our ongoing process and commitment. There will be an evaluation of these resources and that will inform our ongoing strategy. Effective leadership is to make sure people are linked to training and that someone is responsible for coordination. There should be a steering committee set up and that should comprise senior managers and middle managers that could then cascade down policy and help put it into practice. Training should then be cascaded throughout the institution and every single month staff should be sent for essential training, much like what happened with the SENDA model of training. Every member of staff, from engineering to the cleaners, should be trained. It needs to be an SMT-driven agenda and it should be made compulsory for all staff irrespective of departments. SMT have to be made aware of the possibilities for litigation. Litigation is the bullet that can move mountains. Litigation can move mountains and I do not think SMT are fully aware of what needs to be done. (Manager)

I would want to know that if anything happened to me that I could go to a tutor or someone higher up and that they would deal with it. I would want support and something to be done. I am not sure if this would happen. Do they really care? I hear stuff about "Queers" all the time, not just in the canteen but in class as well. The lecturers don't do anything about it. So you kind of think there is no point saying anything 'cos they can't be bothered. When I did say something to a tutor, I was told I was being too sensitive and to stop making a fuss. I kept being called "dyke" and nothing was done about it even though it was happening in front of my lecturer. The name-calling got worse. I would be walking down the corridor and people would call out "lezzer." I then got my head knocked against a wall and that was when I decided to change course and move to another campus. The trouble is, I wasn't out and the last thing I was going to do was to go up to someone and say I was a lesbian. (Student)

When I first started work at the college I was working with a group of students and there was this one individual who had strong views about particular groups of people and would often talk about inflammatory subjects. There was one occasion when the conversation between him and another male member of the group was about his hatred of homosexuals, and very loud comments were made that were offensive. He was talking about how he couldn't understand why they did what they did; how it was unnatural and that it wasn't in the Bible, and so on. I had challenged him throughout the morning in a friendly way on his use of language but I wanted to challenge him whilst keeping the peace within the group. It was quite a difficult situation and, one that, to be honest, I didn't feel fully prepared for dealing with. There were several factors: I didn't feel prepared for dealing with the aggression, and at that point there wasn't any presence or any mention of the college being strongly anti-discrimination on the basis of sexuality. We had zero-tolerance posters up on racism for a short time and I remember thinking at the time, "what could I do?" I was not entirely sure of my position in how to challenge the remarks and that made me angry and I don't think I reacted in the best way. I look back at that situation now and I think, had I been prepared ... had he been racist or sexist to the extent he was being, I would have felt prepared and I would have known how to deal with it. It is having a policy and knowledge that it is something the college takes a stance on. At that point there was no visibility in the college's stance on homophobia. I didn't think it was a part of what we did. We challenged other forms of discrimination ... I think it has definitely changed over the last couple of years. LGB issues have been raised formally; they have been part of management discussions and training. Very recently there has been a strong understanding, in a managerial context, about LGB discrimination and some excellent training that has been embedded as part of a college drive for retention. We need, as managers and lecturers, practical strategies to tackle LGB discrimination. I still don't think it is something that we do well enough. I have not heard of any training for new members of staff for challenging inappropriateness, they are sort of left to their own instincts. There needs to be a policy and training to back you up. It can be quite daunting when you have to deal with an aggressive person. To know that there is a policy, to know what you can say and how to challenge homophobia, is needed. (Lecturer)

There was an incident in my curriculum area in which a young man who had just come out was receiving some very homophobic remarks. He had come to see me and was absolutely beside himself. He was not a confident person and was very upset. He was feeling challenged and intimidated. It turned out the person making the remarks was an ex-student so I sought him out and politely asked him to leave the campus after explaining that his remarks were unacceptable and would not be tolerated. He refused to leave so I asked security to escort him off the premises. I think that has to be the only way to deal with someone if they cannot curb their homophobic opinions in an environment that does not accept that kind of outpouring. If they refuse to alter their language or behavior then you have to remove that person. The visibility surrounding that incident was very important, as many people were aware of it happening. It sent a very clear message to all students that his behavior was not acceptable. So often snide remarks can build and they can have a debilitating impact if not challenged. For me, it is important to challenge homophobia in everyday language and challenge, wherever we can, the prejudice that students sometimes bring to an institution. (Lecturer)

Conclusion: Reflections

The chapter has intimated how the discourses that surround, constitute, and privilege youth are routinely only heterocentric, and despite the rhetoric of policy statements, the work of Queer acceptance and celebration is still not being heard at senior leadership levels. The U.K. *14–19 Education and Skills White Paper* (Department for Education and Skills, 2005) stated:

> Our final key task is to tackle disengagement … By tackling the personal problems of young people through the "Every Child Matters" programme, we will progressively lower the barriers to their achievement. And we will seek to make sure that we develop options for the most disengaged young people which gradually draw them back into learning, with support … We will make sure that the organisational arrangements follow the needs of learners and reflect their diversity.

It is perhaps not the youth that need to be re-engaged, but the institutional structures and professional practices that intersect, coalesce, and separately construct a collective and individual sense of Queer belonging. In the context of investigating educational leadership and Queer youth, we have drawn on Tierney and Lincoln (1997), whose use of narratives as a form of social inquiry gave space to empathic engagement in the research encounter. Ellis (1999) also noted that we must "come to understand [our] self in deeper ways. And understanding of self comes from understanding others … [and our research is] … an avenue for doing something meaningful for self and the world" (p. 672). The Queer space and the research practice presented in this chapter remind us that as researchers, we are inside what we are studying, and that we must sustain a professional and pedagogical curiosity. It also reminds us, 25 years on, that we still have a long way to go to realize the "commitment to creating space to generate, share knowledge and theory about lesbian, gay, bisexual, and transgender issues in education" ("Lesbian, Gay, Bisexual, and Transgender People and Education," 1996, p. ix).

References

Alexander, B. (2005). Performance ethnography: The reenacting and inciting of culture. In N. Denzin & Y. Lincoln (Eds.), *The handbook of qualitative research: Third edition* (pp. 411–441). Thousand Oaks, CA: Sage.

Department for Education and Skills. (2005, February). *14–19 education and skills*. Retrieved from http://www.educationengland.org.uk/documents/pdfs/2005-white-paper-14-19-education-and-skills.pdf

Ellis, C. (1997). Evocative autoethnography: Writing emotionally about our lives. In W. G. Tierney & Y. S. Lincoln (Eds.), *Representation and the text: Re-framing the narrative voice* (pp. 115–139). Albany, NY: State University of New York Press.

Ellis, C. (1999). Heartfelt autoethnography. *Qualitative Health Research, 9*(5), 669–683.

Lesbian, gay, bisexual, and transgender people and education [Special issue]. (1996). *Harvard Educational Review, 66*(2).

Luke, A., & Carrington, V. (2002). Globalisation, literacy, curriculum practice. In R. Fisher, M. Lewis, & G. Brooks (Eds.), *Raising standards in literacy* (pp. 231–250). London, England: RoutledgeFalmer.

McKenna, T. (2009). *Heteronormativity—Workplace discrimination in Australian schools: Gay and lesbian teachers in Australia*. Saarbrücken, Germany: VDM Verlag Dr. Müller.

McKenna, T. (2012). To begin the day—An introduction to our Australian "scene": Emergent reflections on the consultation feedback report on the DRAFT shape of the Australian curriculum: The arts. Creative Approaches to Research, 5(3), 7–20.

McKenna, T., & Vicars, M. (2013). Sexualities: Gays and lesbians as outsiders. In T. McKenna, M. Cacciattolo, & M. Vicars (Eds.), *Engaging the disengaged: Inclusive approaches to teaching the least advantaged* (pp. 178–194). Cambridge, England: Cambridge University Press.

Ricoeur, P. (1995). *Figuring the sacred: Religion, narrative, and imagination*. Minneapolis, MN: Fortress Press.

Seale, C. (2001). The body and death. *Explorations in Sociology, 61*, 98–116.

Sedgwick, E. K. (1990). *Epistemology of the closet*. Berkeley, CA: University of California Press.

Tierney, W. G., & Lincoln, Y. S. (Eds.). (1997). *Representation and the text: Re-framing the narrative voice*. Albany, NY: State University of New York Press.

Wolfe, M. (1992). *A thrice-told tale: Feminism, postmodernism, and ethnographic responsibility*. Stanford, CA: Stanford University Press.

Wright, L. W., & Cullen, J. M. (2001). Reducing college students' homophobia, erotophobia, and conservatism levels through a human sexuality course. *Journal of Sex Education and Therapy, 26*(4), 328–333.

· 1 4 ·

WHERE WE @?

Blackness, Indigeneity, and Hip Hop's Expression of Creative Resistance

Audrey Hudson and Emmanuel Tabi

To me, Hip Hop says, "Come as you are." We are a family. It ain't about security. It ain't about bling-bling. It ain't about how much your gun can shoot. It ain't about $200 sneakers. It is not about me being better than you or you being better than me. It's about you and me, connecting one to one. That's why it has universal appeal. It has given young people a way to understand their world ... That's what I hope the Hip Hop generation can do, to take us all to the next level by always reminding us: it ain't about keeping it real, it's about keeping it right.
—Clive Campbell (aka DJ Kool Herc, 2005, pp. xi–xiii)

When it comes to Hip Hop, it seems, the obvious is not that obvious, so it needs to be stated over and over: *Hip Hop is both an art and a form of resistance*. Hip Hop is, to quote Kool Herc again, "a platform to speak our minds" (p. xiii); it has been and continues to be a voice for the voiceless, a way for marginalized and racialized, especially, youth to demonstrate their agency in oppressive conditions. In this chapter, we begin with a genealogy of the academic literature that describes the ways Hip Hop serves as a form of resistance, in general, but particularly for historically marginalized and racialized youth in Toronto (aka Tdot), Ontario, Canada. Following a brief description of the Tdot context, and using the lens of two Black male youths who use rapping to paint a picture of their social and political environments, we discuss how Hip Hop becomes a form of resistance, "a medication from reality"

(p. xii). Always within the Tdot context, we explore the different ways Indigenous youth use dance and visual art as forms of creative resistance to "claim their turf." Finally, we offer a conclusion on the pedagogical and educational implications of Hip Hop as resistance, particularly, for educators of urban youth.

From the Bronx to Hong Kong to Tdot: Hip Hop (is) Mobilizing Youth

Although the rhyme began as a democratic declaration for disenfranchised Black youth in post-industrial America, Hip Hop has transformed into a groundbreaking tool for educators. Hip Hop's beginnings are multifaceted and politically conflicting (Chang, 2005; Rose, 1994). Hip Hop was born in the Bronx, New York, in the 1970s, when Black youth who existed within the lowest socioeconomic spaces sought to speak to their situation and creatively express themselves with two turntables and a microphone. Since then the world has witnessed the impact of this music and has listened to how various racialized and marginalized groups use this art form as a means to actively declare their unheard voices. From Brazil to Japan, Egypt to Australia, France to Canada, and back to the U.S., Hip Hop has made its mark in history. Hip Hop is much more than a passing fad: for many young people, Hip Hop is a reflection of their political, economic, social, and cultural lives (Clay, 2003). Throughout our engagement with Hip Hop, we have come to view Hip Hop culture as a means of resistance.

Rose (1994) and others after her (Alim, 2006; Asante, 2008; Chang, 2005; Emdin, 2010; Ibrahim, 1999, 2014a, 2014b; Imani, 2004; Low, 2010; Morrell & Duncan-Andrade, 2002; Petchauer, 2009; Walcott, 2003) have come to define Hip Hop culture as a composition of four creative elements: MCing/rapping (writing and singing); graffiti art (visual art); breakdancing (movement and dancing); and DJing (the beats/music that accompany the rapping); and an added fifth element: knowledge. Hip Hop has become one of the most influential artistic, social, and cultural movements for youth globally. Alim (2006) stated that Hip Hop culture is now a billion-dollar industry, while also receiving an extraordinary amount of attention from scholars within the academy. In the following sections, moving from the global to the local, we will provide three examples of how Black and Indigenous youth in the Greater Toronto Area use elements of Hip Hop (rapping, knowledge, dance, and visual art) to put forth a "creative insubordination" as a means of resistance against systemic oppression.

Understanding the Genesis and Global Influence of Hip Hop as Resistance

Resistance, Campano and Simon (2010) argued, is most effective when people working in solidarity actively aspire and move toward a vision of social justice. When it comes to Hip Hop, it must be read as both a form and an act of resistance as it has been, and continues to be, a voice for the voiceless. Hip Hop is both an address to issues surrounding silence and to those who have been historically silenced (Ibrahim, 1999). What we know today as Hip Hop was born in response to social atrocities such as the death of civil rights and liberties, joblessness, declining schools and youth programs, drugs, gang violence, and the growth of the prison industrial complex (Akom, 2009; Emdin, 2010). As such, Hip Hop emerged as both a creative and cultural space of resistance (Ibrahim, 2004), thus becoming a proper (capitalized) noun: Hip Hop (Alim, Ibrahim, & Pennycook, 2009). Black youth began to merge the art of speaking over beats, rhythm, and rhyme with dancing and visual art, inventing a force that shapes the identity and expression of youth culture today (Emdin, 2010; Ibrahim, 2004; Lashua, 2006; Low, 2010).

As a cultural response to oppression—through dance, language, and music—Hip Hop amalgamates knowledge, which can serve as communal and generational resistance (Rose, 1994). Stemming from James Scott's (1990) work in *Domination and the Arts of Resistance: Hidden Transcripts*, Tricia Rose (1994) considered rap music as a "hidden transcript." As she put it (and she is worth quoting at length):

> [Rap] uses cloaked speech and disguised cultural codes to comment on and challenge aspects of current power inequalities. Not all rap transcripts directly critique all forms of domination; nonetheless, a large and significant element in rap's discursive territory is engaged in symbolic and ideological warfare with institutions and groups that symbolically, ideologically, and materially oppress African Americans. (pp. 100–101)

Admittedly, not all rap critiques all forms of domination and oppression. In fact, some factions of rap music reinforce it (Pennycook, 2005). Still, a substantial amount of rap resists the notions and ideologies put forth by institutions and groups that oppress Black people, making rap music an important conduit of communication for oppressed people (hooks, 1992; Miller-Young, 2007; Rose, 1994).

While Tricia Rose (1994) wrote of an African American context, we extend her concept of rap as hidden transcript to include Indigenous and African Canadian contexts. Despite historical and geographical differences, we draw attention to similarities in the social, political, and economic oppression these populations face.

The global expansion and manifestation of rap music carries with it principles of resistance (Pennycook, 2005). Rap music and Hip Hop culture played an important part in fueling, documenting, and producing a culture of opposition in the face of systemic oppression, fueling riots in the United States (Martinez, 1997). In France, Hip Hop has been mobilized by African and Arab youth as a means of resistance against the state (Alim, 2009). In Tunisia, a rap song, "Head of State" by 21-year-old Hamada Ben Amor, better known as El General, helped to spark the Arab Spring revival (Ibrahim, 2014a). Moreover, in Brazil, youth used the lyrics of Public Enemy as a means to establish meaningful dialogue surrounding race and racism in public discourse (Ibrahim, 2014a). In Canada, several Indigenous rappers, Plex, Eekwol, JB the First Lady, and A Tribe Called Red, used Hip Hop as a platform to spread the word of "Idle No More," a protest movement started by Indigenous women as a reaction to Bill C-45. The movement was a fight for sovereignty, respect for treaties, and environmental issues ("The Story," n. d.). With these examples we see how the power of Hip Hop has been embraced as a medium of resistance, both globally and locally. In this chapter, we take to the local turf of the Tdot, to reflect on how Black and Indigenous youth have taken up Hip Hop as a form of resistance.

Case Studies of Youth Resistance
Tdot Context—Take I: Diversity in Your Face!

Toronto is Canada's largest city, and its residents reflect a diverse population of approximately 2.8 million people. Of Toronto's population, 47 per cent (1,162,635 people) reported being a visible minority, and half of Toronto's population (1,237,720) were born outside of Canada. Black people make up 8.4 per cent (208,555 individuals) of Toronto's population. Aboriginal people make up 0.5 per cent (13,605 individuals) of Toronto's population ("Toronto Facts: Diversity," 2014).

Toronto is also Canada's cultural capital and is home to an extensive, cosmopolitan, and complex arts and culture community ("Art Toronto," 2014), of which Spoken Word venues and Hip Hop shows play a large part. Cultural festivals such as *Afrofest*, *Canada Music Week*, *Luminato*, *Manifesto*, *Canadian Spoken Word Festival*, *When Brothers Speak and When Sisters Speak* often showcase Canada's best poets and rap artists. Toronto houses Canada's largest collecting institutions and exhibiting spaces, which include the Art Gallery of Ontario, the Royal Ontario Museum, the Museum of Contemporary Canadian Art, and the internationally admired contemporary art exhibition space, the Power Plant Art Gallery ("Art Toronto," 2014), which for 6 months housed the *Beat Nation* art exhibit (one of the spaces discussed in this chapter). This exhibit describes a generation of artists who remix Hip Hop culture with Indigenous identity in order to communicate the most current realities of Indigenous people.

Tdot Context—Take II: Black Youth's Counter-Narratives and the (Re)imagination of Space

Rappers are often portrayed and represented within the media as embodying violence, not only in their music but also in their lifestyle. Such stories help to reinforce crime as a racially coded entity associated with young Black men (Giroux, 2004). Though rap music is used at times as a tool to communicate radical political views (Ibrahim, 2014b; Martinez, 1997), it is also used as a tool to exploit Blackness in stereotypical ways (hooks, 1992; Rose, 1994). In my work with young rappers in Tdot, this was definitely the case. Khalfani Nassor and Kwadjo are members of the Hip Hop syndicate Empty Handed Warriors (EHW). EHW is a Toronto-based rap collective that is known for its dynamic and intense stage presence. Khalfani Nassor and Kwadjo are both in their mid-20s and reside in the Greater Toronto Area (GTA). Khalfani Nassor and Kwadjo are best described as being opposite sides of the same coin. Both of these young men are powerful individuals that exude confidence in every interaction. Khalfani Nassor personifies the popular adage "still waters run deep." He is quiet by nature, often the last to speak in social gatherings. Though reserved, Khalfani Nassor is aware of everything that is occurring around him, and if called upon, will offer insight and wisdom. Khalfani Nassor's onstage presence could not be farther from his offstage personality. Khalfani Nassor greets his audiences with lyrical jabs, dissecting words and serving the crowd with a wild and contagious bravado. Kwadjo greets his audience with controlled rage and unbridled passion. His raspy baritone voice lends itself to both laughter and pain, often shocking his audiences into a trance. Kwadjo is an extremely honest individual who will not shy away from offering his opinion both publically and privately. The combined fearlessness and talent of these men always leaves their audience captivated and thoroughly entertained. Both of these men began rapping at an early age, often imitating the older youth in their neighborhood.

As young men, Khalfani Nassor and Kwadjo used their lyrics not only to speak about their current circumstances but also to express their dreams, painting pictures with words of the men they hoped to one day be. Currently, both men are writing new material for their individual and collective projects. Khalfani Nassor is currently performing throughout Toronto. Kwadjo, unfortunately, is currently being held in a Canadian Correctional Penitentiary. Due to the nature of the case, further details cannot be provided. The co-author of this chapter, Tabi, met these two rappers through his work as an arts educator, community activist, and musician within the city of Toronto. Being a Black male born to a Grenadian mother and a Ghanaian father, Tabi has shared much of the social familiarities Khalfani Nassor and Kwadjo address with their rap lyrics. As artists who offer extensive and complex critiques of the Canadian urban environment, the lyrics of these youth paint murals with words and guide their audience through the urban settings in which they circulate their identities and desires.

Khalfani Nassor: Redefining Adjectives

In Hip Hop culture, the term "remixing" is in reference to the manipulation, and, in some senses, blending of cultural artifacts to create a new entity (Knobel & Lankshear, 2008). The term "flip the switch" quite literally means turning on the light switch so the room becomes illuminated. Flipping the switch is often used in reference to receiving new knowledge, or perceiving a concept, person, or object in new ways. In the passage below, Khalfani Nassor remixes or flips the switch on the youth of color's incarceration experience. By doing this, Khalfani Nassor provides counter-narratives concerning incarcerated youth, particularly youth of color, as he communicates his conversation with an imprisoned friend. In so doing, Khalfani Nassor displays a more complete, and even horrifying, picture of incarcerated youth. These youth remain as friends, brothers, sons, and confidants to those who know and appreciate them:

> I catch the zone watching my friends grow old/behind a thick glass wearing orange clothes talking through a phone/to see your future kidnapped/love is what you show me homie/that's what I give back/and I can't forget that knowing that you live by a code if anyone breaks that you take aim and unload/I sit back and wonder how these kids are taught to make crack then pay back/you caught a sentence in court rooms they talk condescendingly/but never taught accession in schoolyards/from experience I can say that/because our success was not to be mentioned/I don't care how much you got homie/let me know how much you give back/we running out of time.

Khalfani Nassor describes the future of many youth in prison as being "kidnapped" or stolen from them. Despite this situation, Khalfani Nassor expresses love, loyalty, and friendship to a friend regardless of the social stigma of his imprisonment. Furthermore, Khalfani Nassor attaches adjectives not often associated with prison inmates, such as love, loyalty, and honor. Khalfani Nassor then moves to explain that these young men live by a code of honor and loyalty, privileges not extended to them by society; yet they display such concepts to one another and violently defend their rights as human beings to be shown respect. Khalfani Nassor communicates that youth both on the streets and behind prison walls are running out of time, for they will not be young forever. Through his hidden script, Khalfani Nassor creatively tells the story known by too many youth of color (Ibrahim, 2014a). He refuses to allow imprisoned youth of color to be seen or perceived negatively, but instead tells the story of their situation and (re)presents these youth as loyal, loving, and honorable individuals who do the best with what they have been born into.

Kwadjo: "We Know the Prognosis"

In the following passage, Kwadjo presents his outlook on the social landscape of Toronto's urban communities and their residence. He states:

> We gotta make the best out of bad situations that we facing … the block's Jurassic, it's hard to stop it we know the prognosis but got no answer for synopsis Black, White, Asians, Natives, Hispanics face the same … all nations are oppressed in chains … it's these positions that leads to crime decisions or to amplify the mind within them … the time is ticking.

Here, much like Khalfani Nassor, Kwadjo acknowledges that, though it is tough, many youth are making the best out of bad situations. Kwadjo admits that putting an end to crime within communities is hard. He continues explaining that all ethnic groups represented within Toronto face the same oppression, that it is not a racial situation as much as it is a class situation. As such, class disparity leads to crime and the cycle continues. Similar to Khalfani Nassor, Kwadjo also warns that time is running out.

When stating that the block is Jurassic, Kwadjo is making reference to the movie *Jurassic Park* to explain the size and fierceness of the urban community. When referring to "the block," Kwadjo not only makes reference to Toronto's urban communities, but also to communities that share similar social, economic, and political outcomes. As Kwadjo reminds us, we know the problems these communities face, but we have yet to develop and apply solutions that effectively support underprivileged and underserved communities.

Khalfani Nassor and Kwadjo use the art of rapping to paint pictures with words, communicating the stories of Toronto's urban communities and their youth. The hidden transcripts of these youth flip the switch and shine light on the social condition known to many of Toronto's urban communities. Simultaneously, Khalfani Nassor and Kwadjo resist popular stereotypes of urban youth by presenting a more complete story of marginalized youth. These young men use their gifts as storytellers to communicate hegemonic and oppressive messages that reinforce how the members of their communities are imagined. Instead, they choose to speak to the barriers they and youth like themselves have to navigate, for a seed must first survive the ground before it can grow into a tree and produce its own fruit.

Tdot Context—Take III:
Hidden Transcripts: Blackness Meets
Indigeneity—A Personal Story

Building on the notion of *hidden transcript* in rap music, I, co-author Hudson, will highlight how Black and Indigenous youth are using hidden transcripts as a form of creative resistance, allowing for the repositioning of how they are viewed in gallery settings. The cultural responses of the youth through dance and music, challenge power inequalities through the cultural codes of Hip Hop, where "the frontier between public and hidden transcripts is a zone of constant struggle between dominant and subordinate groups" (Rose, 1994, pp. 100–101).

Beat Nation: Art, Hip Hop, and Aboriginal Culture

To illustrate how Hip Hop acts as a means of resistance, I use the past exhibition at the Power Plant,[1] Beat Nation, as my example. From December 2012 to May 2013, Beat Nation: Art, Hip Hop and Aboriginal Culture[2] was on display at the Power Plant. Beat Nation describes a generation of artists who juxtapose urban youth culture with Aboriginal identity to create innovative and unexpected new works—in painting, sculpture, installation, performance, and video—that reflect the current realities of Indigenous peoples today. To me, this exhibition was a vital means to actively resist the traditional narrative of the "Indian of the past," which is often depicted in art history (Leuthold, 2011, p. 35). This show was pivotal in remixing, retelling, and reimagining Indigenous culture into the very contemporary art form of Hip Hop. For us, this is an example of "flipping the switch" in Hip Hop culture.

The artists in this exhibition told their own stories from their own cultural backgrounds, using multimedia techniques to express the re-mix of cultural forms while combating existing images to create new ones mixed with Hip Hop. The artists were juxtaposing primitivism and urbanity to engage conversation around identity as an Indigenous people, demonstrating an "Othering" in visual cultural narratives between white and Native relationships (Leuthold, 2011, p. 37). And at the same time they are talking back to colonial powers and reclaiming their Indigeneity. The exhibition prompted discussion around representation and cultural appropriation, validating a place in contemporary studies that moves from the margins of being represented to representing self in an urban landscape.

For over a decade I have been working in the field of art education and I have accompanied many school groups through galleries and museums, but the enlightenment I recently (winter 2014) experienced is the one I am going to share. It is a memory that is rooted in my psyche, and I know it will stay with me for a long while. The emotion, education, and light that came from this experience I felt privileged to be a part of. It is a story that is personal and involves a group of Black and Indigenous students from an arts program in Toronto. In this work, I discuss the relationship Black and Indigenous youth have with Hip Hop music and consider how this can be conceived as a contemporary means of resistance. From a personal point of view, similarly to Recollet (2010), I use the term Indigenous to refer to a similar historical memory and consciousness that is common amongst African and Caribbean cultural traditions and Indigenous traditions in the context of music and oral storytelling. Growing up, my household was always filled with animated storytellers, rhythmic beats of music and rich cultural traditions from my Jamaican heritage. My identity was being formed by my surroundings, as I came to identify as a mixed-race Black Canadian woman, who has Jamaican, German, African, and Arawak ancestry. My identity also grew through my love of art, which is why I am so honored to see these youth growing in a similar trajectory.

As a whole, we (youth and educators) walked into the gallery space and navigated our way around the terrain in small groups. The exhibition was entitled *Beat Nation: Art, Hip Hop and Aboriginal Culture*. There was a lot to take in, but one group of youth stopped abruptly as they discovered the Nicholas Galanin video stills, entitled *Tsu Heidi Shugaxtutaan Part 1 and 2*. Initially, they were captured by the sound, their heads turned towards the piece, and they gazed at the break dancer on the screen moving to the beats of a traditional hand drum. The perplexity of this image provided a platform for the youths' expression. At first, I witnessed their small controlled movements, stilted and unsure, then, to the beat of a drum, the small actions became brilliant, confident, bombastic expressions of converging cultures.

The youths' bodies moved with the dancer on the screen, their hands shifted in rhythmic motions to the sky, their legs formed into right angles and then popped into a fluid shrill that made its way up their bodies and out into the sway of their heads. It was contagious. The movements began with one student and ended with a group of five, all interacting and communicating with their bodies to traditional Tlingit beats. It was a rhythmic envelopment of poignant communicative dance. In contrast to their movement—I stood still—captivated by their spirit, creativity, and freedom. Stilted in the moment, I reflected on the pedagogical potential of the Galanin piece, what my students already knew, and the experience they created. It aroused vivid, reflective experiences that move students to come together (Greene, 1998).

In retrospect, this kinetic group of youths triggered the pivotal work of Afrika Bambaataa and the Zulu Nation. As a prominent figure in the early establishment of Hip Hop culture, Bambaataa recognized the advent of gang violence, and took it upon himself to form the Zulu Nation. The mandate of the Zulu Nation was to get youth off the street by getting them involved in Hip Hop (Chang, 2005). Bambaataa would put youths into a cypher to battle, with elements of Hip Hop instead of weapons. Many youths who joined the Zulu Nation found a role model and means to direct their creative energies into positive rather than negative. With the youths in question, there was a definitive silent conversation with dance to the rhythmic beats of the Galanin piece. This discourse provided a platform for embodiment of their kinesthetic learning about culture, relationships, movement, and history.

There is work to be done around telling stories through dance, which was proven with the impromptu beauty of the student's movement to Galanin's piece. This notion of taking up or claiming space or "turf" can be viewed as an act of resistance against settler colonialism and a reclamation of space. "Thus, in terms of an art of being in a particular space such as 'turf' or imagined cipher," Lamotte (2014) argued, "Hip Hop practices are really about trying to find alternative affiliation within, and in, the city. Resistance is then less a resistance 'against' or 'to,' but the building of a way of being, anchored in the city's sound and movement" (p. 688). The youth in the gallery space felt the creativity of the artwork and in solidarity. The Black and Indigenous youth participated in reclaiming the space and made it their own, as an act of defiance in the pristine, often quiet, gallery space of careful gestures.

The video stills from artist Nicholas Galanin, *Tsu Heidi Shugaxtutaan Part 1 and 2* (2008) were composed of three artistic elements: sound, video, and dance. The sonic elements of this piece permeated the large gallery space, with echoes of tradition and images of convergence culture. The captivating images projected onto the white gallery walls were hypnotically achromatic, and the dancer's movements on the screen were visually stunning to observe. Galanin juxtaposed two forms of dance: traditional Tlingit dance and the freshness of break dancing. This piece was an eclectic convergence of traditional and contemporary, young and old, sonic and visual. The artist's dedication to traditional music and artistic elements is juxtaposed with his connection to the urban art form of Hip Hop. Galanin created a stunning relationship of the two worlds to represent himself as an Indigenous artist whose identity is formed by both traditional Tlingit culture and his alliance with breakdancing, rooted in African American youth culture of the 1970s. In a way, the youth articulated a means of claiming space, and inserted their voice to the piece.

Turf! Taking up Space

As a settler colonial nation, we are on this land by treaty, whereby Canada's borders extend to absorb Indigenous people without regard for their sovereignty (Sehdev, 2011). "Treaties," Sehdev continued, "are/were sacred relationships between settlers and Aboriginal people … The government violated deeply the spirit and intent of the most important (to the Indians) promise with residential schools" (p. 270). As Indigenous and non-Indigenous people, this requires a shift or change in understanding Canada's history of colonization on education. To initiate this groundwork, we can look towards the arts, Hip Hop, here, as a means to further question the discourse of resistance.

Amsterdam (2013) claimed that Indigenous Hip Hop artists are "Refusing to be restricted by geographies of dislocation ... mapping cartographies of continuity over stolen lands and constricted latitudes of existence, and using beats and break-dancing to navigate new places, sacred places, and dismantled places" (p. 54). The artists are spreading the word about their lived experiences and using dance as a nuanced method of storytelling. The youth at the gallery exemplified this notion of mapping cartographies on stolen land. They resisted the space that was allowed for them, and took over the gallery turf, reserved for a certain type of viewing in a formal gallery setting, speaking back to the traditions of what O'Doherty (1976) termed, "the white cube." Born out of a modernist concept of art,

> The work [in these white cubes] is isolated from everything that would detract from its own evaluation of itself. This gives the space a presence possessed by other spaces where conventions are preserved through the repetition of a closed system of values. Some of the sanctity of the church, the formality of the courtroom, the mystique of the experimental laboratory joins with chic design to produce a unique chamber of esthetics. (O'Doherty, 1976)

As I have witnessed it, youth are negotiating boundaries of space, engaging with the work on an intuitive level, because the work speaks to their lived experiences, in an active post-modernist fashion. This act of resistance against "the white cube" becomes an act of questioning authority and resisting the status quo.

Here, as well as elsewhere, youth are making challenges to the system and resisting the education system. Andreana Clay (2006) made a case for youth resistance struggles and moved to argue that Hip Hop is a means of organizing for social and political change. Evidence of this can be seen throughout the exhibition. Indigenous artists in *Beat Nation* were finding connections with struggles in the music, as they created rhymes, images, and visuals that made transformative strides to pay homage to histories of Indigenous resistance and traditional culture. Other examples from the exhibition are numerous, including *Assimilate This!* by Bear Witness; *Wasco* by Corey Bulpit and Larissa Healey; and Jordan Bennett's *Turning Tables*, to name a few. Indigenous artists have remixed Hip Hop with their Indigeneity to produce a creative identification with Black communities, having a shared, yet different, history of oppression. By allowing this organic act and acknowledging the lived experiences of these Black and Indigenous youth, we validated the youths' rich cultural knowledge of storytelling through dance, which becomes an important site for examining resistance and settler colonialism through Hip Hop.

As mentioned above, many artists around the globe (France, Tunisia, Brazil, etc.), and locally, have embraced Hip Hop as a means of resistance. Much like artists around the world Hip Hop became a means of resistance for Indigenous artists in this exhibition. Indigenous artists flipped elements of Hip Hop and made it an art form that speaks to their specific lived experiences, while still paying homage to the African American originators of the culture. In the gallery space, it was a sober moment for Black students in the group. They had just witnessed a postmodern moment where Hip Hop culture and Indigeneity mixed, dialogued, and met in a true moment of struggle and solidarity. Black students made the connection between the similar struggles both Black and Indigenous people face, and recognized that Hip Hop had just become an Indigenous art, an outlet for claiming turf and resistance for both groups. The Black youth in the group knew the artwork had a different vibe than what they were accustomed to; however, they also realized the authenticity of the Indigenous artists and felt the beats of the music. Acceptance was natural once these youths observed the honesty in their collective expression. This was evident in the dance piece I witnessed.

> Hip-hop is a family, so everybody has got to pitch in. East, west, north, or south—we come from one coast and that coast was Africa. This culture was born in the ghetto. We were born here to die. We're surviving now, but we're not yet rising up. If we've got a problem, we've got to correct it. We can't be hypocrites. (DJ Kool Herc 2005, p. xiii)

After critical engagement with *Beat Nation* as a form of resistance, I was left with more questions about the representation of historically marginalized communities in the gallery, specifically the representation of Black and Indigenous peoples. Following this observation, I was also left with hope and slight trepidation that this work can continue to be a catalyst to pedagogy in gallery spaces, showing Indigenous culture as a vibrant, contemporary one that is still very much alive and present. But what happens when this exhibition is over? Where does the knowledge lie and how do we keep these conversations alive as artists, educators, and scholars? What is our responsibility as creative critical educators to acknowledge the lived experiences of youth to prompt learning about race, Indigeneity, and settler colonialism? I believe the arts have the power to do this work, inside and outside of formal places of learning.

Although my experience with the youth from the art program was over a year ago, the organic element of how the youth expressed their creative resistance had such an impact on the way I experienced the exhibition. The rhythms of their fluid, yet controlled, bodies shaped a new critical space of belonging for youth in the traditionally pristine, uninviting terrain. Black and Indigenous worked in solidarity with each other to claim their "turf," the youth using Hip Hop, which provided a memory for the otherwise sterile white walls of the gallery.

Conclusion

While we acknowledge the importance of doing this work, we also acknowledge the risks and barriers that come with such topics and understand that subject positionality needs to be handled with grave respect and sensitivity. The studies we provided made these considerations and also acknowledged the power of youth voices. Using Hip Hop as creative resistance, we provided exemplars of how youth have utilized Hip Hop as an interruption of the hidden transcript and a means of resistance that speaks back to colonial powers.

The Black and Indigenous youth in this chapter use elements of Hip Hop to communicate their lived experiences. The lyrical and dance performances of these youth are often efforts to reclaim "turf." Working outside of the formal classroom prompts critical examination of the pedagogical work that is yet to be taken up. The expressions of these youths call into question the chronological role of resistance to education that is often expressed within the lyrics of rap music. With Freire's (2000) notion of critical pedagogy, we are made aware of how vital it is for educators to look to the lives of their learners as a valued means of teaching and learning. Based on our case studies, we consider ways in which we can take the knowledge we received from these experiences into the classroom, and question why this is important to our work as educators.

Educators cannot negate and should not forget about the lives of youth outside of the classroom. On the one hand, many underserved youth are heirs to rich literary and activist legacies, yet on another, these youth continue to experience injustice firsthand and have to negotiate political boundaries such as race, class, and gender (Campano, p. 50). As critical educators, we can assist these youth in providing a forum for their nuanced, intelligent, and insightful voices, engaging them with the knowledge production of decolonizing educative spaces. By developing literacy around their own experiences, cultural resources, and interests, educators can mobilize Hip Hop culture to create spaces for a more culturally relevant pedagogy (Ladson-Billings, 1995) that includes voices of diverse peoples.

One of many effects of settler colonialism is that Black and Indigenous bodies/voices have been marginalized in curriculum studies (Battiste, 2013; Dion, 2009; Hill, 2009; hooks, 2003; Ladson-Billings, 1995; Morrell & Duncan-Andrade, 2002; Smith, 2012; Swartz, 1992) and have had to use other means to have their voices heard. Rap artists have used music as an avenue to speak to lived experiences of many Black diaspora youth while also capturing the imagination of young people throughout the world (Gilroy, 1997; Rose, 1994). Rap music has also been an important lens into the political critics and ideas of Black youth, motivating many young people to speak political agendas and influence their worldview (Clay, 2003). The Black male youths in our study, Khalfani Nassor and Kwadjo, *choose* to express their lived experiences through their rap lyrics and poetry. This is because many youths feel safe and free from judgment when expressing themselves through these media (Kirkland, 2013).

Thus, it is imperative that educators continue being culturally responsive and attempt to meet each of their individual needs, breaking down the "master script" (Swartz, 1992) in the curriculum. In education, the "master script" refers to classroom practices, pedagogy, and instructional materials—as well as to the theoretical paradigms from which these aspects are constructed, grounded in Eurocentric and White supremacist ideologies (Swartz, 1992, p. 341). This master scripting is evidenced in all aspects of pedagogy. By breaking down elements of the master script and being culturally responsive, it enables us to better teach our students in a context they understand.

The Black and Indigenous youth in these case studies danced their stories and moved their bodies in solidarity with each other to claim turf in a gallery space that was not historically representative of their contemporary cultures. Their expressive movements resisted the current power inequalities often faced by Black and Indigenous youth to fully engage with the art work in a spontaneous and instinctive manner, which is not often encouraged in gallery settings. In this case, the power lay in the hands of the youth who resisted/pushed back the institutional colonial powers by flipping the role of *silent* viewer into an active, engaged young viewer in a contemporary art gallery.

In our practice as arts educators we aim to bring means of creative resistance to youth, where Hip Hop acts as an interruption of Trisha Rose's concept of the hidden transcript. In our work, we aim to interrupt this dominant framework, using the artistic methods of Hip Hop. In many cases, youth are making challenges to the system and resisting the education system. Andreana Clay (2006) made a case for youth resistance struggles and moved on to argue that Hip Hop is a means of organizing for social and political change. This resistance is evident in how Black and Indigenous youth claimed their "turf" through dance in the traditionally sterile Eurocentric museum setting and how Black youth are using their rhymes to voice their socio-political terms on stage for audiences to hear.

In the case studies presented, we have shown how Black and Indigenous youth use Hip Hop as a form of creative resistance and engage with critical issues prevalent in the broader realm of the presented case studies. As educators, it is vital that we recognize what hinders Black and Indigenous learners to excel to their greatest potential and push for their voices to be heard. Moments such as the ones presented in the case studies reveal that these youth are actively taking strides to have their life experiences heard and also claim spaces that are rightfully theirs. The pedagogical issues presented point us to the abundance of work that still needs to happen as we remix Hip Hop culture in the classroom as a means to speak to our youth. While we acknowledge that Hip Hop does not appeal to *all* Black and Indigenous youth, educators should recognize that it is now an option to ignite learning in otherwise disengaged students. Bringing Hip Hop into the classroom encourages the potential for critical learning experiences of and with our students as we enter the pedagogical cypher and think outside of traditional boundaries.

Notes

1. The Power Plant is a contemporary art museum located in Toronto, Ontario, dedicated to showcasing artists working in various media from all over the world. http://www.thepowerplant.org

2. http://www.thepowerplant.org/Exhibitions/2012/2012_Winter/Beat-Nation--Art,-Hip Hop-and-Aboriginal-Culture.aspx

3. Throughout my research I choose to use the term Black to describe the varied mix of people that are of African descent, before colonization. I will use this term throughout the project.

References

Akom, A. A. (2009). Critical Hip Hop pedagogy as a form of liberatory praxis. *Equity & Excellence in Education, 42*(1), 52–66.

Alim, H. S. (2006). The natti ain't no punk city: Emic views of Hip Hop cultures. *Callaloo, 29*(3), 969–990.

Amsterdam, L. J. (2013). All the eagles and the ravens in the house say yeah!: (Ab)original Hip Hop, heritage, and love. *American Indian Culture and Research Journal, 37*(2), 53–72.

Art Toronto. (2014). Retrieved from http://arttoronto.ca/about/

Battiste, M. (2013). *Decolonizing education: Nourishing the learning spirit.* Saskatoon, Canada: Purich.

Campano, G., & Simon, R. (2010). Practitioner research as resistance to the normal curve. In C. Dudley-Marling & A. Gurn (Eds.), *The myth of the normal curve* (pp. 221–240). New York, NY: Peter Lang.

Chang, J. (2000). *Can't stop, won't stop: A history of the Hip Hop generation.* New York, NY: St. Martin's Press.

Clay, A. (2006). All I need is one mic: Mobilizing youth for social change in the post civil rights era. *Social Justice, 33*(2), 105–121.

Emdin, C. (2010). *Urban science education for the Hip Hop generation.* Boston, MA: Sense.

Freire, P. (2000). *Pedagogy of the oppressed* (2nd ed.). New York, NY: Continuum.

Gilroy, P. (1997). After the love has gone: Bio-politics and etho-poetics in the Black public sphere. In A. McRobbie (Ed.), *Back to reality? Social experience and cultural studies* (pp. 83–115). New York, NY: Manchester University Press.

Giroux, H. A. (2004). Doing cultural studies: Youth and the challenge of pedagogy. *Harvard Educational Review, 63*, 233–260.

Greene, M. (1998). Introduction. In W. Ayers, J. A. Hunt, & T. Quinn (Eds.), *Teaching for social justice: A Democracy and education reader* (pp. xxvii–1). New York, NY: New Press.

hooks, b. (1992). Eating the other: Desire and resistance. In *Black looks: Race and representation* (pp. 21–39). Boston, MA: South End Press.

Ibrahim, A. E. K. M. (1999). Becoming Black: Rap and Hip Hop, race, gender, identity, and the politics of ESL learning. *TESOL Quarterly, 33*(3), 349–369.

Ibrahim, A. (2004). Operating under erasure: Hip Hop and the pedagogy of affective. *Journal of Curriculum Theorizing, 20*(1), 113–131.

Ibrahim, A. (2014a, May). *Creative ways to engage youth: Notes on critical youth studies.* Paper presented at OISE Alumni Spring Reunion, Toronto, Ontario, Canada.

Ibrahim, A. (2014b). *The rhizome of Blackness: A critical ethnography of Hip Hop culture, language, identity, and the politics of becoming.* New York, NY: Peter Lang.

Kirkland, D. E. (2013). *A search past silence: The literacy of young Black men.* New York, NY: Teachers College Press.

Knobel, M., & Lankshear, C. (2008). Remix: The art of craft of endless hybridization. *Journal of Adolescent & Adult Literacy, 52*(1), 22–33.

Lamotte, M. (2014). Rebels without a pause: Hip Hop and resistance in the city. *International Journal of Urban and Regional Research, 38*(2), 686–694.

Lashua, B. D. (2006). "Just another native?": Soundscapes, chorasters, and borderlands in Edmonton, Alberta, Canada. *Cultural Studies—Critical Methodologies, 6*(3), 391–410.

Leuthold, S. M. (2011). *Cross-cultural issues in art.* New York, NY: Routledge.

Low, B. (2010). The tale of the talent night rap: Hip Hop culture in schools and the challenge of interpretation. *Urban Education, 45*(2) 194–220.

Miller-Young, M. (2007). Hip Hop honeys and da hustlaz: Black sexualities in the new Hip Hop pornography. *Meridians: Feminism, Race, Transnationalism, 8*(1), 261–292.

O'Doherty, B. (1976). Inside the white cube: Notes on the Gallery Space. Retrieved from http://www.societyofcontrol.com/whitecube/insidewc.htm

Pennycook, A. (2005). Teaching with the flow: Fixity and fluidity in education. *Asia Pacific Journal of Education, 25*(1), 29–43.

Petchauer, E. (2009). Framing and reviewing Hip Hop educational research. *Review of Educational Research, 79*(2), 46–978.

Recollet, K. (2010). *Aural traditions: Indigenous youth and the Hip Hop movement in Canada* (Doctoral dissertation). Trent University, Ontario, Canada.

Rose, T. (1994). *Black noise: Rap music and Black culture in contemporary America.* Middletown, CT: Wesleyan University Press.

Sehdev, R. (2011). *People of colour in treaty.* In M. DeGagne, A. Mathur, J. Dewar, Aboriginal Healing Foundation (Canada), & Canadian Electronic Library (Firm) (Eds.), *Cultivating Canada: Reconciliation through the lens of cultural diversity* (pp. 263–275). Ottawa, Canada: Aboriginal Healing Foundation.

The story [Blog post]. (n.d.). Retrieved from http://www.idlenomore.ca/story

Toronto facts: Diversity. (2014). Retrieved from http://www1.toronto.ca/wps/portal/contentonly?vgnextoid=dbe867b42d853410VgnVCM10000071d60f89RCRD&vgnextchannel=57a12cc817453410VgnVCM10000071d60f89RCRD

· 1 5 ·

INTERRACIAL CONSCIENTIZATION
THROUGH EPISTEMOLOGICAL
RE-CONSTRUCTION

Developing Autobiographical Accounts of
the Meaning of Being Black and White Together

Paul R. Carr and Gina Thésée

The two authors—one a White male, and the other a Black female—propose to illuminate some of their reflections, experiences, and circumstances that led to their coming together as a couple. Seeking to understand the meaning of race within diverse contexts, the two authors underscore the complexity of their own, and everyone else's, identities, attempting to develop a more enhanced and nuanced understanding of the meaning of race in what some have claimed is a "post-racial" or "color-blind" society. Their autobiographical meandering is not intended to be a chronological listing of all of their experiences, but, rather, the highlighting of a few themes and moments in time that led to different levels of thinking on the subject of race. This is not to say that their experiences are superior to others, only that everyone's experiences are unique in some way, and that race not only need not be a barrier to human and humane contact, but that it also should be considered more appropriately as another layer onto which diverse, complex, and meaningful reflections and relations can be developed. Therefore, race, albeit a central feature to the sociological construction of identity, is considered to be but one dimension, and the authors delve into how such experiences—including dance and poetry, volunteering with Haitian and Hispanic communities, formative defining moments in diverse countries, cultural development, and connecting with diverse social classes—play a fundamental role in shaping our minds, attitudes, behaviours, and actions as we age. The authors also consider how democracy, transformational change in and through education, and science can play a role in how we are further enmeshed in the project of developing as individuals and collectivities in relation to racialized identities. In thinking about cross-racial dynamics, which the authors connect to love, inspired by Paulo Freire's work, they conclude the chapter by providing some thoughts and analysis in relation to interracial conscientization in connection to youth studies and the formative period framed within the context of the youth experience.

Introduction

Re-thinking the thinking about how we have thought about, or not thought about, race for some time is, concurrently, a daunting, problematic, exhilarating, and cathartic exercise. Without peeling back the layers of the race onion, we remain locked into the utopian world of post-racial fantasies, and by entrenching oneself in the murky waters of the pain and suffering of acknowledging that race has been fundamental to everything we know we then risk further obfuscating our own daily cultural, professional, amorous, and other lives. But we see no way around this paradox: to deny race is to deny history and the lived experiences of us all, and to ingratiate it is to plunge into an area that risks being filled with discomfort, tension, and controversy. It is almost commonplace to believe that we are "color-blind," that Obama believes that we are in a "post-racial society," and that we are all just people. While working toward the bona fide reality that we truly do live in a "color-blind" society, and while acknowledging the historic salience of an African American president of the U.S.A., we are, individually and collectively, obliged to accept that, despite the globalized neoliberalism that preaches materialism and individualism, we have all been affected by race, racialization, and racism.

We present in this chapter a rather personal analysis and discussion building on the framework introduced in the first paragraph related to our own racialized awakenings and experiences as a White male (Paul) and a Black female (Gina). Undoubtedly, as a couple, two people in a marriage, we profoundly and vehemently believe that we are both individually and collectively more than two people of different races. To diminish us, or anyone, to a skin color, to a set of phenotypes, to a series of myths and stereotypes constrained by racialized thinking would be inadequate, unacceptable, and problematic.

We elaborate below on some of the events and happenings that have shaped and re-shaped our thinking around a racialized being, and also discuss the notion of interraciality.

This is a cumulative and evaluative process, without an endpoint but an ever-developing logic, thinking, epistemology, and a set of experiences that frame our beliefs. While race is an obvious center-piece to our work, we believe, as will be elaborated on throughout the chapter, that people from all sectors, social classes, religions, linguistic groups, ethnicities, cultures, and, with specific reference to our focus, racial groups, share human values and should naturally engage with one another. This is not a revolutionary statement, far from it, but it is one that needs to be re-positioned within the micro-, macro-, and meta-spheres of epistemological thinking. In sum, race, or the lived experience of race, is man-made, a social construction, and there is no legitimate, reasonable, persuasive reason as to why there should not be huge waves of interracial connectivity throughout the world. In many societies, such mixing is commonplace, and not questioned with the same vigor as it is in supposedly "developed" "Western" societies. We might even argue that the norm should be interracial relationships within a multicultural society. To only wish to be, for example, with a White person, a group that constitutes only 20 percent of the world's population, would seem extremely limiting and almost nonsensical to eliminate the other eighty percent of humanity. In other words, race is often over-conflated for everything, and having a relationship is complicated enough without having to be consumed with the dysfunctional foibles of a society that places too much credence on race while denying its very existence.

The connection between our work, experience, and theorization of interraciality and youth studies is that, at any point during the formative years, our individual and collective thinking could have been dissuasive or contorted, leading us to different decisions, thoughts, meetings and finalities. What happens in the formative years of constructing identity for the long-term takes place within the formal and informal constructs of classrooms, communities, and cultural venues in the years leading up to adulthood. Thus, we believe in the power of formal education to lead to a more decent society, while at the same time advocating for a healthy and transformative conscientization through non-mainstream and counter-hegemonic activities that help validate, shape, and cultivate identities for years to come. We hope that our own reflections, and critiques and analysis of those reflections, will help shed light on the meaning of interracial conscientization, in the spirit of Paulo Freire's work and others who have contributed to the field of critical pedagogy.

Culture Without Borders

We have both learned over the years that culture cannot be, nor should it be, constrained to hermetically sealed borders enclosed around racialized groups. Rather, as is a testament to mass concerts around the world in favour of the environment, peace, live-aid, Haiti, and other noble and worthwhile events, music, in all of its dimensions—whether it be classical, jazz, rock, experimental, or Hip Hop, not to mention all of the wonderful sounds and vibrations emanating from ethnocultural and other groups around the world who participate in Montreal's International Jazz Festival and other similar events speckled throughout the human universe—brings people together. Literature also travels across boundaries, as does cinema. In the technological age, many people around the world develop their own media, producing videos, news, blogs, and networks through the internet, social media, and other virtual means. We have the capacity, some more than others, to connect with others, and to engage with what may have seemed impossible a generation ago.

Through poetry, the male side of this equation was able to read the words of those from other locations and experiences, especially in Spanish from those in Latin America. This opened the door to thinking about how identity is shaped throughout chaos, oppression, and conflict in societies imbued in the web of American imperialism. I (Paul) did not have pity or guilt and shame for the works of Gabriel García Márquez and some of the great poets of Cuba, including Nicolás Guillén and José Martí, among others. I felt an enormous sense of joy in being able to attempt to understand the intricate complexity of realities that oozed and flowed through the almost-impenetrable tectonic plaque of U.S. hegemony on my thinking as a young Canadian trying to understand the world. Race seemed, concurrently, more nuanced, more accepted, and more ingrained with the Aboriginal historical reality while still being an obvious issue of concern.

In my mid-30s I started to write poetry, primarily in English but also in French and Spanish, and I could see a progression in the cadence, rhythm, and musicality of the words. The more I wrote the more I became interested in reading the words of others, which offered an escape from the monotony of the mainstream news, endless government policy documents that I read at that time in my day-job as a senior policy advisor in the Ontario government, and the deluge of endless scholarship on racism that I waded into incessantly as part of my doctoral studies at OISE at the University of Toronto. Poetry became a surreal and euphoric way to experience the world, outside of the strictures of the mainstream society and mainstream way of thinking, and I met a number of people from different racial origins, but, beyond that, from different ideological and theoretical vantage-points.

I wrote a book of poetry in English and Spanish in 2000 around my experiences in Cuba, documenting the many wonderfully nuanced experiences I had on the island, which were largely at odds with the supposed official version of the truth I had been led to believe through mainstream channels in North America. This project then led to two edited books with Cuban colleagues, joint Canada-Cuba anthologies with 10 Canadian poets writing in English, and 10 Cuban poets writing in Spanish, with me and my Cuban co-editors writing a series of poems in both languages. Launching one of these books in the downtown square in Holguin late in the evening, with some jazz music in the background, palm trees, a little rum, and typical Cuban hospitality, made it a very fond memory to this day. I then edited another book of poetry in both languages with 10 Canadian poets of Hispanic origin or those who had relationships with Latin America. The book we produced, with the publishing support of Hugh Hazelton in Montreal, who also contributed engaging poems and superb editing, was celebrated in Toronto at La Cervejaria, where all of the poets read, and where we interspersed those readings with dance, music, and song. A final project was completed in mid-2013, a book with two Canadian poets (Hugh Hazelton and myself) and two Cuban poets, with all of the poetry being translated into the other language. In sum, poetry—reading, writing, performing, and engaging with it—has been an enormously transformative vehicle, dynamic, and experience, and one that I believe has been instrumental in presenting me with visions, sounds, themes, and identities that further my appreciation for, and engagement with, people from all over, including within the racialized confines we know of.

The female side (Gina) of this equation has had a long relationship with dance, and this experience, similar to the poetry experience above, has transcended cultural, political, and racial boundaries. My journey into the world started with dance, which I undertook as a form of language (self-expression), a form of communication (with the Other), a sort of ritual (with the World); in other words, a universal movement starting with the body to embrace the cultural and cultures in all of their dimensions. Driven by music stimulated by a range of instruments, dance can transport you, exalt you, and provide happiness and joy. Regardless of the shape, form, or phenotype of the body, the body that dances can release itself from constraints to be free and present, joyous and comforted. The dancing body need not stop to be judged by a particular aesthetic or value-set; it is simply an individual (and even collective) trance, something that liberates.

Within this metaphor of the dance, all cultures have a choreographed place, all with their music, rhythms, and sounds. This is how I first encountered the world, including Latin America (salsa, samba, tango, and other dances), the Caribbean (folkloric dances from Haiti), Africa (dances especially from West and Central Africa), United States (ballet-jazz, disco, Hip Hop), the Middle East (baladi), and Asia (dance from Bali). However, the origin of the dance should not leave the impression that there is a geographic enclosure around cultures. I have danced African dances in Montréal, New York, Brussels, and Paris; the tango in Geneva, Montréal, Paris, and Buenos Aires; and Haitian folkloric dances in Montréal, Toronto, and Rouen, etc. Regardless of where I dance, I appropriate my body, incorporate it into who I am, and it becomes part of my being. My dance space is a cultural identity space open to diverse linguistic, communicative, mythological, and transcendent spaces. Beyond the racial, linguistic, and cultural barriers, dance is a fundamental cultural manifestation that celebrates life in all of its forms, including love, fertility, liberation, planting and cultivation periods, illness, war and conflict, suffering, famine, and death. Some dances are festive, suggestive, and even militant. Dance has always been a tension-point for me in relation to my academic studies, with the former being an expression of liberation, teaching me a great deal about myself and the Other.

Volunteering Without Borders

Another lens through which we have observed and experienced human dynamics and efforts at social-justice engagement is through volunteer experiences. However, volunteering is not necessarily the most complete, appropriate, or effective label for giving one's time, energy, and effort to a cause. For both of us, we engaged in endeavours that had great meaning for us, and we both felt transformed by the experiences of working with others, learning of the sensitivities and sensibilities of those around us, which also delved into racialized identities, whether people in these circumstances spoke of the concept and reality of race or not.

For Gina, volunteering at "Sant Na Rive," the Center for Haitian adult literacy at the Bureau de la Communauté Haïtienne de Montréal (BCHM), was a determining step in her entry into the world, and later in relation to her professional orientation. As a volunteer for seven years in the 1980s, I taught French as a second language to adult Haitians who were largely uneducated in the formal sense. At that time, and still today, the linguistic position of the Center was somewhat revolutionary in the sense that it privileged learning via Creole, which is imbued within the political-linguistic struggle of Haiti from its foundation. The adult students would start in Creole, and then move into French, which we believed made sense for people whose first language was Creole, not French. We sought to break down colonial barriers and divisions that have penetrated Haitian society forever.

I discovered anti-colonialism and liberation pedagogy in 1981 at a lecture given by the Guadeloupian sociolinguist Dany Bébel-Gisler at the Sant Na Rive during one of our annual reflection days or retreats. It was a complete revelation for me to see this beautiful Black woman, dressed in African garb, with exotic jewelry, walking about in a self-assured yet simple way, open to the Other, and making us laugh at the same time. When she started to talk, it was as though all of our knowledge(s) began to crystallize in Creole: she spoke of our peoples, our languages, our difficulties, our struggles, our education, and our liberation. With great acumen and skill, she demonstrated to us how total domination of a people is generated and maintained through language, and how Creole, within the Caribbean context, continues to be played out through political, economic, and symbolic power relations between people and their choice of language. Being accused of retarding immigrants with learning in Creole was now clearly exposed, and we had a better understanding of the roots and tentacles.

At the Center, I read Paulo Freire's *Pedagogy of the Oppressed* and many other important works, *Les damnés de la terre* by de Frantz Fanon, *Portrait du colonisé* by Albert Memmi, *Gouverneurs de la rosée* by Jacques Roumain, *Compère Général Soleil* by Jacques Stephen Alexis, and *De l'égalité des races humaines* by Anténor Firmin. My identity as a young Black Quebecoise woman of Haitian origin became more Haitian and connected to my roots during the seven years at the Center. I became more concerned and engaged with equality between men and women, between peoples and cultures, and between all human beings. De-colonization now became a key part of my epistemological journey.

For Paul, non-paid experiences similarly involved a connection to social-justice activities, such as with UNICEF Canada working on a development education curriculum, with the Centre for Spanish-speaking Peoples assisting Latin American refugees and immigrants to settle in Toronto, and undertaking a range of participation in my daughters' school related to a human rights committee and school council functions. However, the action that most shaped my thinking concerns the roughly 10-year experience within the Cuba solidarity movement, as a member of the Canada-Cuba Friendship Association (Toronto) and the Canadian Network on Cuba, a pan-Canadian network of all the Cuban solidarity associations in the country.

Working within the solidarity movement involved myriad formal activities—sitting as a board member, running meetings, writing reports, liaising with the media, organizing conferences, visits, and campaigns, strategic planning, and other tasks—and informal undertakings—including socializing, planning, networking, and developing solidarity. I learned about the meaning of solidarity, where it came from, what it consists of, and how it works. Of course, there is no one answer, and never an outright consensus on every point in the process, but the key is always to bring people together, despite ideological and experiential differences, to move forward in unison for the greater collective good.

The Cuba solidarity movement builds on sentiments of social justice across a broad spectrum of political and socio-economic concerns that mesh with other significant causes, such as feminism, anti-racism, and de-colonization. It is not necessary here to make the case for Cuba but to simply underscore that the Cuban Revolution has made explicit and long-term efforts to create a society that diminishes and even removes social class and racial barriers. Conditions before and after the Revolution for Afro Cubans are incomparable, and, yet, removing the entrenched, systemic, authoritarian, and viscerally discriminatory mind-sets and social conditions that ensured physical, mental, political, and socio-economic barriers at the formal and informal levels has been a challenge. I met numerous individuals, groups, and bodies, inside and outside of Cuba, who fought and advocated for the virtues of a socialist society in which all people of all races could live in dignity, together, and could also share in the fruits of the entire society as well as being responsible for decisions that affect all people. This sustained exposure to all kinds of outings, evenings, events, campaigns, movements, and processes deeply affected my psyche and consciousness, and I experienced many fundamental and transformative contacts with people from a range of backgrounds and racial origins working in solidarity.

Knowledge Without Borders

Our own formal education has also been instrumental in sensitizing and re-positioning our thinking about racialization. Along with much of the informal education outlined above, we believe that what we learn and do not learn, through formal learning, is fundamental to assisting us to process, conceptualize, theorize, and image differently, and in more complex and nuanced ways, the meaning and experience of race in multicultural societies. We were both transported to different levels of understanding and engagement throughout our university studies.

At university, my (Gina) studies in biology seemed to be a fluid choice as my mother was a nurse and my father a doctor. We had daily discussions around the dinner table related to science, and I naturally believed that biology was the most important scientific discipline. However, my courses in socio-biology altered the rosy image I had of the discipline when I learned that some racist, sexist, and colonialist ideologies were maintained and validated by this field of study. My master's degree in toxicology enabled me to question the pharmaceutical industry and its relationship to food, health, and the security of the most vulnerable workers in our society. Yet, this was not enough to fully develop an analysis of the sciences.

When I shifted from the natural to the social sciences, I was confronted with an epistemological conflict. Despite my varied experiences in education and in life, including with the Haitian community as a volunteer, I had still been largely influenced by the positivist epistemological stance. I began to question the social representations of natural science when I became a secondary school teacher. My students in a multi-ethnic school in Montreal helped me understand many things and inconsistencies, which led me to a master's degree in education, and then to the doctoral program to study our relationship to knowledge within an intercultural vantage-point of marginalized minorities. I became sensitized to socio-critical perspectives of research, thanks in large part to Dr. Lucie Sauvé at the Université du Québec à Montréal (UQAM), who specializes in environmental education. When I became a professor, I was immediately accorded a 6-month leave, which I took to do research at the Ontario Institute for Studies in Education (OISE) in Toronto, and there I met two highly influential colleagues who furthered my epistemological renaissance (Dr. George Dei from Ghana, and Dr. Njoki Wane from Kenya). With George and Njoki, my research, readings, lectures, writing, and teaching took on a more antiracist, anti-colonialist, feminist, and indigenous perspective and posture. At McGill University, along with Paul, I found, or was found by, Drs. Joe Kincheloe and Shirley Steinberg, who left an indelible mark on my thinking. With Paul, who is a sociologist in education, I began to question my earlier scientific orientation and experience, and evolve to a more critical level of inquiry.

My evolving consciousness has been continually questioned, especially within the francophone academic world. During conference presentations in a number of countries though the Association pour la Recherche Interculturelle (ARIC), I experienced a number of polarized reactions: in general, people from the South were quite favorable, even enthusiastic, with what I had to say, but many people from the North were less charitable and generous, and many denounced my notion of race or the use of the term Whiteness; many thought that this was activism, not serious, scholarly work, and some even said that this was "abrasive." It is not always easy or comfortable to know that peers wish to denounce you because of ill-ease at the notion of our complicity in race and racism, and, further, that this can have damaging professional consequences, for example in relation to tenure, promotion, grants, awards, etc. When these comments and reactions have arisen, especially within the francophone context, they have served to further compel me to construct and reconstruct my thinking, to advance it, to understand it, and to more fully engage with it, thus altering and advancing my epistemology. Together with Paul, we are working on models to further advance our own thinking, and hopefully that of the field, in relation to Democracy, Political Literacy, and Transformative Education, which involves myriad concepts, concerns, and human dimensions, and which we are hopeful will contribute to building more meaningful educational experiences for everyone concerned.

For Paul, the progressive exposure to anti-hegemonic theories throughout undergraduate and, especially, graduate students provided him with a discomforting and somewhat jarring sensation that the world he thought was supposedly just and commonsense was, in effect, something that needed to be deconstructed and reconstructed. Studying anti-racism undoubtedly laid some important groundwork for reconsidering how "color-blind" we really are. Being introduced to a multitude of theories, concepts, studies, and arguments about how racism has structured and grounded contemporary realities was a pivotal and transformative learning experience. Studying with many wonderfully engaged colleagues, many of whom are now leading scholars in the field of cultural studies, critical race theory, media literacy, and the sociology of education, was complemented by the generous and wide-reaching influence of the faculty and scholars I met at OISE and elsewhere. I would like to highlight here, in particular, Dr. George Sefa Dei, whose work has had, and continues to have, a significant impact on my thinking and intellectual development.

Continuing my reflections throughout my years in government and in academia, I have become painfully aware of the hegemony of knowledge production, what counts, who is considered more credible, how ideas are given credence, and the salience of inequitable power relations in the process of legitimating epistemological knowledge. My work on Whiteness with Darren Lund and others made me understand that Whites must be more of the racial equation in seeking to engage and render them materially involved in the project so as to accept that they are implicitly and explicitly responsible for undoing racism. This is not to say that this is not a complex sociological venture, but it is to acknowledge that, along with other kinds of inequities and injustices, Whites must work to end racism, and feigning that other problems exist, that racialized peoples also must take responsibility, and that their lives are also difficult can no longer be used as a defence to shield them from action.

My work these past several years looking at and into democracy and its meanings, potential, and realities has led me to better appreciate the myriad informal and counter-hegemonic movements that flow outside of the formal trappings of elections, governments, laws, parliamentary procedures, and normative power structures. Much is being done to counter, undo, challenge, and transform situations that are unjust, including those related to racism and racialization. I have explored these margins and central configurations to multicultural societies through my research related to the *Democracy, Political Literacy and the Quest for Transformative Education* project, which is funded by a Social Sciences and Humanities and Research Council of Canada grant. Democracy is an important organizing reference point to understand how social justice is possible in and through education, and the framework that I have developed, which brings together pedagogy, curriculum educational policy, institutional culture, and epistemology within a critical pedagogical umbrella, has helped me better grasp the centrality of race, of identity, of marginalization, and of the intersection with neoliberalism and globalization. The work of surveying and interviewing students, educators, and others about the experiences in and through education related to democracy has led me to formulate a theorization about the silencing and systematic closing-down of deliberative democracy and engaged, participatory, critical manifestations of transformative education. Learning to not engage with controversial concepts, problematic notions, and experiential learning in schools and at the university level can lead to a further re-production and essentialization of identity and the problems we face, including—albeit within a more sophisticated, less Jim-Crow-ish lens—racism. What happens in education, in the classroom, in the cafeteria, in the assemblies, in the staffroom, during recess, during school trips, during parents' nights, and in all other ways, has an effect on the potential for how we understand, experience, and *do* democracy, and this work has been fundamental to my reflection on Whiteness, racism, and, for the purposes of this chapter, interraciality.

Interraciality Without Borders

The concept of interraciality seems, concurrently, one of great intrigue, something that may appear to be elusive, ill-advised, and threatening, a concern for many people, some of whom invoke religion and/or social conventions, and a phenomenon that should be entirely normal for people—human beings—to come together. Why should it be abnormal or inacceptable for two people to join in solidarity, union, and/or marriage? Trying to keep people apart seems counter-productive, counter-intuitive, and counter-human. Excessive efforts are required to instill intolerance, disrespect, and disdain in people, and these efforts need to be further cultivated in and through education. Epistemologically, we can learn racism, indecent behaviour, and discrimination, and we can also unlearn these attributes, actions, and experiences.

Along with the multitude of international and national covenants, laws, protocols, and narratives that preach human rights, anti-racism, social justice, and the progression toward a more decent global and local society, despite the visceral reality of globalization and neoliberalism, there are many individual and collective efforts to build more sustainable, uplifting, and emancipatory societies. However, there is still ample empirical, anecdotal, and lived evidence that racism and racialization are imbued within the contemporary as well as previous socio-political realities. Yet, there is not the same tendency, movement, and reasoned deliberation in every context for what race means, and how it is conceptualized and experienced in every culture and society.

The mixing of the races, which has long been contested in many societies, is, we would argue, not only inevitable and desirable, but, importantly, also a false paradigm. Why should people not interact based on race when the whole premise of race is smothered in the real and perceived historical and contemporary cultural practices, idiosyncrasies, and power relations that have divided people based on phenotypes, skin color, and nonsensical inter-pretations of what race actually is. There is more variation within races than between them; when stretched back several generations most people have people of different races within their own families. All racial groups share the same blood types, there is no evidence of moral, cognitive, and behavioural superiority of any racial group, and the social construction of race provides relevant and critical interpretations of how race plays out in societies struc-tured around racial categories and hierarchies. In short, sustaining race as an organizing principle for society is not beneficial for anyone.

As a couple who does not negate its racial origins but who, at the same time, does not believe that it frames all that constitutes their individual and collective personal, emotional, social, political, and cultural beings, we understand that, while we believe that interracial relationships are increas-ingly inevitable and evident, there may be some, or many, who contest this reality. Although such relationships were considered unthinkable in historical times, and even though they were even once illegal and attacked through violence and shunning, the reality of people coming together is evident when attending any classroom in a Toronto school, for example, where a number of children of mixed origin is but one of the characteristics that underpins the diverse, socially constructed, fluid and complex identities forming our con-temporary society.

Discussion

Our discussion above, and the examples and elaborations on our identities and experiences related to race and interraciality, provide a backdrop to this last section, which attempts to unpack and make sense of what it means to rethink our thinking on such issues. What is the connection to education, and, importantly, to youth studies? Is it helpful to interrogate and critique one's own identities to be able to reconsider what race means in the contem-porary context? How might our own experiences be helpful when they are so unique and isolated? Where do we go from here?

We would like to start by re-emphasizing that the notion of interraciality is a social construction, and its meaning varies widely from place to place. Context is fundamental here, and, although the American reality is often conflated to vastly disproportionate international dimensions, the world is different outside of the United States, which is not to say that similar problems may not exist, or that racism is not a reality, but, rather, that different cultural, social, political, and national contexts may shape realities quite differently. In the U.S., in particular, it is important to note that the relationship between Blacks and Whites is firmly anchored within a legacy of formal, institutionalized, and viscerally evident racism. Blacks and Whites together can sometimes be considered a cornucopia of deception (Where do you live? Will you be accepted within the community? Is the local church segregated or open? What will the parents and family think? What will happen in school? etc.). The gender issues related to Black-White relationships have also been fraught with the lingering gaze of slavery: Is the Black man turning his back on Black women when he is with a White woman, and is the Black woman an object of fetishized desire when with a White man, along with other stereotyped inquiries that cloud what should be thought of men and women being together (and also same-sex relations, although that is not the focus of our chapter). The complexity of what people see on the outside compounds all of the normal and nuanced debates, foibles, and concerns that couples have on the inside.

What interracial relationships are, then, more common, comfortable, and less provocative to the Other's eyes? Is it White men and Asian women, or White men and women of all types? Does this underscore and exemplify the inherent capacity of Whites to be good, and to override the scorn of history? Or does it mean that White men are drawn to the Other? Or is it that people want to find other people, and it is senseless to always question why? Interracial relationships take on a compounded sense when one of the partners comes from abroad, from the country of origin that has a relatively clear and distinct notion of identity, and then drifts into a more-or-less multicultural "new society." Power relations may or may not be established, and levels of dependency and autonomy will also be determining factors on what happens with the couple. Whiteness, power, and privilege exist, but, at the micro level, how do they function? This opens up discussion on the micro- versus macro-levels of interracial partnering, identity, and consciousness. When are we most aware of our racial identities, with whom, how, and where?

In Canada, despite the numerous concerns, critiques, and problems about which we have written and have been engaged, including our own racialized, or interracialized, identities, we spend time with our families, many of whom are in interracial relationships, and with friends and colleagues who work in areas of common interest, and we engage in many other activities, like anyone else. We talk about the phenomenon and also try to contribute, in our own individual and collective ways, to make for a more decent society. Are we privileged to not be plagued by thinking about racial identities all of the time? Are we distressed by this aspect of our multi-layered identities? Are all of our problems, or any of them, connected to racialization? How do we consider those close to us who are so infinitely wonderful and beautiful, and also of mixed race, knowing that race is but one aspect of who they are? Ultimately, and we do not say this to diminish the debate, or to somehow lead readers into believing that race is of no consequence, but, rather, to simply illustrate the positionality, the intersectionality, and context for such debate by noting that race plays out, and has played out, differently for us in a large, urban, multi-cultural, predominantly French-speaking city like Montreal, or like Toronto, where we also spend time, than it has played out for us on our numerous trips to the United States over the past 10 years. We are not stating that racism does not exist in Canada, but that it has not impacted us in the same way as it has during our time in the U.S. Our social class undoubtedly plays a role, our status as university professors also gives us access to resources and cultural capital, and our own experiences, personalities, and networks have also shaped how we live, all of which can lead to differentiated and extremely nuanced racialized realities.

In the U.S., where Paul was a professor at Youngstown State University in Ohio for 5 years, where Gina has family in Chicago and Miami, and where they have attended the annual American Educational Research Association conference every year for about a decade, we have encountered extensive and heartwarming solidarity related to anti-racism work. The issues are often defined differently, and it is clear that racialization functions in a different way south of the border, as evidenced by the residential housing situation in almost every city. Our own experience has been favourable when with colleagues and scholars, and it has been truly uplifting to engage in important work with such committed individuals; this is a political project, and not a simple professional task. However, at the personal level, we have felt the gaze, the intrigue, the sometimes uncomfortable swagger, and many other reactions that have been sent our way when in primarily White or primarily Black areas in the U.S. Speaking French to each other, and perhaps relating to each other in the way we normally do, may not mesh well with the stereotypical regard of the Other.

Travelling in Cuba, where most of the population is mixed at some level, brings a different regard, especially since most Cubans believe Gina to be Cuban and are surprised when they discover that she does not speak Spanish but her "Gringo" husband does. Travelling in Romania brought a different type of reaction, not always a comfortable one, and we are not sure if it is because of our interraciality, our foreignness, our willingness to be there, or some other factor. Travelling in Australia, where there is a growing Asian population in Melbourne and Sydney, and where Aboriginal peoples have a claim on the land and society despite the obvious Whiteness, seemed effortless, but we may be seen as harmless scholars, and not as part of the small wave of Sudanese refugees who are constructed in a less-beneficial way. Travelling in Brazil, with its large Afro Brazilian population alongside a quasi-official ideology of integration, acceptance, and a society without racism, we are more keenly aware of who has power, and how our movements are considered. Travelling in Argentina has also been extremely invigorating, and we have made friends there and in all of the other places we have visited. Oddly, many places, such as Argentina, claim that there are no Blacks in the country, yet a vivid history of African heritage is evident throughout Latin America. Have we been accepted because we are, or are perceived as, nice people, because there is no reason not to accept us, or because we have a certain status, which may or may not mean much, or some other reason? There are many nuances and differences to various cultural milieus, but race need not be the only defining issue, and, in our minds, it would be an overwhelmingly sad reality if that were the case.

This brings us to youth and youth studies, and the prospect for education. Our mildly ethnographic strolls through some of the components that have shaped and structured our present realities serve as a backdrop to the issue of education. We have learned much and continue to do so; we have engaged in studies, projects, causes, and careers that aim to take anti-racism seriously, and, yet, we have also engaged in many other experiences that may or may not have been influenced by the racialization project. Here is where we believe that education can and should play an important role, because we cannot easily dissect or liquidate, at this time, when and where the racialization project starts and stops. While we are critical of our own educational experiences, and have serious concerns about what is happening in schools today, we also believe that formal education must address serious concerns at diverse levels related to race and social justice. If formal schooling does not, then the project of building a more decent society becomes all the more complex. We learn about ourselves and others/Others in school; we learn how to relate, how to engage, how to question, how to function, and how to construct knowledge. What teachers do, what the curriculum requires, what happens generally and specifically within the four walls of the school, what the educational policies are, etc., all come together to help us individually and collectively make sense of the world, and possibly change and transform our life situations.

More specifically, however, related to youth culture, we would like to enlarge our analysis to emphasize that what happens outside of the school is equally as important as what happens in the school. Making the connection between the two would seem pivotal and fundamental. Tethering the formal with the informal is necessary because too many young people are abandoned or let go or pushed out of the way. Similarly, if education is not about anti-racism … then it must be about … (at some level) racism. Indeed, there have been many changes over the years, and they all came through struggle. Conversely, compliant, docile, patriotic, non-questioning education would seem to be an extremely deleterious way of achieving a supposedly post-racial or color-blind society. Bringing people together is important, but what is critical here is what people do when they are brought together: what type of engagement, what type of solidarity, and what type of knowledge construction.

In sum, placing a premium on skin tone is an extremely disenfranchising way of developing a better society. But this is the reality we live in, and this is manifest in myriad explicit and implicit, as well as institutional and cultural, ways. Race morphs into culture, and social class is intertwined with racialization, and gender becomes political labelling for other racialized identities. Interraciality will continue to increase over time, Whites will continue to decrease as a percentage of the global population, and the need to find people of different races connecting and working together will become more and more necessary. We do not say this in an upbeat, Pollyannaish way so as to prove our point, because we are aware of the vast and entrenched complexity of the issue of interraciality. But we do believe that there is much good work taking place, there is much good will in many quarters, and that struggling with those working for change is a noble, worthy project. Our own story, as incomplete as it has been recounted in this text, is but an anecdote of the vast number of people enmeshed with interraciality. Becoming conscious and developing a conscientization about interraciality requires engaging with—stripping it of its *half-breed, mulatoo, metis, mestizo* taboo—and seeking to look beyond the outer layer of pigmentation that has so shrouded the universal mind-set, learned through endless cultural manifestations that have been replayed before the world's stage but that have been stridently denounced by people from all over … who love each other.

ABOUT THE CONTRIBUTORS

Mary Frances Agnello is currently an associate professor at Akita International University in Japan. She has been faculty in Foundations of Education, Teacher Education, and Curriculum Studies at The University of Texas at San Antonio and was tenured at Texas Tech University. She is teaching writing and literature in the English for Academic Purposes Department as Liberal Arts faculty at AIU and continuing to research discourses of language, literacy, and culture, as well as educational policy and comparative education.

Adriana Alfano is a French immersion teacher at the elementary level in the Hamilton Wentworth District School Board. She has a background in English and French, and is a graduate of the University of Ottawa and Glendon College of York University. Her interests include: languages, music, dance, improv comedy, integrated arts education, and critical pedagogy.

Marcelle Cacciattolo is a sociologist and an Associate Professor in the College of Education at Victoria University. Marcelle teaches in both preservice teacher and postgraduate teacher education programs. Marcelle's particular research interests are cross-disciplinary involving health sciences and education-based research. Her research is linked to wellbeing, inclusive education, social justice, and authentic teaching and learning pedagogies.

Paul R. Carr is Professor in the Department of Education at the Université du Québec en Outaouais, Canada. His research is broadly concerned with political sociology, with specific threads related to democracy, media literacy, peace studies, intercultural relations, and transformative change in education. He has approximately fifteen co-edited books and a single-author book, and roughly a hundred articles and book chapters. He is the Principal Investigator of a five-year Social Science and Humanities Research Council of Canada (SSHRC) research project entitled Democracy, political literacy and quest for transformative education (www.education4democracy.net).

George J. Sefa Dei is Professor of Social Justice Education at the Ontario Institute for Studies in Education of the University of Toronto (OISE/UT). He is the Director for the Centre for Integrative Anti-Racism Studies at the University of Toronto, Canada. He is also a 2015 Carnegie African Diasporan Fellow. Professor Dei's teaching and research interests are in the areas of Anti-Racism, Minority Schooling, International Development, Anti-Colonial Thought and Indigenous Knowledges Systems.

Emmanuel Tabi is a doctoral candidate at OISE/University of Toronto. His work examines how race, gender and class dynamics intersect within Toronto and how they are performed through various forms of cultural production such as spoken word poetry and rapping. Emmanuel is in the midst of writing his Ph.D. thesis, which explores how Black male youth in Toronto use spoken word poetry and rapping as a form of both community organizing and education.

Audrey Hudson is a Ph.D. Candidate at the Ontario Institute for Studies in Education at the University of Toronto (OISE/UT). Her research considers Hip Hop as a means of solidarity between Black and Indigenous communities and how this can be used to decolonize education. Hudson is also an Instructor at OCAD University.

Awad Ibrahim is Professor of Youth, Cultural, and Curriculum Studies. He is a Curriculum Theorist with special interest in sociology, cultural studies, Hip Hop, youth and Black popular culture, social foundations (philosophy, history and sociology of education), social justice and community service learning, Diasporic and continental African identities, ethnography and applied linguistics. He has researched and published widely in these areas. His books include: *The Rhizome of Blackness: A critical ethnography of Hip Hop culture, language, identity and the politics of becoming* (Peter Lang, 2014); *Critical* *youth studies: A reader* (with Shirley Steinberg; Peter Lang, 2014); and *Global linguistic flows: Hip Hop cultures, youth identities, and the politics of language* (with Samy Alim & Alastair Pennycook, Routledge, 2009).

Carl E. James teaches in the Faculty of Education and the Graduate Program in Sociology at York University, Toronto, where he is also Director of the York Centre for Education and Community. In his research and teaching, he takes up questions of accessibility and equity in schooling and education that address the needs, interests and aspirations of students. In this regard, he pays attention to issues, programs, and structures that enable, support and encourage the academic performance, participation and attainment of students. One of his recent publications is: *Life at the intersection: Community, class and schooling.*

Patricia Krueger-Henney is an Assistant Professor at the University of Massachusetts Boston in the Leadership in Urban Schools doctoral program. Through participatory action research and visual research methods she examines how young people perceive and experience social injustices produced and reproduced by current purposes of education.

Tony Kruger is Adjunct Associate Professor in the Victoria University College of Education. From 2006 to 2011 he was Head of the School of Education. His research and teaching have focused on the ways in which forms of education affect and are affected by social and economic relationships, and to establish how education can contribute to a socially just society through practices. With colleagues, over many years he has led the development of partnership-based teacher education at Victoria University and the application of collaborative practitioner inquiry approaches in research and professional development projects.

Haidee Smith Lefebvre is a Ph.D. candidate with the Faculty of Education at McGill University. Her research and publication areas focus on b-boy/b-girl culture, Hip Hop, Indigenous girlhood, kinship and youth culture.

Michael B. MacDonald is Assistant Professor of Music at MacEwan University in Edmonton, Alberta. He teaches courses in musicology and cultural studies and publishes widely on topics in popular music with special attention to Critical Youth Studies, Community Learning and Development, Aesthetic Systems, and the critical pedagogy of music education. Michael's ongoing research explores the connections between youth music learning practices, community sustainability, creative industry economic development, and (semio)capitalism. twitter: @prof_macdonald

Tarquam McKenna is Professor in the College of Education, Victoria University, Melbourne, Australia. Tarquam has been active as a Teacher Educator and an Arts Psychotherapist for thirty years. He is immediate past president of the Association for Qualitative Research (AQR) and an honorary life member of the Australian and New Zealand Art Therapy Association. He is keenly interested in educational research methods, social justice and especially research approaches using artful practices, which aim to redress the life world challenges of those people with whom he works.

Maryam Nabavi earned her doctorate in Educational Studies at The University of British Columbia. Her research interests in the areas of social citizenship, inclusions and exclusions within "the nation," and migrant identities are motivated by a commitment to advancing educational and social policies in the same area. In addition to her academic research, Dr. Nabavi works as a Research Associate with the Social Research and Demonstration Corporation in Vancouver.

Elizabeth P. Quintero has worked as teacher (Pre-K to Grade 2), curriculum specialist and university teacher educator. Her passion is programs serving families from a variety of histories in multilingual communities. She is Professor and Coordinator of Early Childhood Studies at California State University Channel Islands. Publications include: Elizabeth P. Quintero and Mary K. Rummel. *Storying, A path to our future: Artful thinking, learning, teaching, and research* and *Critical literacy in early childhood education: Artful story and the integrated curriculum*, both by Peter Lang Publishing.

John M. Richardson teaches English and Drama at a Canadian independent school, speaks at educational conferences across North America, has been published in journals such as *Learning, Media and Technology* and *English Journal*, and has appeared as a youth culture commentator on CBC radio's flagship arts show, "Q", and in *The National Post*. His research interests include youth responses to live theatre, digital culture, critical pedagogy, and identity formation. john.mathew.richardson@gmail.com.

Shirley R. Steinberg is Research Professor of Youth Studies at the University of Calgary, and Director of the Institute of Youth and Community Research at the University of the West of Scotland. She is the executive director of freireproject.org. She is the author and editor of many books on transformative leadership, critical pedagogy, urban and youth culture, and cultural studies. Her most recent co-edited books include: *Critical youth studies* (2014); *Critical qualitative research reader* (2012); as well as her edited volumes: *Kinderculture: The corporate construction of childhood*, 3ʳᵈ edition (2011); and *19 Urban questions: Teaching in the city* (2010). A regular contributor to CBC Radio One, CTV, CJAD Radio 800, *The Toronto Globe and Mail*, *The Montreal Gazette*, and Canadian press, she is also a weekly columnist for CTVNEWS Channel's Culture Shock. The organizer of the International Institute for Critical Pedagogy and Transformative Leadership, she is committed to a global community of transformative educators and community workers engaged in radical love, social justice, and the situating of power within social and cultural contexts.

Gina Thésée is Associate Professor in the Department of Education and Pedagogy at University of Quebec à Montreal (UQAM), Canada. She is the past Director of the Bachelor in Secondary Education program at UQAM and is currently a member of the Teacher-Education Committee (CAPFE), an advisory committee to the Quebec Ministry of Education in Quebec, which reviews all teacher-education programs in the province. She is a past laureate for the Montreal Black History Month, which honoured her for her work in the Black community. Her research focuses on interculturalism, epistemology, democracy, environmental education, and science education, and she has published widely in these areas in both French and English.

Mark Vicars is a teaching and research academic in the College of Education at Victoria University, Melbourne. His research is focused around the inter-connectivities between literacy and identity practices in everyday life. In 2010, he was awarded the Australian Learning and Teaching Council Citation for pedagogical approaches that motivate, inspire and support socially disadvantaged and culturally diverse students to overcome barriers to learning and to experience and attain success.

Jo Williams began her career in education as a secondary school music and drama teacher and has been working in Teacher Education since 2001. Her research interests include critical pedagogy, teacher education, comparative education and Latin American education systems. Her doctoral research focused on critical educational partnerships in an era of neoliberal crisis.

Handel Kashope Wright has been Canada Research Chair of Comparative Cultural Studies and David Lam Chair of Multicultural Education; he is currently Professor and Director–Centre for Culture, Identity and Education, University of British Columbia. He has published extensively on Africana cultural studies, cultural studies of education, multiculturalism and its alternatives, and qualitative research. He is the author of *A prescience of African cultural studies* (Peter Lang, 2004) and his recent publications include the co-edited books *Africa, cultural studies and difference* (Routledge, 2011); *Cultural studies of transnationalism* (Routledge, 2012); *Precarious international multicultural education* (Sense, 2012) and *The Promised Land: History and historiography of the Black experience* (University of Toronto, 2014).

INDEX

A

Action Research 29, 39, 44, 52–53, 67, 69, 98, 107, 287
Addiction 155, 157, 159–161, 163
Adorno, T. 29–30, 43
Aesthetic education 27–31, 46
Aesthetic experience 28, 31–32
Aesthetic function 31
Aesthetic value 30–31
Aesthetics 27–32, 39
African Youth 53, 74, 183, 205–231, 252, 258
Afrika Bambaataa 258
Agency 10–11, 22, 32, 75, 86, 147, 162, 168, 177, 185, 208, 220, 236, 249
Agricultural workers 196–197
Alarcón, Francisco X. 195
Anzaldúa, G. 191–193, 198, 202
Anesthetized learning 29, 43
Liberation 213, 216, 272–273, 278

Anti-colonialism and liberation pedagogy 273
Apple 22
Aspirational, navigational, and resistant capital 75
Assu, S. 111–114, 117, 119–121–127
Australian Disadvantaged Schools 93
Autobiography 46, 267
Autoethnography 40, 248
AVID 96

B

Bacon, F. 28
Baldwin, J. 66–67
Barbie and Ken 22
Barthes, R. 119, 127, 156
Baudrillard, J. 23
Beat Nation: Art, Hip Hop, and Aboriginal Culture 111–114, 116–119, 125, 127–128, 253, 257–258, 260–261

Beatles 158
Berleant, A. 31
Biesta, G. 37, 38
Black youth 206, 208–209, 211, 216, 223, 250–251, 263–264
Black culture 208, 266
Black youth's counter-narratives 253
Blackness 128, 164, 249, 253, 256, 265, 286
Blue epistemology 31
Blues aesthetic-knowledge 31
Boal, A. 167–168
Bonding and bridging social capital 75
Book club 34–35, 39
Bourdieu 75, 93–94, 107
Bowie, D. 156
Boy scouts 7
Breakdancing 118, 250, 259
Buckingham, D. 12, 18, 24, 131, 146, 176
Butler, J. 171

C

Canada's colonial and White supremacy history 113
Capital 12–13, 16, 18, 21, 51, 63, 66, 71, 74–76, 80, 82, 85–86, 88, 96, 106, 130, 137, 173, 175, 238, 251, 253, 288
Cartography 55
Cellphones 136, 140
Character education 208–209, 231–232
Chief Billy Assu 120–121, 123, 126
Childhood 4–24, 68, 169, 192–193, 203, 222
Chomsky, N. 23
Church 157, 164, 175, 240, 260, 280
Cipher5 27–43
Citizenship 97, 164, 168, 177
Civil Rights Movement 181
Class (social) 6–7, 10, 13–14, 18, 21, 35, 37, 41, 51, 53–54, 62, 64, 76, 79–80, 84–86, 89, 95 192–193, 199, 214, 216–217, 223, 232, 241–242, 256, 263, 274, 281, 283
Collaborative Practitioner Research (CPR) 98–99

color-blind society 267, 269, 283
Common Core 17, 201
Common Hour 72–73, 77, 82, 86
Communities of learners 230
Community knowledge 33, 37–38, 207
Conocimiento 191–202
Conscientization 28, 152, 267–273
Corporate cultural pedagogy 16
Corporate power 12, 18
Correspondence 94
Cosmos Kinship (CK) 114–115
Creative Resistance 249–250, 256, 262, 264
Crisis of childhood 13, 15
Critical consciousness (Freirean) 23, 32–34, 38, 44, 69
Critical engagement of proverb 220
Critical inclusion 212
Critical literacies 23
Critical literacy 192, 195, 201
Critical media literacy 12, 146
Critical pedagogy 24–25, 28, 36, 45, 131, 177, 262, 269
Critical pedagogy of childhood 24
Critical theory 38, 97, 192, 194, 195, 201
Critical Youth Studies 27–43, 66, 128, 265
Criticality 12
Cultural circle 32
Cultural curriculum 16
Cultural pedagogy 3, 16, 19
Cultural politics of schooling 214
Cultural studies 18–20, 22, 24, 25, 29–31, 45, 46, 146, 169, 265–266, 276, 287, 289
Cultural studies of consumption 22
Culture and pedagogy 18, 202, 216
Culture as site of empowerment and source of disempowerment 215
Curricular justice 95, 97, 105–106

D

Dance 32, 126, 228, 134, 147, 172, 199, 207, 239–240, 250–251, 256, 258–264, 267, 271–272, 285

De Boever, A. 36, 44
De-academization of theory 193
Descartes, R. 28
Decolonized research methodology 51
Democracy 212, 268, 276–278
Democratic pedagogy 20
Dewey, J. 31, 145
Discursive practices 19
Disney 22
Disney English Schools 17
Disneyland 3
Disposability 49–66
Disruption 136, 236
DJing 34, 250
Drama 129, 144
Dreamworks 22
Dual nature of kinship 124

E

Education as a right 210
Ellipsis 111–114, 119–126
Elvis 158
Emceeing, graffiti, b-goying/b-girling DJing 34, 118, 250
Emigration 167, 170–176
Empowerment 9, 12, 25, 88, 98, 107, 118, 128, 208, 215, 217–218
Epicurus 28
Epistemology 28, 31, 334, 52, 54, 218, 230, 238, 248, 269, 276–277
Equity 87, 91, 107, 182–184, 208–210, 215, 216, 222, 227, 229, 232, 237–238, 265
Erikson, E. 5
Exchange value 31

F

Facebook 131, 139–142, 147–149
Failing school 52
Felman, S. 154, 164
First Nations 41, 112, 117, 133, 231
Fiske, J. 21–22

Flip the switch 254, 256
Fluck, W. 30–31
Foucault, M. 27–28, 31, 35, 37, 39
Frankfurt School 30
Freedom of speech 212
Freire, P. 32–36, 38, 44, 91, 95, 98–99, 107, 153–154, 162, 195, 202, 213, 262, 268–269, 273
Freire's situations 34

G

Galanin, N. 258–259
Gender 6–7, 21–23, 45, 51–52, 54, 62–63, 65, 68, 80, 214, 216, 216, 228, 235–247, 263, 280, 286
Gender Queer 235
Genealogy Kinship (GK) 114–115
Gesell, A. 5
Ghana Proverbs 223–224
Girl scouts 7
Giroux, H. 16, 25, 36, 49, 52–53, 64, 67, 95, 107, 169, 253
Gladwell, M. 156
Globalization 3, 8, 277–278
Gosine, K. 80
Graffiti 34, 112, 118, 250
Greene, M. 27–28, 46, 145, 152–153, 155, 258
Guillén, N. 270

H

Halloween 13
Hegemonic curriculum 97
Hegemony 209, 238, 270, 277
Hidden transcript in rap music 256
Hip Hop 29, 33–34, 36–37, 39, 41, 43, 111–114, 116–121, 125, 127–128, 151–158, 161–164, 249–254, 256–266, 270, 272
aesthetics 112
as Resistance 251

culture 33, 118–119, 125, 127–128, 158, 163–164, 250–254, 257–258
elements 118
genealogy 158
headz 118, 125
industry 163
Kulture 29, 33–34, 36–37, 39, 43, 45
practices 118
producers 119
products 119
scholars 113
sensibility 113
Hiphoppas 33–34, 36–37
Home country 167, 172, 174–176
hooks, b. 29, 32, 36, 45, 211, 232, 252–253, 263
Hyperreality 23

I

Ice T 36
Identities (transnational, cyber, diasporic, religious) 168
Identity 6, 14, 16, 19, 22–23, 25–26, 41, 42, 79, 84, 109, 116, 122, 127, 128, 132, 148, 153, 157, 161, 164, 167–169, 171–177, 186, 206–207, 209, 215–219, 227, 229–230, 238–240, 251, 253, 257–259, 265, 267, 269, 272–273, 277–278, 280
Immigrant parents 71, 75
Immigration 167, 169–170, 172–174, 176, 182, 202
Impression management 132
Indian identity 122
Indigeneity 127, 129, 229, 249, 256,
Indigenous African proverbs 205
  Americans 50
  communities 116
  cultural activities 122
  Peoples 111
  teachings 209
Interraciality 269, 278–279, 282–283

J

Jabari 160
Jacotot, J. 38–39
Jenkins, H. 9, 24, 131,
Jurassic Park 256

K

Kant, E. 28
Kenway, J. and Bullen, E. 12–13, 25, 215
Kenya Proverbs 220–221
Kincheloe 3, 5–6, 9, 11, 13, 22–26, 28, 31, 36, 92, 95, 107, 195, 276
Kinderculturated kid 15
Kinderculture 3–26
Kinship as literacy 124
Kinship narratives 110–127
Knowledge 4, 6, 8, 10, 13, 16, 19, 22, 24, 27–29, 31–39 42–45, 49–51, 54–55, 68, 73–75, 82–84 87, 91, 93, 95, 97–100, 113, 117, 119–125, 128, 132, 148, 152, 155, 158, 168, 171, 193, 195, 197–199, 201–202, 206–212, 214–216, 218–220, 223–231, 236–237, 242, 246, 250, 254, 256, 261–264, 273, 275, 277, 282–283
KRS-ONE 34, 45
Kwadjo 253–256, 263
Kwakwaka'wakw 111–112, 114, 119, 121–123, 126

L

Ladson-Billings, G. 73, 195, 202, 263
Lewis, R. 81–82, 152–153, 156, 159, 160–165
LGBTQ 53, 237, 238, 242
Live theater 129–146
Low Income Awareness Checklist 97, 100, 107

M

Macklemore 152–165
Maps 49–50, 52, 54–56, 63–64
Marginalization 71–86, 277
Marketization of education 215
Márquez, G. G. 270
Martí, J. 270
Marxist notions of false consciousness 38
Marxist political economic language 31
McDonald's 17
McGraw-Hill 17
Media Literacy: A Reader 23
Mental mapping as research methodology 55
Mexican Americans 181–189
Microsoft 22
Migrant youth 191, 201
Mixtec 191–198
Mobilizing youth 250
Multicultural nation 169
Multiculturalism 167–169, 172–173, 176, 177
Mungo Martin 120
Mythologies 119

N

Nassor, Khalfani 253–256, 263
Navigational capital 75
Neoliberal 55
Neoliberal agenda 91, 95
  education 51–52
  ethos 80
  ideology 51
  policies 54, 65
  regime of high stakes testing 52
  schooling practices 64
  social order 56
  strategies 96
  times 49
  world 66
  world order 50

Neoliberalism 56, 64, 268, 277–278
Networked public 132–134
New childhood 4
New immigrant youth 168, 176
New paradigm of childhood 8
New Youth 167–177
Nigeria proverbs 221–222
Nike 17
Notion of youth 169

P

Participatory culture 129–132
Payne, R. 96
Pearson Publishing 17
Pedagogical sites 16
Pedagogy of the Oppressed 107, 153, 164, 213, 273
Pedogogy of pleasure 19
Piaget, J. 5
Pixar 22
Pizza Hut 17
Plato 28, 35
Plurality 212
Poetry 151–162, 263, 267, 270–271
Popular culture 3, 13, 18, 19, 20, 23, 25, 117, 124, 132, 202–203, 208
Positivism 6–8, 10
Positivist 6–10, 24, 171, 275
Post-racial society 267–268, 283
Potlatch 120, 126,
Poverty 6, 10, 14, 90–91, 93, 94, 97–98, 106–107, 196, 214–215
Power 6–7, 9–13, 16, 18–27, 31, 33, 38–39, 44–45, 49, 55, 61, 63–64, 73, 78, 85, 92–93, 96, 98–99, 105, 107, 112, 116, 118, 128–129, 132, 135, 138–139, 142, 144, 152, 155, 157, 162, 171, 173, 188, 192, 195, 200, 202, 208–209, 211–218, 220–221, 224–225, 228, 230, 238–239, 244, 251–252, 256, 262–263, 273, 277–278, 280, 282
Power and knowledge 212

Power bloc 21–22
Power relations 21, 37, 93, 99, 132, 211,
    273, 277–278, 280
Proverbs 219
    the study of proverbs 227
    as acquisition of power 228

Q

Queer differences 236
Queer issues in practice 236
Queer space 247
Queer students 241
Queer talk 239
Queer youth 235–238, 241–242, 247,
Queer youth sexualities 235
Queer-positive strategies 237
Queerly embodied counter-narratives 241

R

Race 277
Racialized 62, 65–67, 72, 74–75, 80, 84,
    87, 155, 157–158, 171, 207, 213–216,
    232, 249–250, 268–272, 277,
    280–281, 283
Radical love x1
Radical reform 91
Radicalization 154, 278
Ranciére, J. 27, 29, 31, 37–39, 44, 46
Rap artists 253, 263
Rap music 157, 162, 251–253, 256,
    262–263, 266
Rapping 153, 156, 161–162, 249–250,
    256, 277
Reconstruction Era 64
Remixing 254, 257
Reproduction 94
Resiliency and resistant capital 74–75
Resistance 19, 23, 49, 69, 76–77, 122, 125,
    127, 138, 159, 207–208, 216, 220, 229,
    232, 236–238, 249–252, 256–257,
    259–262, 264–265

Respect 15, 58, 79, 83, 158, 171, 173, 195,
    201, 209, 217, 219, 223, 226–228, 238,
    252, 255, 262
Revolutionary 34, 38, 151–152, 157,
    269, 273
Rorty, R. 152–153, 162

S

School Disinvestment 50
School justice 92
School-to-prison pipeline 52–53, 56, 61, 64,
    65, 69
Scientific dimensions of child
    development 8
Sedgwick, E. 238
Self-discipline 208
Self-empowerment 98, 217
Settler colonialism 49–51, 259, 261–263
Sexualities 235, 238, 248, 266
Skin tone 183
Smartphones 129, 131, 135, 143–144, 147
Social class 21, 79, 86, 106, 274, 281, 283
Social justice 20, 24, 90, 92–94, 97, 105–7,
    202, 208–209, 212, 227, 229, 251, 265,
    274, 277–278, 282
Social media 16, 18, 129, 131, 133, 138,
    140–142, 270
Socially Committed Research
    Methodology 97
Solidarity 165, 251, 259, 261–263, 274, 278,
    281, 283
Solidarity movement 274
Sonny Assu 111–112, 121, 123–127
Spivak, G. 27
Standpoint Project 90–107
Structuralists 11–12
subject-of-aesthetic system 32

T

The Art of Rap 36
The Dream Act 186

The Gospel of Hip Hop 36
The Heist 152
The Indian Act 112, 114, 120–124, 126
The new theater 135, 140
The United States of Africa 36
Theatre of the Oppressed 167–170, 176
Traditional ecological knowledge (TEK) 33
Trans-Atlantic Slave trade 50
Transformative Artful Praxis 238
Transformative 10, 42, 76, 195, 201–202,
    212, 238–239, 260, 269, 271, 276–277
Treaties 252, 259
TV 8, 13, 15–16, 23–26, 67, 157, 165,
    174–175
Twitter 141

V

View of childhood, positivist 7
Volunteering 267, 272
Vulnerable child, positivist construction 7
Vygotsky, L. 15

W

Waiting for Superman 51
Web 2.0 129, 131, 135
White rapper 158
Wireless generation 130–131

Y

Yosso, T. 73–76
Youth activism, research and pedagogical
    space 42
Youth culture 111, 206, 251, 257, 259, 283
Youth identities 169
Youth Participatory Action Research
    (YPAR) 53
Youth resistance 252, 260, 264
Youth theater-goers 131
Youth-co-researchers 52, 54–55, 59, 62–63

Z

ZPD 15–16
Zulu Nation 258

critical qualitative research

Shirley R. Steinberg, *General Editor*

The Critical Qualitative Research series examines societal structures that oppress and exclude so that transformative actions can be generated. This transformed research is activist in orientation. Because the perspective accepts the notion that nothing is apolitical, research projects themselves are critically examined for power orientations, even as they are used to address curricular, educational, or societal issues.

This methodological work challenges modernist orientations and universalist impositions, asking critical questions like: Who/what is heard? Who/what is silenced? Who is privileged? Who is disqualified? How are forms of inclusion and exclusion being created? How are power relations constructed and managed? How do different forms of privilege and oppression intersect to affect educational, societal, and life possibilities for various individuals and groups?

We are particularly interested in manuscripts that offer critical examinations of curriculum, policy, public communities, and the ways in which language, discourse practices, and power relations prevent more just transformations.

For additional information about this series or for the submission of manuscripts, please contact:
Shirley R. Steinberg | msgramsci@gmail.com

To order other books in this series, please contact our Customer Service Department:
(800) 770-LANG (within the U.S.)
(212) 647-7706 (outside the U.S.)
(212) 647-7707 FAX

Or browse online by series:
www.peterlang.com